HAND ON MY HEART

Caitlin Press Inc.
3375 Ponderosa Way
Qualicum Beach, BC V9K 2J8
www.caitlinpress.com

Text and cover design by Vici Johnstone
All photos copyright Maureen Mayhew unless otherwise noted
Edited by Pam Robertson
Printed in Canada

Caitlin Press Inc. acknowledges financial support from the Government of Canada and the Canada Council for the Arts, and the Province of British Columbia through the British Columbia Arts Council and the Book Publisher's Tax Credit.

Library and Archives Canada Cataloguing in Publication

Hand on my heart : a Canadian doctor's awakening in Afghanistan / Maureen Mayhew.
Mayhew, Maureen, author.
Canadiana 20220429685 | ISBN 9781773861029 (softcover)
LCSH: Mayhew, Maureen. | LCSH: Médecins sans frontières (Association) | LCSH: Women physicians—Canada—Biography. | LCSH: Women physicians—Afghanistan—Biography. | LCSH: Medical care—Afghanistan. | LCGFT: Autobiographies.
LCC R464.M42 A3 2023 | DDC 610.92—dc23

Hand on My Heart

A Canadian Doctor's
Awakening in Afghanistan

by Maureen Mayhew

CAITLIN PRESS
2023

*For the many Afghans who shared their lives and their trust with me
and by so doing helped me become a better person*

For my mum, who gave me more than I realized

PRAISE FOR *HAND ON MY HEART*

"*Hand on My Heart* gives us a literally behind-the-veils view of life in one of the world's least understood countries. Maureen Mayhew writes with a doctor's precision and a novelist's sense of story about her decade on the ground in Afghanistan as a physician, gaining rare access to the family and intimate lives of people caught up in the tides of history. The story is by turns sad, wise, and joyful, leaving the reader deeply moved by Mayhew's personal story, the story of Afghanistan, and the deep thread of shared humanity running throughout both."

—Thomas Hayden, Stanford University,
author of *Sex and War* and *On Call in Hell*

"From first touchdown on a desolate airfield, *Hand on My Heart* travels beyond the journalistic and political images of Afghanistan and lifts the veils to reveal the hearts of the Afghan people. Through the lens of a physician, Dr. Maureen brings the reader on her daily adventures, confronting fears and isolation with respect and joy. Building trust and learning the language, she bonds with men and women to confront the web of religion, gender, and health. Always teaching yet learning even more, she explores the relationships of men and women and sees herself. The book demystifies the human side of Afghan life and reminds us of the universal connections we all share."

—Thomas A. Burke, PhD, MPH, Professor Emeritus, Johns Hopkins University, Bloomberg School of Public Health

"A remarkable and revealing journey into the heart of both Afghanistan and the insightful narrator. As this compassionate and nonjudgmental narrative unfolds, Dr. Mayhew immerses herself in Afghan customs, including the importance of family and belonging, and discovers a new way of seeing and knowing herself. *Hand on My Heart* is a compelling story of medical aid, of discovery, and personal growth."

—Barbara Sibbald, former MSF volunteer, medical humanities editor and author of *The Museum of Possibilities* and the forthcoming *Twelve Annas to a Rupee*

In remote Afghanistan, these nomads moved with the seasons in search of pasture for their animals.

CONTENTS

PROLOGUE

I wrote this book to share the sense of wonder and the wealth of learning that I experienced over ten years in the one country I vowed I would never visit. In 2000, I was en route to Afghanistan for the first time. Curiosity about what I might encounter had overtaken my prejudices because I had heard that Afghans were incredibly kind and dedicated, even though they lived in a country reminiscent of a patient with enormous festering wounds. I had very few expectations. When I let go of my preconceived notions and opened myself to what was, Afghans demonstrated a level of commitment and a sense of belonging to their communities that was inconceivable to a nomad like me.

As a child, I dreamed of becoming a hobo, the romantic storybook kind who travels from town to town with her possessions wrapped in a handkerchief dangling from a sturdy stick balanced on a shoulder. I didn't need much to be happy, and I was already practised at moving from place to place. As a kid, I didn't know that people spent their entire childhood in one house or that children attended all elementary school grades with the same friends. Wouldn't that be boring?

As a teenager, I flip-flopped between wanting to become a modern-day Florence Nightingale, an oboist in an orchestra and an astronaut. On my medical school application, I wrote that I would use my medical skills to work internationally and help those in great need. I wanted to give a voice to the voiceless, to help people who suffered be their best. Just before completing my training, I beelined to a Médecins Sans Frontières (MSF) office, keen to offer them my brand-new knowledge and skills. And they refused to give me an application! They said they might consider me after two years of work experience. I felt crushed. What about my dream?

One and a half years later, I was studying a map of Africa, anticipating where MSF might send me, when a man walked into my life. I was smitten.

For nine years, he and I worked in rural and remote clinics and hospitals across Canada. I lived like a nomad, novelty popping up at every curve in the road. When we decided to commit to each other, moving our minimal possessions to Whistler by Canada Post, fate intervened. Under a star-studded sky in a pool in Columbia, our dream together withered and died.

Months later, in Vancouver, I locked my bicycle to a signpost and walked into the local MSF office. After I told her my story, the girl behind the desk slid a thick application package toward me. Surrounding her were posters of the people who had inspired me to become a doctor.

"Your experience is perfect. And there happens to be room in the next orientation course in Apeldoorn, the Netherlands."

A new but hazy chapter in my life shimmered exotically. My entire body tingled. Little did I know then that this simple interaction heralded the beginning of a ten-year journey into Afghanistan, a place so few foreigners understand, and decades of mastering concepts in a burgeoning field called global health.

It took years of soul searching to comprehend how my experiences in Afghanistan shaped me, and to learn to write about them in ways that people who hadn't been there might understand and appreciate.

Throughout the book, I have spelled Dari words phonetically using Roman characters the same way I recorded them in my journal when, with no access to a Dari-English dictionary, I was creating my own. Dari-English dictionaries, with their inconsistent phonetical spelling in Roman characters, became available to me on my third trip to the country, but to remain true to the local dialect, I have retained most of the spelling and phrasing that I learned early on.

I hope that by fictionalizing names, I am protecting those who gave me their trust, since conflicts still rage on in the country. After twenty years of foreign aid being received by Afghanistan, the Taliban have once again seized power, and the country's story twists yet again.

To help readers situate the story visually, I have inserted photographs throughout the book that I shot while living in Afghanistan. Exceptions are those of me that were taken by colleagues (pp. 15, 213 and 235). Given the current danger to Afghans who are affiliated with expats and who are still living in the country, I have done my best to protect them by deliberately selecting images of people not featured in my memoir. To enrich the reader's experience of my narrative, I chose to illustrate events that were too dangerous for me to photograph by selecting images taken at another time or place.

It gives me great pleasure to share this journey of exploration, revelation, joy, confusion and pain—but also great big belly laughs.

CHAPTER ONE

A DREAM

— Rumi

"Out beyond ideas of wrongdoing and rightdoing, there is a field. I'll meet you there. When the soul lies down in that grass, the world is too full to talk about."

Holding my breath, I licked café au lait foam off my upper lip and hovered the mouse over the envelope icon, but my finger doggedly refused to press the button. A prayer came unbidden, one of those selfish negotiations that some of us make with God when we pine for something so badly that we think our life will be ruined without it, or when we are utterly terrified. I don't recall what my promise was, but God must have known that my pledge was hollow because when the little mouse opened the envelope, AFGHANISTAN bellowed at me from the first paragraph. Below it in bold script, "nine months" caused my heart to beat double time. What were they thinking?! When answering the question in the application to Médecins Sans Frontières (MSF) about where I would refuse to work, Afghanistan was the only country that I had listed. I hadn't minced words. I had plainly printed "Afghanistan" on that line and nothing else. You would think that organizations like MSF would respect a volunteer's request, wouldn't you? At the time, the amount that they offered to pay me wouldn't even cover my furniture storage fees and professional dues.

Two months earlier, in January 2000, I hadn't even known where Afghanistan was on the globe. During the orientation course for new MSF volunteers, a psychologist had introduced me to the country by mentioning that women were forced to wear head-to-toe coverings called burkas that hid even their faces. She said that Sharia law involved thieving hands being sliced off at the wrist and women being stoned to death for having sex out of wedlock. Her contract was already signed. She would counsel Afghan women who had been locked in compounds or widows who the society discarded like used baggage. Despite her expectation of being stuck in a compound most of the time, her voice bubbled with excitement.

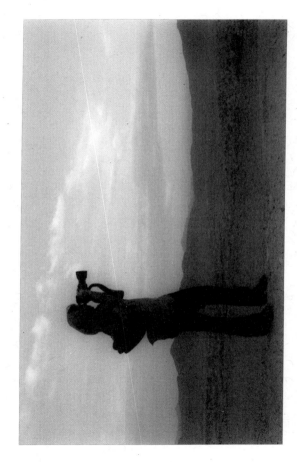

Travelling the world as a doctor, camera in hand, I wanted to understand everyone I met.

Gosh, the job sounded dreadful. Why give up nine months of your life to live like a prisoner? And how on earth would she meet these persecuted women?

Hoping that the email might have been addressed to the wrong person, I verified the name written in the salutation. "Maureen Mayhew" stared brazenly at me from the top of the page. I placed a hand on my heart, breathed in deeply and tried to calm its rapid rhythm. With more than two hundred countries in the world, how did they manage to assign me to the only one that I had vowed to refuse? You don't have to go, I told myself. But what if they stopped offering me positions?

Three documents were attached to the email, a fact sheet from the Central Intelligence Agency and two MSF documents describing the war in Afghanistan and the project. Afghan men and women lived an average of only forty-one or forty-two years. The average mother had nine pregnancies, and very few women could read. A place couldn't get much worse than that, could it?

I was being offered a position as medical lead in a four-person expat team based at a refurbished primary care clinic in a remote part of Western Afghanistan, near the border with Turkmenistan. Getting there involved at least four flights, then a two-day drive to a village with no other foreigners. What if the team didn't get along? The driving distance was said to be 180 kilometres. How could it take two days to drive a distance that I usually covered in less than two hours?

I learned that the civil war had been fuelled for years by a long list of other countries and that Afghanistan was one of the most heavily mined countries in the world. As a result, a mine-awareness course was mandatory.

I thanked my lucky stars when I read "under no circumstances will any expat woman wear a burka." Apparently the Taliban insisted that foreign women wear a *shalwar kameez*, a pajama-like outfit from Pakistan that would distinguish us from them. Every time she left the compound, a foreign woman was to be escorted by a foreign man, not an Afghan. No exceptions. The "male escort" was referred to locally as a *maharam*.

I squinted at the words as if they were the enemy and my eyes were the barrel of a sniper's rifle, primed to shoot them off the page. How could an independent doctor and outdoor enthusiast survive under rules like that?

With a huff, I stood up, then slipped into a pair of spandex tights and a long-sleeved, skin-tight shirt. I ran down the street to the beach, then upped the pace. My muscles pumped hard and my breath found its rhythm. Inside me, a battle raged. I swore. I bargained. I dreamed. I criticized. And eventually, the blustery March wind blew my thoughts away.

An hour later, as sweat trickled down my temples, my head was clear and I felt at peace. Kneeling before my newly acquired, second-hand computer, a bargain at $100, I crafted a response.

Dear Sir/Madam:

Thank you for considering me. I feel honoured at having received this offer. But Afghanistan really isn't a good fit for an athletic woman like me who needs to go outside every day, especially when feeling stressed. Perhaps a more sedentary person would be a better fit. I hope that refusing this offer does not jeopardize my chances for a different mission. I look forward to hearing from you in the near future.

Sincerely,
Maureen Mayhew, MD

If they didn't offer me something more suitable, I would give up on the idea—which would delight Peter, my boyfriend at the time. Although our relationship was pretty good on many fronts—we both loved cooking, reading, entertaining and spending weekends exploring the outdoors—it wasn't enough for me when, over the previous two years, I had felt so stifled by my life as a family doctor in Vancouver. Another opportunity would appear. I was certain of that. I just needed patience.

Over the next week, MSF recruiters somehow convinced me to speak with volunteers in Canada and in Amsterdam who had worked in Afghanistan. They expressed either love or contempt for the experience. There was no middle ground. A call from a Dutch woman in Herat, Afghanistan, nudged the door wide open. The far-away voice with the eight-second delay told me how much the team on site loved their work and how fantastic the Afghan staff were. The outgoing team swam, hiked and visited villagers! My heart swelled when she told me that the three years I had spent in the Canadian Arctic was the best preparation for this kind of mission, and that the physician's position in Bala Morghab was made for someone like me. I knew she was selling hard, yet I latched onto her words. I so wanted to believe her!

Intrigue and adventure finally won. I could add a novel country to the list of forty-five that I had already visited. The following week, I signed a contract. From that point, my life moved along a conveyor belt as I acquired vaccines and visas, packed my belongings into a storage locker and said goodbye to friends in a whirlwind of events. In the end the decision to go had been quite simple.

In Afghanistan, a land so different from Canada, how would I fit in? Photo credit: Kareem

Making up stories about people I know nothing about is easy to do. Staying open and avoiding stereotypes can be challenging.

CHAPTER TWO

My Neverland

"When I let go of what I am, I become what I might be."

— *Lao Tzu (attributed)*

In early April 2000, a King Air turboprop propelled us west of Peshawar, Pakistan. Through the scratched window of a porthole, I stared far below at the reddish-brown landscape of Afghanistan, a lifeless desert with deep, parallel fissures that resembled wounds from a knife blade. Squinting, I searched the ground for armoured vehicles and tanks, even snipers. Of course, I didn't see any. True to his word, the pilot flew high, supposedly out of range of whatever weapons the Taliban possessed. To anyone on the ground, our plane would appear as a tiny speck speeding across a vast, blue sky.

The civil war awaited, and as a first-timer, I was sweating. Travelling alone, I knew nothing about the other passengers, the six men who dressed in Central Asian garb and the one Caucasian female in a shalwar kameez like me. In Herat, someone bearing a sign that featured the world-renowned logo of Médecins Sans Frontières would meet me in the airport parking lot.

Getting a seat on the plane had been a crapshoot, even when I possessed a ticket. In 2000, only the International Committee of the Red Cross flew into Afghanistan. It had taken five days of negotiations to get a seat on the aircraft, which had me wondering whether MSF ranked rock bottom in some obscure but important hierarchy. Once, I was summoned to the office only to wait for two hours before being told that they had cancelled the flight with no explanation. Our staff told me that the unpredictable schedule was a safety tactic. Although annoying for passengers, it kept the pilots alive.

"Maybe tomorrow." The agent's voice had sounded tired but, for some reason, I hung on to the hope that I heard in it.

The next morning, the ticket agent weighed each passenger along with their carry-on bags and luggage. Not a kilogram beyond the twenty kilos per person limit was permissible because the plane had to carry enough fuel in jerry cans for the return trip. Apparently, the Taliban stole petrol.

I had left every stitch of Western clothing behind in a box labelled with my name and return date at the MSF guest house in Peshawar. For nine months, I would wear my three new shalwar kameezes with matching chadors that the organization had purchased for me. Dressed in my new garb, I felt lighter somehow, as if my costume gave me freedom to explore forgotten remnants of myself. Heading into Afghanistan, I felt like a neophyte actress without a script who was about to step onstage to perform in a play, only the plot was still a mystery.

Wrapped in my new outfits, my Nikon FE2 and twelve rolls of Fujifilm Velvia were tucked away at the bottom of my seven-kilogram carry-on knapsack. Under Taliban law, taking photographs of people was illegal. MSF had told me to keep the camera out of sight or risk it being confiscated. As a traveller, I was drawn to snapping images of people in their daily lives. I was keen to document as much as I could since I didn't expect to return. My contract clearly stated that neither the camera nor I was insured, yet there was money available to repatriate my body to Canada if required. That had been sobering to read.

The King Air had a crimson Red Cross logo painted on its belly that was hard to miss. Male passengers had boarded first. I had followed the other foreign woman, who looked twenty years my senior. Crouching in the narrow, metal tube, we had taken the two remaining seats, one behind the other, right beside a propeller. While one pilot flipped switches and turned knobs, the other one twisted around to give a brief safety demonstration that lasted about a minute. That's when he mentioned that we would fly at an altitude above target range and that the greatest risk of attack was at takeoff and landing so ascents and descents would be rapid.

As our seat belts clicked closed, the propellers cut the air—the deafening noise of the engines leaving me alone with my thoughts. When the plane rattled to altitude, I said goodbye to the safety that I had known in Pakistan.

Glancing around, I felt like I was in a makeshift office, its mood sombre. Notebooks and reports lay open on passengers' laps, their pens poised to scribble in margins. I was reading a second-hand copy of Ahmed Rashid's book Taliban. The Pakistani journalist claimed the Taliban had been trained by the Central Intelligence Agency as a weapon against the Soviets. He said their tutelage had been so effective that, when the two superpowers abandoned the country, the Taliban easily conquered it. Given this information and how secretive the military is, would the pilots even know what weapons the Taliban possessed? For a moment, I pictured a missile, launched by an unseen tank, heading directly at us, and I drew back from the potential impact.

Stretching out a kink in my neck, my head fell back. With a jerk, I remembered that this plane had no luxuries like headrests. I shifted in the torn canvas seat, trying to avoid the dig of the metal bar pressing into my shoulder blades.

In preparation for the trip, I had read Dervla Murphy's book from the 1960s *Full Tilt: Ireland to India with a Bicycle*. Sleeping in a tent with a gun under her pillow, she had cycled solo through Afghanistan, where she developed a deep attraction to Afghan masculinity. Hard to imagine that now, after so many decades of war and extremism! Since that time, millions of people had left. No longer did hippies board Magic Buses headed there in search of cheap Afghan weed. I wasn't brave like her. I had bike-toured countless times in Europe, for up to three months at a time, and trekked up mountains in Asia, Europe, and Central and South America. Multi-day kayak camping trips had been fun, and so too had been my escapades in the forests, jungles and deserts of several continents. But heading to Afghanistan, I felt like I was jumping to a new rung in the traveller hierarchy.

The silver hair of the woman in front of me was cropped short. A head scarf of silky, pale blue fabric nestled on her shoulders. From the back, she looked peaceful and small, like a nun or a missionary. As I studied her, she turned around and smiled, the fine lines in her cheeks and around her eyes crinkling, her ears rising a millimetre or two. Unadorned, her grey eyes struck me as both kind and wise, and I immediately felt attracted to her.

She spoke in a gentle voice like a grandmother's that I could hear in spite of the rattle of the plane, the roar of the engine and the whoosh of the propellers. "Is this your first time… going in?" She paused. One eyebrow twitched.

I nodded while trying to identify what had advertised my inexperience. Had my anxiety permeated my new clothes? Could she smell my fear? I glanced behind me to cover up taking a surreptitious whiff of my armpits. Everyone else looked relaxed.

"I used to live in Afghanistan." Her eyes sparkled. "My husband was a diplomat. In 1962, we moved to Afghanistan. At that time, Afghanistan was where expats in Pakistan went for R&R. Kabul was known as the City of Flowers. It was, at the time, very beautiful." She sighed and continued. "In Kabul, I met the love of my life, an anthropologist who had been studying Afghan sociology for some years. He has written several books on Afghan culture. When we met, we were both married to other people. I couldn't help myself. We became involved and a few years later, after our divorces, we married." She looked wistfully at the floor. "Our affair rocked Kabul. We became the talk of the town, although not always in a nice way." She laughed playfully. "Divorces weren't common then." Her voice trailed off as she looked into my eyes. "We used to meet in the beautiful garden, Bagh-e-Bala. It's where we were married. At that time, Kabul had many wonderful buildings, gardens and palaces. The city was decimated during the civil war that began after the Americans left. It is totally destroyed now and the gardens are mined, so you won't be able to visit them even if you reach Kabul."

Wow! What an adventurer! I had often heard Kabul described as wartorn but never as beautiful. "When were you last in Afghanistan?" I wanted to drink the nectar from whatever fruits she would share!

"Last year. I go once a year. My organization is based out of my home in Peshawar. We preserve Afghan artifacts. I still find it strange that Afghans require aid. I would move back to Kabul in a heartbeat but not the way it is now." She paused. "Do you speak Dari?"

I shook my head.

"I learned Dari in the 1960s and Urdu as well. Dari is the easiest Afghan language. What would you like to know?"

I hesitated. With so many unformed questions, where could I start? Were the Taliban as bad as I'd heard? How hard was it to adapt to life in Afghanistan? What does it take to succeed in such a place? Did I really have to follow all the rules? What should I do if someone points a gun at me? I blurted out one at random: "What is Afghanistan like now compared to the first time you went in?" MSF staff in Peshawar had taught me that people didn't visit Afghanistan, they "went in."

"My first impression of the country was very different from what yours will be. History has been unkind to Afghanistan." She faced forward for a moment, as if resting her neck. I sensed sadness. How many deaths had she witnessed during these four decades?

"Are you afraid?" she asked, turning back. Her eyes seemed to peer inside my head, as if searching for the emotions that I tried so hard to conceal.

I nodded. In Peshawar, excitement had overridden any notion of fear. But on the plane, I felt insignificant. If we crashed, who would know that I had died? My family was spread across North America. We were an independent lot who fended for ourselves. My friends would miss me until they didn't. So many people I knew were neck deep in the daily grind of raising kids, building careers and making enough for retirement. They had little room for anything else. A student in Nova Scotia once asked me what I was running from. He had decided that I was afraid of commitment. On the plane, I pondered his question. Wasn't I running toward excitement, exploration and novelty? That day I felt like I was flying out of the world's consciousness, farther than I'd ever gone. I pictured stepping through a curtain that closed behind me, the world that I knew disappearing from view. My next trip out was in twelve weeks. A lot could happen during that time.

My stomach grumbled. I had hardly eaten that morning. Slowly, I sipped water from a small plastic bottle courtesy of a cooler between the pilots' seats. Before the flight, I had avoided coffee. There was no toilet on board and who knew if the Herat airport housed one.

Watching my face, the woman in front of me seemed to read what I felt. "Rules in Afghanistan are very foreign to Westerners, and often difficult for us to accept. When we arrive in Herat, you will see no women. None. Afghan men won't look at you. It's not meant as an insult, even though you may take it that way. The North American habit of looking directly at someone is not normal here. My best advice is that you consider their disregard as the highest form of respect that they can offer. That's what I do. Many foreign women become upset with the way Afghan men treat them, which is a waste of energy. Taking their disregard of you—remember, they won't look at you or speak directly to you—as a form of respect will save you from yourself. It does take practice." Her face was only a foot away from mine, and she spoke passionately.

I pasted a smile on my face. My cheek muscles felt strained but I was afraid that if I let them relax, tears might flow. I felt like a clown with sad, droopy eyes. "Thank you. The advice is helpful, although it'll take some practice for me to be able to do that. I will think about this."

She faced forward again, moving her head to the left and rolling her shoulders. What would it be like to not be noticed? For the first twelve years of my life, our family had moved every year or two. I had been the new kid at school, the brainy one with the big nose who was adept at fitting in and not being noticed. That might be a useful skill for what was to come.

She turned toward me again. "Most Afghans who remained in the country are religious, and they use literal interpretations of the Koran. Avoid looking directly at them so they do not assume unkind thoughts about you. In their view, *any* interaction between men and women, unless the man is her husband, brother, son or father, defiles the woman. Therefore, men and women should not acknowledge each other unless they are in the same family. Interactions include touching, conversing, looking at each other and pretty much anything that connects two people. If you keep this in mind, you are likely to feel more comfortable when you are in their company." As she spoke, sunlight streamed in the opposite window and her eyes turned to silver.

The pilots announced our upcoming descent.

Don't look at them. Don't greet anyone. Don't shake hands. Don't touch them. Yeesh! But she had lived in Afghanistan for decades and still loved the place.

It was years later that I discovered who she was. Nancy Dupree had authored several guidebooks on the culture and history of Afghanistan. She had married Louis Dupree, the anthropologist and archaeologist whose book *Afghanistan*, a bible for scholars, was published in 1973. I used it five years later when researching my master's thesis. Her teachings that first day were a gift that, unbeknownst to me then, would allow me to return to Afghanistan again and again. And later, as a veteran aid worker in the country, I would dish out the same counsel.

"It's alright if I look at women, right?" It might be a rare event but when I did see one, I would surely want to peek at her.

"Of course, but you won't see any unless you go inside compounds. The rare time a woman is in the streets, she will be covered with a burka."

Our small plane dropped quickly, just like the pilot had forewarned. We flew over the battered carcasses of a helicopter gunship and a gutted plane. At the far end of the runway lay the remains of an airport. A metal roof covered only a quarter of the building. Clustered nearby on the tarmac, a group of men wearing turbans stood waiting. Our tiny aircraft rolled toward the crowd, whose long beards and turban tails rose in the wind in unison as if choreographed. We taxied by the phantom aircrafts. Kalashnikovs slung over shoulders, the men stood quietly waiting. When we stopped, they moved toward the tail of the plane.

Rooted to my seat, I sensed a rumble of curiosity, but my gut ached for the safety of Pakistan. I had never been to a country like this one. Biblical came to mind. One propeller sped up while the other slowed down, and then the plane was poised to leave. The pilots announced that loading and unloading would occur quickly so they could return to Pakistan as soon as possible.

"What are they waiting for?" Looking at Nancy, I tilted my head toward the turbaned men. I rubbed my fingers together to distract myself from a gnawing fear.

"They wait for supplies. This is the only reliable transport route from Pakistan. No one uses trucks anymore. They'd be vandalized."

Didn't the Taliban cut off thieving hands?

In a surprisingly graceful movement, she unwound her chador, placed it over her hair and tucked in the ends. Only her finely lined face with the silver eyes was visible. She tipped her head in my direction.

I flipped the polyester scarf over my head. It slid down my hair and onto my shoulders. I pulled it back up, fastening it tightly around my face and tucking strands of hair underneath it. I cinched it again. I thrust stray curls beneath it. The scarf loosened. Locks sprung out. I coerced them into compliance, pulling the material tight. Letting my breath go, my face felt like a pimple ready to burst. She had made it look so easy!

Nancy put the finishing touches on my scarf and suddenly, it felt like it might stay on my head. She tilted her head. "Cotton chadors stay on. Polyester always slips. Indian cotton is the best."

Through the window, the apostles looked ready for a day of judgment. How would I fare?

The two pilots strode purposefully between our seats, and one of them tossed out the short metal ladder so it hung out the door. When he descended, the turbaned men moved closer. Two figures strained against a wooden cart with wooden wheels, loaded higgledy-piggledy with a tower of boxes. What Afghan goods were exported? Opium? Wouldn't they ship that by land in the dark of night?

Male passengers disembarked first. Draped in my chador, I felt like a maiden in a fairytale. I watched through the window. Some men shook hands, but no one hugged, slapped backs or smiled. They looked directly into one another's eyes, as if reading words that weren't said. Was smiling in public taboo too?

"Remember, look down. You'll do fine." She patted my shoulder. Standing up, she smiled like a saint. So many years later, that's how I remember her.

Through the aisle of empty seats and out into the sunshine, I followed the tiny, elegant woman who looked so self-assured, even comfortable, in a place that was so foreign and foreboding to me. As I exited the plane, I vowed to heed her advice. Disregard was respect. With each step, over and over, I repeated my new mantra. As we walked toward the building, no one seemed to notice us, yet a mysterious path through the men opened, guiding us to the destroyed building.

Seen and unseen at the same time. If I approached a man, what would he do? I shifted my eyes to the ground. I focused on their bellies but it felt rude. What if they thought I was looking lower than that? I repositioned my backpack. A shoulder cramp released, and I counted my steps to keep my rebellious thoughts at bay.

Nancy climbed the pockmarked cement steps toward a Taliban guard, then disappeared inside the bombed-out building. Subconsciously, I sped up, like a kid with separation anxiety chasing her mother who had just stepped out of sight. Up the steps I went and, as I did, I realized that those pockmarks were bullet holes! Hundreds of them. I slipped through the doorway, past the sturdy guard wearing a black turban and an AK-47. He studied the plane, as if I was invisible. I felt like a ghost. Or maybe a spy?

Inside, large strips of greyish-green paint, the ubiquitous colour of hospitals in rural Canada, peeled off in strips. The bullet holes reminded me of chicken pox scars. At the centre of the room, a feminine-looking man sat behind a large wooden desk. Kohl outlined his eyes, and coal-coloured hair framed his face, the fringe of it just

Had I taken a photograph of the decaying Herat airport and nearby aircraft carcasses, the Taliban would have confiscated my camera, destroyed my film and possibly done something scary to me. So I didn't. This photograph, taken outside of Kabul in 2005, portrays my first impression of Afghanistan.

touching his ears. On his head sat a large jet-black turban with so many layers that it looked like a beehive. He gazed disinterestedly at the documents strewn across the desk. Behind him, another Taliban man, who looked like a brother, stood beside a Kalashnikov that was propped, muzzle up, against a metal filing cabinet. Standing behind him, a man sporting a dark beard and a magnificent white turban leaned his AK-47 against his leg and drank a glass of tea. The MSF workers in Pakistan had told me that the Taliban were hard to distinguish from other Afghans. Typically, they wore voluminous white or black turbans and outlined their eyes with black kohl.

Nancy placed her passport on the closest side of the desk, crossed in front of it, then stopped to wait on the far side near a long hallway. To the men, she seemed invisible. Placing my passport beside hers, I paused for a moment, uncertain whether I wanted to give to this man the one document I needed to exit the country. Would he steal it? The Taliban agent's wrist waved me toward Nancy. So he did see me! Ignoring both documents, he handed a haphazard stack of papers to the man with the dark beard, who passed them on to the next man, and so on, until they arrived at the guard, who disappeared with them. A few minutes later, he resumed his position at the door and continued to study the plane. It was easy to criticize their crude methods. They might be uneducated and bull-headed, but they had survived rebel warfare and I hadn't, so I was cautious. What could I learn from them?

Dragging our passports closer, the Taliban official leafed through both of them back to front, and he never once looked at the photo page. I could have been anyone. In a way I was glad. I'd heard that some Taliban placed a giant X through passport photographs. He left ours unscathed. He stamped the Afghan visa and left the others alone. I had one for India and another for Turkmenistan in case we needed to escape. Sliding the passports over to us, he flicked his wrist as if batting a fly. We were dismissed. Not once had his eyes strayed from his desk.

With documents in hand, we headed down the hallway, then Nancy stopped. "The drive to Herat takes about half an hour, sometimes longer. The road is very bumpy. Would you like to use the toilet before you go?"

I could have kissed her! There was a functioning toilet in this derelict building?! One that women could use? My aching bladder was grateful.

Staring at the wall, she walked toward the seated Taliban official and muttered something in a foreign tongue. He waved to the guard, who approached and bent over so his ear was close to the other's lips. After listening for a fraction of a second, the guard walked out the door. Nancy nodded. I scurried after him, my backpack straps draped over a shoulder. Passing through two rooms, I saw the sky above and large blast holes in the walls. Stopping, he drew a key from an inner pocket, unlocked a padlock, then promptly turned around and disappeared. The sun's rays, beaming through bullet holes in the tin roof, decorated the fractured, cement floor. Using my index finger to nudge the door open, I peered into a sun-dappled space. At the far end, near the wall, was a hole encircled by darkened cement. Sticking out of the wall, a broken pipe spewed a stream of clear water onto the floor. Was that the faucet?

My bladder was bursting and there was no clean surface on which to place the backpack with my precious camera, so I opted to wear it while disrobing. The many layers and the need to squat complicated what usually was a simple task in Canada. I tucked the back of my kameez between me and the backpack. The front end of it, I tucked into my bra. Pulling the cuffs of the shalwar up over my knees so they didn't drag in the puddles, I undid the drawstring and slipped my underwear down. Squatting, I hoped that I wouldn't pee on my sandal. What a relief!

Of course, there was no toilet paper, only a plastic container with a long spout for washing nether regions. I didn't want to touch the hordes of cooties on it. Balanced in my squat, my thighs started to complain. I told them to hush as I clicked open the clasp of the pack's waist belt to slip an arm out of the strap so I could access the topmost pouch. From there I withdrew the tiny supply of toilet paper safely contained in a Ziploc bag. The used tissue I tossed into the void, grateful for my foresight. While hiking the shalwar up to my waist, the cuffs had fallen into a nearby puddle. Dampness, like a dead fish, brushed against my ankle. Yuk!

While repositioning the tails of my kameez, I blindly verified that they were still dry. Hoping the gushing water was clean, I rinsed my hands several times. There was no soap. Oh well. Smoothing my kameez with wet hands, I checked that both tails hung all the way down. I had once walked out of a bathroom in Pakistan without noticing that the back of my kameez was tucked into my shalwar's drawstring, which is akin to tucking your dress into your underwear. Embarrassing but common amongst foreigners, I was told. I pulled on my chador and wrapped the ends tightly around my face. I checked to see that I had left nothing and then walked out, thankful that no one had entered the unlocked door with the empty socket where a doorknob had once been.

At the end of the hall, Nancy looked like a guardian angel. Together, we walked into the scorching sun. I wished her safe travels. Smiling, she voiced the same hope for me. Devoid of luggage, she scooted into the back seat of a waiting white Toyota Corolla and disappeared from my life. I searched the parking lot. Where was that MSF sign?

CHAPTER THREE

TWO TEACHERS

"The beginning is the most important part of the work."

— *Plato*

After a two-day journey on narrow paths with herds of sheep and goats, and deep ruts that threatened to overturn the vehicle, I stepped out of a white MSF Land Cruiser onto a countryside so remote and barren that it reminded me of the Canadian Arctic, except sweltering heat replaced frigid temperatures.

Bala Morghab, a village of about five thousand inhabitants, felt like the biblical backdrop for a play. I could imagine a manger in one of the rooms of the adobe compound where MSF expats lived and worked. In the courtyard of my new home, I met the outgoing foreigners and our all-male Afghan staff, who waited in a reception line as if at a wedding or a funeral. I was the first of the incoming team to arrive. Vicky, an English midwife, and John, a Canadian logistics technician, made the introductions. Martin, the project coordinator from Quebec, had said hello earlier and then disappeared through a doorway.

First up was Momo Rahim, the clinic manager, who was a slim man in a grey shalwar kameez onto which was sewn a panel of fine embroidery. Beneath his striped turban, I saw the copious wrinkles and thickened skin of a chain-smoker.

"Welcome, Dr. Murreen. Welcome to Bala Morghab!" His eyes twinkled. "*Momo* means uncle. I am everyone's uncle." He offered his right hand with its nicotine-stained fingers and waited expectantly.

Dusty, thirsty and tired, I uttered the one Islamic word that I had learned in Herat: "Salaam." Then I thanked him in English. John told me that Momo Rahim had escaped the Taliban's threats in Kabul by fleeing to Bala Morghab, where his extended family lived. He looked honest and kind, so I grasped the outstretched hand. His handshake was firm. I saw sadness in his eyes.

Next up were office staff: a manager, a logistics assistant and two interpreters who provided verbal and written translation. There were also three drivers and several guards. I followed each person's lead. If they extended a hand, I shook it. If their hand went to their heart, so did mine. The greetings went on and on and so did the handshakes, like old friends seeing each other after many years. I understood "Salaam" and "Allah." The rest was incomprehensible but they seemed to mean every word. From their sad glances at John and Vicky, I concluded that the entire team hesitated to trade in the old expats for an unknown crew.

"This is Habib, the cook." John pointed to a boy who looked about fourteen and sprouted only two chin hairs. "He is Momo Rahim's nephew. Except for barbecuing kebabs in the bazaar, cooking is considered women's work. The Taliban forbid us to employ women, so his mother teaches him at home. He has learned a lot of dishes over the last several months, even vegetarian ones and chocolate cake." John's narrative continued. During wartime, jobs disappear, and an MSF salary is welcomed by most households. Another of Momo Rahim's relatives was our cleaner, a wiry, feminine teenager who looked like he might get into mischief.

I was fascinated by the simple daily tasks of villagers in Bala Morghab, such as using a homemade tool to load animal feed onto a donkey.

Vicky took me on a tour of the house. Our first stop was my spacious yellow bedroom with its domed ceiling, located as far away as possible from the office where most of the staff worked. Inside it, my maroon duffel bag sat on a small carpet by the bed. Vicky's bedroom was next door. Both rooms overlooked a fledgling orchard of plum, peach and pear trees whose miniature fruits were dark green and rock hard. John had built a sauna among the trees. Apparently winters were cold, which was difficult to fathom. From behind a nearby wooden barricade, a generator roared. It was silenced each evening at 9 p.m. when kerosene lanterns lit up the compound. A pit latrine and a shower with cold water were for expats only. At first glance, they looked clean. My favourite was the boudoir-like living room that resembled the interior of a wealthy Bedouin's tent. Wine-coloured velvet drapes arced across windows and were held open by black sashes. A burgundy wool carpet with a black floral design covered the dirt floor. On velvety mattresses, piles of plush pillows and cushions invited me to lie back, relax and imagine being fed plump green grapes by a magnificent stud. The cubbyhole kitchen contained a sink, a gas stove and a refrigerator. In the courtyard was a mechanic's pit and a parking lot. Beyond that was the three-room office. All in all, it seemed comfortable enough.

That first evening, a million stars twinkled in the black sky. The North Star, which I had relied on while on adventures in Northern Canada, blinked hello. Seeing it nestled between the Big Dipper and Cassiopeia just like it always was gave me a sense of peace. The Milky Way was so vibrant that it really did look like a smear of milk on a child's lip.

John and Vicky waved at me from a blue and white mat made of woven plastic where they lounged cross-legged on pillows they had fetched from the living room. Across from them sat two Afghan men I didn't recognize, their dusty brown turbans and shalwar kameezes blending into the earthen wall. One of them was short and round. The other was tall and slim. Laurel and Hardy in *Lawrence of Arabia?*

Heartbeat pounding in my throat, I approached. At the mat, I removed my worn leather shoes and left them in the dirt. Like many of my possessions, they would be donated at the end of the trip.

Where should I sit? According to the MSF rule book, an expat woman wasn't supposed to sit beside Afghan men. Vicky patted the mat beside her. At the far end, Laurel and Hardy were illuminated by flickering lantern light. I stared at them, then shifted my eyes away, but they drifted back again, as if defying my brain's orders.

We had four days for a handover and then John and Vicky, and whatever knowledge they had gained over the previous nine months that wasn't recorded somewhere, would be gone. Hopefully, their replacements would soon be found.

As I sat down, John made unintelligible, guttural sounds. I only understood "doctor" and "Maureen." For my benefit, he translated. "This is Miss Maureen, Khonum Maureen. She is a doctor from Canada, replacing Marie-Claire."

Maire-Claire and I had met for a two-hour handover in Herat. By now she was home with her son in sub-Saharan Africa. During our encounter, I had tried to organize the avalanche of information by scribbling bullet points as fast as I could in my new MSF agenda. It felt as if I knew nothing.

Hardy nodded, spluttering sounds so strange that I had no point of reference for them in English or French or in the smattering of words that I knew in other languages. At times, his voice was strained, like at the beginning of a cough that never comes. Sometimes a "g" stuck in his throat, momentarily cutting off sound before being forcibly expelled. Then there was the sound like "rr" in French and the voice-clearing one in Dutch.

While Hardy spoke with John, Laurel sat tall and remained silent. Only his eyes shifted.

Turning toward the two men, John spoke first in English and then in the foreign tongue. It was difficult for me to reconcile the throaty phonetics with his obviously laid-back, outdoorsy British Columbia appearance.

"These are our night guards." John extended a hand toward Hardy. "This is Asif." In the lantern light, an exuberant smile lit Asif's face. Touching his heart with his right hand, he bowed his head slightly and uttered a word that sounded like he was expelling a wad of phlegm. His hand looked like that of a farmer—big, meaty and strong. If we had met in Canada, his hello would have been accompanied by a great big bear hug and a slap on the back.

"Welcome!" John interpreted. I nodded, a smile spreading on my lips.

John motioned to the tall, slim man with hooded eyes, who looked like the Taliban at immigration only his turban was grey like

Momo Rahim's and he wore no kohl makeup. MSF wouldn't knowingly employ Taliban, but anyone can make mistakes. Did his angular face make him look like one of them or was it something else?

"This is Kareem." John extended a palm toward Laurel.

While I wondered about the possibility of Kareem being the enemy, he raised a long-fingered, well-manicured right hand to his heart, quietly muttered a phrase that made no sense to me, then bowed his rectangular head on his bean pole neck far enough so his chin touched his chest. Something intangible about him intrigued me. It was as if I'd glimpsed beyond his mask for a split second.

John said that MSF employed night guards to do odd jobs, to patrol the compound grounds and to answer the door when someone knocked. Bereft of guns, they were a deterrent. Their late afternoon to early morning shift was split in two so they could each sleep for a few hours in a small cupboard-like room beside the kitchen. He mentioned that surprises did happen. Once a deactivated grenade had been lobbed over the exterior wall. Everyone but the expats had laughed. Gosh, how do you know if a grenade has been deactivated?

John's lighthearted tone turned serious. "These two men are my teachers. Without them I would not speak Dari."

Laurel and Hardy had taught John a local language? Not wanting to offend anyone, I covered my surprise by donning the neutral mask that used to help me disappear when I was the new kid at school.

John's soft baritone continued. "You can trust them. They helped me understand a lot about this p-p-place." As the word stuck in his throat, I sensed that he was attached to these two.

With a paw-like hand, Asif slapped John's shoulder. John returned the gesture just as hard. Back and forth they jousted, the play escalating in intensity, just like that of two adolescent boys struggling with feeling vulnerable. Muttering additional foreign sounds, they shoved each other and emitted big, round belly laughs until they bent over in joyous agony. Kareem sat quietly, the corners of his thin lips turned slightly upward, a look of enjoyment in his eyes, as if he too shared their pleasure.

Gasping, Asif used the tail of his turban to wipe his eye, then he faced me. A short torrent of sounds sprang from his lips, beginning with "Asalaam," which means hello. Then he switched to stilted English. "Tea... green tea. Woman's tea." More laughter oozed from the corners of his mouth, as if he was trying hard to contain himself and failing miserably. Handing me a glass filled with steaming yellow-green liquid that looked like what my grandmother called gnat's pee, Asif eked out another word that began with "b." Twice bringing an empty cup to his pudgy lips, he appeared to be demonstrating how to drink tea. As if I wouldn't know!

Once again, John came to my aid. "Asif gave you green tea. Some people call it women's tea. Black tea is known as men's tea, but men drink both kinds, the green variety especially at night because it has less caffeine."

Women's or men's? Who cared as long as women could drink both? Later, I learned that black tea was more expensive than green, which is why, in most households, green tea, called *chai saps*, was more commonly consumed—and perhaps that also explained the his and hers labels.

Asif pointed a meaty finger at his chest and slowly enunciated. "Aw-sif." Opening a palm to the night sky, his index and third fingers pointed at me. "Khon-um Muurr-een."

The way he spoke my name reminded me of the word "myrrh," the essential oil in the story of the Three Wise Men. I liked the way the long "r" rolled off his tongue. The way he pronounced my name sounded softer than the English version of it. Having travelled to many countries, I had long ago decided to accept however my name was pronounced—which, in my opinion, made travelling more fun. Once, in Spain, I had even changed my name to Marina because the villagers' tongues seemed to twist into knots when they tried to pronounce Maureen. Maureen in Afghanistan would do.

"As-sa-laam-a-laik-um." His index finger struck the air as he conducted each syllable from his mouth. He waited a moment before repeating the sounds and baton motions several more times. Once done, he raised a palm upwards, as if anticipating my participation in the lesson.

"Asalm-oo-lake-em," I said, parroting what I remembered as I sang to the beat of his baton. The order of the sounds was next to impossible to retain because I hadn't yet catalogued them in my brain. Salaam was much simpler. Asif nodded and repeated the same sounds again, keeping the beat going with his finger while emphasizing the round "o-like" phonetics of the long "a." Three tries later I had mastered one phrase and was madly trying to figure out how to retain it for future reference before he moved on to the next one. Asif handed a pencil to me and tore out a page of lined paper from his pink cahier like the one I had used in grade two.

"Khonum Murreen, goot." Again, the invisible conductor's wand tapped the air and a different word was spoken. "Wa-a-laik-um-e-sa-laam." John said it was the response to the first word.

The back and forth continued until Asif judged that my pronunciation had met some invisible standard. When he was satisfied, he moved on to "How are you?"; "How is your family?"; "How is your house?" My lesson concluded with a long slurp of tea.

Then he faced John. With their heads close together, words erupted simultaneously from both of them. Urgently they repeated similar sounding phrases in different patterns but at the same time. By their intonations, it sounded like they were asking questions and answering them. It was hard to focus on either voice because the two were so jumbled together. On it went for about a minute. Suddenly, the cacophony ceased. Crickets chirped. Both men ended at the same time. How could they hear what was said by the other person while spewing out so many words? The interlude struck me as rude and disrespectful, but they both seemed happy.

John nodded to me. "That was a typical greeting. How are you? How is your family? How is your house? The children? The farming? The animals? Your father? Your mother? It's a bit long but that's how it's done. It took a lot of practice to say it right. You can learn it too."

I liked that their greeting addressed how a person fared in their environment and linked them to a broader community, but it sure sounded awkward. Our individually focused "How are you?" paled in comparison, but it was a whole lot simpler to say and to disregard.

Asif's smile caused a cascade of wrinkles around each eye. A moment later, his laughter transformed into sternness that didn't really suit him. I almost laughed out loud. When I heard his words, I was glad that I hadn't.

"Khonum Murreen, one wife is good?" He struggled to hold on to his grim expression as a goofy grin threatened to take over. As if shushing himself, he held one finger in front of his impish face.

Should I say what I thought? I had read that Afghan men could have four wives. And women could have one husband. If she was widowed, she couldn't marry again unless his family agreed. I eventually saw this rule in action. The husband of a teacher was reported to have died in battle nine years earlier, but because his body had never been retrieved, his family forbade her to remarry. Eventually, she ran away in the dark of night with a new husband.

That first evening with the guards, I wanted to be careful, to avoid offending anyone. Why had he picked such a minefield for a topic? Of course I believed that one man deserved to have only one wife and then only if he was good to her. "Yes, in Canada one man has only one wife. Here in Afghanistan, it is different. In Afghanistan, maybe one man can have four wives." John interpreted my words while I puzzled over Asif's boldness.

Asif raised his eyebrows and sat upright, his voice insistent. "No, Khonum Murreen. No. Man Kanadayi have two wives." He smiled mischievously. "John is Kanadayi and has two mothers!" He repeated it in Dari for emphasis. Impish eyes dancing in triumph, he raised his glass of gnat's pee, as if toasting a win that no one else had yet recognized.

With a sheepish grin, John expelled a staccato laugh. "My parents divorced when I was young and my father remarried, so I do have two mothers."

Of course, Westerners can remarry after a divorce. At any one time, we think of ourselves as having one spouse. Legally it was true, but emotionally I bet it was all over the map. Children could have many mothers, although one is primary. Afghan men rarely dissolved their old relationships, so their families grew. How many Canadians thought of themselves as having two or more mothers or fathers?

"In Canada, if a husband and wife are divorced, then both husband and wife can marry again, so maybe John has two mothers and two fathers. In Canada, a woman can marry two times just like a man can."

Asif looked from John to me and back again, his grin fizzling. "John has two mothers! No two mothers! Not possible two fathers!" Exhaling a long sigh, he shook his head like a disappointed schoolboy confronted with an impossible answer. Was I pushing him too far this first evening?

"Asif, I have only one father." In the lantern light, John amused himself by making shadow puppets with his fingers. "In Canada, some people have two fathers. If the marriage is broken, a woman in Canada marries another man. He is her second husband." He repeated his words in Dari.

I peered at Kareem, who had remained silent throughout the conversation. At times, a reserved smile had softened his linear mouth and his dark eyes had lit up. Did he know *any* English? MSF paid for language lessons for all Afghan staff, but few of them spoke English well and many didn't at all. Perhaps he was just shy.

"No, wife never marries two men." Whatever battery had fuelled Asif's energy was fading fast.

"A wife does not marry two men at one time. She marries again only after a divorce or if her first husband dies. Just like in Afghanistan, a widow can marry after her husband dies." John translated his own words for Vicky and me.

Asif nodded, but his smile looked forced, as if painted on a clown's face. Kareem, like a tall, straight statue, remained watchfully mute, but his eyes seemed to notice everything.

By learning the language, John seemed to have gained an understanding of who they were and what mattered to them. Did I want to spend time and effort learning a language spoken nowhere else? If I decided to do so, could a lone woman learn it from two misogynous Afghan men like Asif and Kareem? How would that work?

I quickly realized that I wouldn't be able to have meaningful conversations with villagers unless I learned to speak Dari. During an evening chat with farmers, I became acquainted with their process of sifting wheat kernels to remove traces of chaff.

CHAPTER FOUR

FREEDOM

"Freedom lies in being bold."

— Robert Frost

"How do you swim here in Bala Morghab?" It was my second morning in the village. In the living room, I studied the breakfast offerings set out on a plastic tablecloth at the end of a wool carpet. The cook had placed piping hot discs of flatbread beside three blue plastic bowls of gelatinous milk that looked like it was coated with yellow skin and speckled with flecks of what looked like pepper but was probably ash from a wood fire. John, Vicky and I sat cross-legged on large, fuzzy pillows. On the shelves behind us lay a motherlode of goodies furnished by travellers: chocolate, licorice, coffee, pirated DVDs bought for a dollar in a Peshawar bazaar, and dusty second-hand books and news magazines. At the opposite end of the room, concealed behind a heavy curtain, were our illicit television and DVD player, which had to be kept out of sight because they were forbidden under Taliban law.

A subtle popping punctuated our 7 a.m. silence, the kind of sound that you don't notice at first, like the periodic tinkling that sparkling water makes after being poured into a glass. Trying to source it, I scanned the two large white tea thermoses with cutesy pink decals, our teacups—mine full of freshly pressed coffee from the nearby French press—and the jars of jam and Vegemite. Landing on the bowls of milky substance, I noticed tiny bubbles erupting with a pop through cracks in the yellow film. "This is yogurt?"

"Yes, from the neighbour's cow. They make yogurt every morning. Trust me, it's delicious." Vicky pointed upriver. The previous evening when we had walked along raised, muddy banks beside canals, I had noted the cows tethered to trees. They were so bony that it was hard to believe they could generate any milk.

"How safe is it to eat?" The yogurt didn't look very hygienic. Although pasteurized, its surface was reminiscent of a petri dish.

"We eat it every day." Vicky pointed to the actively fermenting bowls. "The bubbles used to bother me. It tastes just a wee bit more

Bathing in the Morghab River was refreshing. I enjoyed many such swims during my first trips to Afghanistan.

tangy when there are bubbles. I've never been sick from the yogurt. We don't drink milk, but yogurt is delicious and a good source of calcium, especially for a vegetarian."

She looked well nourished. I didn't ask how many times she had been sick.

"It must be tough being a vegetarian. Afghans eat a lot of meat, don't they?" I grabbed a loaf of flatbread. It was warm and crusty. When I ripped it open, steam rose up in a puff.

She nodded as she munched on a portion of bread.

Safe for them after living here for nine months, but was it wise for me to consume such a thing this early in my stay? Afghanistan's microbes would be novel to my gut. Perhaps a small bacterial load would build my immunity, but a large one would have me running to the loo. Choosing the most silent bowl, I peeled back the film and spooned about a tablespoon onto my plastic plate.

"You left the best part! The butter!" Vicky grabbed the bowl and scooped out a generous portion of the speckled, yellow skin.

Through the crack in the dark curtain, the sun's rays already felt hot. My memories of running on cool, crisp Vancouver mornings just a month before felt distant. I ate a teaspoon of yogurt, swirling it around in my mouth, ready to spit if necessary. Tasty. Sour. Thick. No grit. Nice. I'd eat it again.

"So yeah, tell me about swimming. Before I decided to come here, I spoke with Josje on the phone and she assured me that you swim and hike here in Bala Morghab." Josje was the medical coordinator in Herat. Our phone conversation had opened the door to this adventure. In Herat, she had told me that MSF didn't officially sanction swimming or hiking; however, given Bala Morghab's remoteness and local security assessments, they considered it a low-risk activity as long as we followed a few basic rules.

"Her assurance that I could be physically active outdoors like you two have been was one of the main factors that led me to accept this mission. Trapped in a compound like the one in Herat, I'd go crazy! I kept imagining myself scaling the walls."

Hearing myself state that outdoor exercise was one of my top priorities sounded really selfish. Hadn't I come to Afghanistan to help the many who suffered so much more than I could imagine from afar? Hadn't I travelled halfway around the world, donating time and skills, so I could witness and give voice to their plights?

I had decided to visit a war zone rather than vacation in Europe or South America. Many people would not have made that choice.

Savouring the taste of freshly cooked bread flavoured with a dollop of sour cherry jam from Hungary, I shrugged off the guilt. Caring for myself, whatever form that took, would allow me to do my best in a place where, from the outside, the needs looked endless. To help themselves cope, some people eat chocolate. Others watch movies. I go outside. I always have. I had an inkling that if I didn't pay close attention to my own needs, the never-ending suffering of the people here would suck the life out of me. I told myself to do whatever it took to top up my energy reservoir. Daily recovery would be important. Exercise had been my therapist for years. When life got tough, running or cycling had always tempered my worries, loosened the constricted sense in my chest and helped me breathe easier.

"Exploring is in my DNA," I continued. "My great-grandmothers were gold rush settlers in the Yukon." I watched them closely to ascertain if we aligned on this topic.

John spooned Vegemite onto a large hunk of bread, then bit into it. "Gold rush folks... sounds interesting."

"Yes, in the late 1890s both of them travelled up there by themselves. One was a chambermaid and the other was a clerk in a store. My grandparents and my mum were born there. So, where do you swim?"

"We drive about ten minutes out of the village, upriver near farmland. One driver mans the radio in the car and the rest of us walk a short distance along dikes to the river. We go in the morning when farmers are busy so we can avoid attracting too much attention. Most Afghans don't know how to swim, so they are curious. I used to be a lifeguard and taught our staff from Herat how to swim. We've never had any problems." He slurped tea, then chewed a piece of bread.

I turned to Vicky, who had finished her bowl of yogurt and was spreading Vegemite on a thick piece of bread. "What do you wear?"

"We swim in a shalwar kameez and chador, like we wear every day. I tie my chador under my chin so it doesn't fall off in the water. It's not so bad. Wearing a swimsuit is not an option. Nor are shorts. You get used to the drag of clothing. You'll see. But you can still swim!"

I imagined the pull of the water causing my gigantic shalwar to slip off and float downriver, the kameez tails winding around my thighs. Not quite what I had hoped for but an adventure nonetheless and, potentially, a good story for later. I spooned more sour cherry jam onto my bread.

"Essentially, we walk upriver and float down." John sucked in more tea, the sound reminding me of Asif the previous evening.

"You just float? You don't swim?" I didn't want to float lazily downriver like people do in inner tubes. My body loved to work hard, to feel that release of whatever was pent up inside it. Floating wouldn't cut it.

"I swim against the current. You can swim as hard as you want, although you don't go anywhere. Most staff just bob downriver to the spot where we get out—the beach. It's refreshing." John sounded tired, or bored.

"What about mines? Has the river been de-mined?" The mine-awareness course in Herat had done its work. Mines could be anywhere, just like avalanches in the backcountry when ski touring. Any good ski slope could slide. You had to assess the risk. Even after de-mining, erosion could cause the explosives that were buried deep to surface. Shifting sands.

Twirling a spoon in the near-empty jar of Vegemite, John smeared a bit more onto a bite of flatbread. "We were told that the stretch of river where we swim was never mined, which makes sense because the closest bridges that the military would have been concerned about are far away. The next upstream bridge is miles away and downstream the closest one is the one you drove over when entering the village. They used to store mines in the old cotton warehouse near the bridge until we told them that location was too dangerous. Initially, we felt excited when the Taliban agreed to move them. Then, we found out that everything was transferred to a rundown warehouse, a two-minute walk from here. If they go off, the whole town is toast."

He shrugged. "We leave that problem with you. A lot of them probably won't detonate anyhow. You just don't know which ones." When he smiled, a lock of curly brown hair fell over his dark eyes. "Now, to swimming. In Afghanistan, nothing is guaranteed. You have to balance the risks. Some people wouldn't feel comfortable swimming at that spot, but we feel safe and so do the staff. You decide for yourself." He looked down.

Had he become complacent? I wondered. In nine months, what would my sense of normal be?

Vicky dribbled preserves onto a chunk of bread. "But we are careful. We jump off a fallen tree and never touch the riverbed, not even with our feet. I swim as far toward the beach as I can and only walk the last few feet. Vicky and I were planning to go this Friday, our last day. Want to come?"

Like a yogi, John gracefully stood up, his legs still crossed. "When walking from the vehicle to the river, we trek along well-trodden trails. Vicky and I were planning to go this Friday, our last day. Want to come?"

Friday, the Islamic holy day, was our one day off each week. Early on Saturday, they would head to Herat, so it was our only chance.

Just then Martin, the project coordinator, walked in, stood in front of the thermos containing hot water and scratched his head, as if trying to kick-start his brain. Vicky had told me that he made moonshine in the sauna. Maybe he was hungover.

"Good morning," Vicky and I called out.

"Another beautiful Afghan morning," he grumbled, his words barely audible. Opening the tin of Lazzaro coffee that I had brought, he slowly ladled grounds into the French press. His hand trembled. Coffee was precious. We couldn't buy it in Afghanistan, so we relied on the charity of visitors. He pumped the thermos, which sounded like a panting pug dog. Hot water billowed out of its mouth. Was this his usual morning personality?

"Want to go swimming on Friday?" Behind Martin, John spoke while shaking his head, as if anticipating a refusal.

"Swimming? What? Non!" Martin tore off a section of bread, throwing the rest of it back onto the tablecloth. He ate it dry.

That Friday at 10 a.m., John, Vicky and I piled into the back seat of a Land Cruiser. Nine Afghan staff from Herat and Qala-I-Nau, who lived together in a nearby compound, filled the remaining spaces in our vehicle and another one just like it. Convoy-style, we exited the compound, following the route that led to the bridge at the entrance to town. At the military checkpoint, Taliban guards waved to us, tea in hand and Kalashnikovs slung over shoulders. Dust, churned up from our tires, sprinkled them like fine, powdery snow.

We passed grazing sheep and goats, then fields of corn and of opium poppies. Arriving in Bala Morghab for the first time a few days before, I had been awed by the showy pink blossoms whose petals billowed in the breeze. On a walk a week or two later, Momo Rahim would demonstrate how opium resin was harvested from seed pods. Each evening, they used a sharp knife to painstakingly score the pods and then, at first light, they harvested the exuded brown goo. While he explained the process, I snapped photos—trying to do so unobtrusively, even though no one else was around. You never knew when the Taliban's morality police would show up and catch you at something illegal like taking photographs that might have a person in the background! John had assured me that no one but the Taliban cared if I took photos; however, if someone was in the image, I had to ask their permission. Some villagers believed that photographs stole their souls.

A few minutes later, we bumped along a winding dirt path bordered by tall adobe walls. The track was just wide enough for our trucks to pass with exterior mirrors retracted. Under a mulberry tree, water tumbled through an irrigation canal. Reza, an interpreter, said that farmers paid the canal owner per unit volume of water flowing into a field, which was estimated by a wooden tool. Canal owners were wealthy because pretty much any land in the desert-like valley required irrigation if crops were to grow. What intrigued me was learning that almost all canals in Afghanistan were gravity fed, silent except for the whoosh of water.

Zia, our head driver, volunteered to stay with the vehicles. His family lived in Qala-I-Nau, the halfway point on our drive from Herat. Like most of our out-of-town staff, he was ethnically a Tajik, spoke Dari and looked Caucasian. Most of the staff from Bala Morghab were Pashtun, a darker-skinned, narrower-faced group, like Kareem and Momo Rahim. Although these ethnic groups had for decades fought against each other in wars, our staff seemed to get along well. From what I could see, the only time that ethnicity seemed to come up was in schoolboy-like jokes.

Having left Zia near the cars, where he covertly watched a young woman wash clothes in the canal several metres away, the rest of us headed single file along one of the dikes toward the sound of rushing water.

John and the Afghans removed their kameezes and carefully placed bundles of clothing on grass near the "beach," a muddy area right beside the river. Vicky and I headed upstream to an area where grass and bamboo provided a semblance of privacy. There, we balanced towels, a change of clothing and a bottle of water on grassy hummocks. Traipsing back through mulberry, bamboo and poplar trees, we eventually caught up to the procession of skinny, barefooted staff, dressed in ill-fitting pants that were cinched in at the waist by drawstrings. They looked like a gang of Tom Sawyers preparing to float downriver on a homemade raft. Some of them covered their scrawny chests with long singlets that extended to their knees like a dress, only the arm holes were so enormous that their undernourished bodies were plainly visible. Scanning their torsos, I searched for battle scars. How many of these young men had been soldiers?

At a bend where the Morghab River's clear water became muddy, we stood on a sturdy tree that shot out of the bank at a thirty-degree angle and extended over the water. Lining up single file, the staff giggled and guffawed, shoving each other like adolescent boys do when they are not sure what is expected of them. When John spoke sternly, they stopped horsing around.

First in line was the logistics assistant. Cinching in the drawstring of his shalwar, he tucked the ends inside the pants and cried a torrent of words wrapped around the only ones I understood, which were "Khonum Murreen." Then, butt first, he splashed into the river. John translated. "He said, 'Look Miss Maureen. It's easy! Come join us.'"

Rising to the surface, he snorted, smearing snot across his cheeks with the back of his hand. A magnificent smile lit up his face, dimples forming in either cheek. While floating, he set to work capturing air in his shalwar until it ballooned around him like a makeshift inner tube, buoying him like a cork that bobbed in an eddy by the tree. One by one his colleagues followed, each performing the same cinching, tucking, ballooning and bobbing manoeuvres. They waited near the tree trunk where John, Vicky and I stood.

John tucked himself into a cannonball and landed with an impressive splash. He floated downstream for a bit before swimming back against the current to the log, where he latched his legs onto a thick branch and waited with the others.

I pulled my shalwar drawstring really snug. I'd seen how these guys unapologetically teased each other and didn't want to be the butt of their jokes. Not yet, anyway. What would they do if I lost my pants?! Next, I knotted my chador under my chin like an old Ukrainian babushka. Vicky nodded. I was ready. Briefly surveying the water for floating debris and rocks, I faced backwards, squatted and tipped in ass first, my hand securing my chador in a modified scuba entry. Refreshing water swallowed me whole. The robes I wore wrapped tightly around me like a second skin. My body luxuriated in the coolness of the moment. Afraid of touching the bottom, I curled into a ball. I shut my eyes in an attempt to avoid any microbes that might cause diarrhea, river blindness or anything else. As I rose in the silty water, my kameez played in the eddies and my shalwar bunched like monstrous balloon shorts. My chador remained tight around my chin, covering any sex appeal represented by my hair.

Fluttering my arms in a simple synchronized swimming manoeuvre, I glided along the surface toward the tree and waited for Vicky. Once she was in, I breaststroked over to where the current flowed fastest. Head above the water, I pumped my arms and legs furiously in a fight against a river that continually pushed me downstream. Refusing to give in, I switched to front crawl and focused. Breathing hard, everything disappeared except the rhythm of the stroke and the might of the current. Through my chador, the sun baked my scalp while cool water and bubbles tickled my bare thighs. In my peripheral vision, a bush on shore stayed at the same point. I imagined a globe with me on one side and Vancouver on the other. I was swimming on the opposite side of the world! Even more cool was the fact that I was swimming in Afghanistan, a country where women don't do that.

Paranoid of the microbes that surely swam with me, I spat twice each time water splashed onto my face. Everywhere I looked, sheep and goats grazed or crops grew. Few houses in Bala Morghab had latrines, so people defecated in fields. Poop was used as fertilizer. The water must have been full of it too.

Suddenly, I was alone. My arms and legs went taut, my breath constricted, and I stroked harder, like I was trying to catch up. As the nerdy second child, I had a fear of missing out, of not noticing a signal that was obvious to everyone else, including my more popular and socially gifted older sister. Consciously, I slowed my movements. Two boys with shepherd's hooks watched me, their nearby sheep chomping mouthfuls of grass. Were the Taliban nearby? Probably not. I turned onto my back and bobbed like a log downstream while water licked my ears and neck and my toes baked in the sun. Gazing at the crescent moon against clear blue sky, I floated toward the distant chatter and whoops that were partially muffled by the babbling of the river. When I arrived at the beach, the staff were shivering on the muddy bank.

John's muscular torso glistened, and puddles formed where his feet had ground into the mud. "Want to do it again?" His voice was calmly excited.

"Absolutely!" I paddled slowly toward him while keeping my body submerged in the shallow water. Then I watched Vicky demonstrate what to do next. Slowly, they moved along the dike, glancing back a few times until they disappeared into the bamboo forest. Only then did he offer Vicky a towel, which he feigned dropping just as she reached out.

"Don't you dare!" She snatched it from him, then shooed him away so she could finish tucking herself into the towel while he followed the others through the bamboo. She wrapped me in a terry-cloth sheet and I began rubbing my body with it. "Now we dry our kameezes until they no longer cling. In such dry air, it takes just a minute."

The staff waited and watched, probably hoping for a glimpse of female nudity, but John growled and his body language told them to scram. Slowly, they moved along the dike, glancing back a few times until they disappeared into the bamboo forest. Only then did he offer Vicky a towel, which he feigned dropping just as she reached out.

Glancing down, I could see my nipples and the small mound of my pubic hair through the garments, but after about a minute of rubbing, the light cotton billowed outward in the breeze and I felt more presentable, once again ready to meet our Afghan team.

"Let's go!" Vicky's excitement mirrored my own. Laughing, we scampered down the path of hard-packed clay, all the while holding our kameezes out like cormorant wings with our fingertips.

While jogging along the path, I once again tightened my shal-war drawstring, and I shook my chador loose so I could retie the ends into a sturdy knot. When we arrived at the tree, the staff were floating lazily in the water nearby and John was swimming stationary laps. They looked up.

Vicky and I each cannonballed into the current. After that, I again pitted my strength against the river, moving into or away from its point of maximum strength, so I could remain parallel to a bush on shore. The song "Flashdance... What a Feeling" by Irene Cara played in my head, as it did during my medical school graduation day when we were all mesmerized by hope, passion and excitement for what was to come. As I swam, I was cognizant only of the moment, until the refrain in my head ended and I noticed five boys squatting on the hillside, silently observing our every move while their sheep nonchalantly grazed. A lamb plaintively baaed. A ewe answered. Rolling onto my back, I relaxed, and the current steered me where it wanted.

"Shepherds. They won't come down." John's voice sounded far away. I lost myself in the moment once more. If I could fill my weekends with rejuvenating experiences like these, I might like it here after all.

When I exited the river for the third time, our staff from Bala Morghab had joined the swimmers on the beach and were setting up a picnic to celebrate John and Vicky's departure the next day. Kebabs, pilau, zucchini, tea and orange pop were laid out on plastic tablecloths on the ground. I would miss their adventurous spirits and sure hoped that their replacements would be just as much fun.

We often celebrated the arrivals and departures of staff with picnics. Here, a splendid soup simmers over an open fire in a pit.

CHAPTER FIVE

A TIME WARP

"The art of simplicity is a puzzle of complexity."

— *Douglas Horton*

John and Vicky's team had refurbished two-thirds of an old hospital to create the clinic. In the dilapidated part of the building, rebar poked through broken concrete walls like toy soldiers. On the disintegrating cement, blue painted letters spelling OMAR in large Roman and Arabic script publicized that mines had been removed from the area. (OMAR stands for the Organization for Mine Clearance and Afghan Rehabilitation, an NGO founded in 1990 that removes mines in Afghanistan and spreads awareness about them.) Less than a month before my arrival in Bala Morghab, a villager discovered an anti-tank mine in the fort, a five-minute walk from our compound. OMAR had already completed its work there. Sometimes deeply buried mines were missed and only later rose to the surface to be discovered. De-miners had to be meticulous. When they messed up, fingers, hands or lives vanished. Their tools were simple: shovels, knives, metal detectors and a good dose of courage balanced with fear.

At the clinic, injuries from explosives, bullets, car crashes and falls were common. We also saw women worried about fertility or giving birth to their umpteenth baby. Infectious diseases such as typhoid, malaria, polio, pneumonia, meningitis and diarrhea were our most frequent guests, along with vague aches and pains that I believed were caused or worsened by anxiety.

At noon one day, a shepherd from a village six hours away pushed a wheelbarrow into the minor surgery room. In it, layers of burlap padded the body of an eight-year-old boy. Not a single muscle twitched. After hearing an explosion, then finding a dismembered goat's carcass splattered on the plateau, the father had found his son far below at the base of a cliff. I imagined the terrified youngster running away from the threat and tumbling down the rock face. Taking a closer look, I noticed brain tissue oozing out onto the burlap. Brain I squashed my impulse to push it back into its rightful home. Brain

One part of the Bala Morghab clinic had yet to be renovated. The writing on the wall in Roman and Arabic script indicated that mines from the surrounding area had been removed.

tissue didn't belong on a burlap bag. The "dresser," the white-haired medic who did minor surgery and dressed wounds, washed the gash with a waterfall of saline that splattered onto his trousers. He had learned surgical techniques while trying to survive in a game of trial and error during the war. He had seen and repaired a multitude of amputations, way more than I had. Consequently, he was hard to rile. As he cleaned the wound, our eyes met. The boy's prognosis was grim.

With a gloved finger, I gently pushed the brain back inside the skull, then palpated the surrounding area for rocks, sticks and other foreign objects. The dresser sanitized the area again, then wrapped a dressing around the boy's head, making him look like a Hollywood soldier. The boy was breathing, but otherwise still. He would never wake up.

"Your boy is with God. We cannot save him, but he can be comfortable." I paused to give his dad time to digest the gut-wrenching message that no one ever wanted to hear. "He will live only a few more days. It is good to sing to him and to pray. He might like to hear stories about memories that are important to you. Hold him. He will know your touch."

His mother cried out, the anguished sound of a heart breaking. An old man watched from afar, his dry eyes relieved that he wasn't a main character in this story, yet he appeared acutely aware of the parents' emotions, as if he too had felt the same sorrow. The dresser handed the father a paper bag brimming with sterile bandages, gauze, tape and antibiotic ointment. It was the least we could do. Momo Rahim gave him another bag with syringes, painkillers and antibiotics. Treating their son would be their therapy. We taught them a clean technique for injecting the drugs that we gave them, and we doled out enough needles so they could use a new one each time. Families often used the same needle until it no longer punctured skin. Not knowing germ theory, they had other stories that described how diseases spread.

Each day, I wondered whether the boy still lived. Sometimes, I imagined a full recovery, the boy waking and running after a lamb that had escaped. I hoped in vain that my medical opinion was wrong, but any other outcome was impossible. What I really wished for was a fast resolution, that he would live just long enough for the family to begin healing.

Five days later, his father returned to request more bandages. Although still breathing, his son responded to nothing, not even pain. With sad eyes, he thanked us for our work and our kindness. We had so little to give a patient with such a severe injury. Hands on our hearts, we shared the farewell greeting "Go with God," as he headed back into the desert, his solitary figure accompanied by a long shadow bobbing along beside him. With a heavy heart, I watched him disappear from my life.

Living in an environment littered with mines changed what I worried about. When out walking, I trained myself to stay on paths and never pick up trash. It might explode. The behaviour was so ingrained that when I later returned to Canada, stepping into the bush for a pee caused my heart to pound. No longer did I pick up litter. You just never know.

In Afghanistan, I kept an eye out for coloured stones. OMAR painted some of them scarlet red to indicate mines had been found nearby. Two white stones meant that the area in between them had been cleared of explosives. I no longer recall what blue meant. I stayed far away from all of them.

One day, an Afghan interpreter and I took a shortcut back to the village through a valley that I had never explored. I revelled in the peaceful solitude there, a sense of contentment welling up from my abdomen. We had been deep in conversation when a chaotic pattern of red, blue and white stones appeared in front of us. Had the area been cleared? Was the work unfinished? Or had mischievous children played a game with the stones? My throat constricted. What if my leg got blown off just because I had meandered meditatively along a goat track. My body felt tense. My feet glued themselves to the ground. Heart racing and fists clenched, I turned to my companion: "There could be mines here. We must walk backward."

Holding my breath, I carefully placed a foot exactly overtop of the print that I had left in the dust moments before. Silence. Whew! Another backward step. We smiled sheepishly at each other. This shouldn't have happened. We were close enough that if one of us triggered an explosion, both of us would be maimed. As the sun hit the horizon, we made it to safety. The entire way back to the village, cold sweat trickled between my shoulder blades as I scanned for ominous stones.

My companion laughed, his eyes trying to read my face. "Khonum Murreen, it is okay. We are safe. We will be just a little late."

I clicked the radio button on the VHF handset and spoke. "Bravo base, Bravo base, do you copy?" When they did, I continued. "It's Maureen and Sahi. We will arrive in thirty minutes." They copied. I relaxed. We knew the way home.

During the summer, cholera grew in the Morghab River. We set up treatment centres in tents with hand-washing stations and disinfectant pools for people to walk through when entering or exiting the clinics. We admitted only the sickest patients, who lay exhausted on cots that doubled as latrines—holes in the canvas that allowed excrement to fall into a bucket that was eventually whisked away by family members. Rows of these cots lay side by side. Privacy was a luxury that MSF didn't offer. We doled out free oral rehydration salts and chlorine so people could disinfect drinking water. Momo Rahim and I identified passages from the Holy Koran that listed simple actions people should do to stay healthy. Blessed by a high-ranking mullah, our notices were posted in every mosque in the valley. Volunteers with loudspeakers, like town criers of yore, visited bazaars and mosques while reciting the Koranic excerpts. Illiterate birthing attendants notified women by going house to house. Cholera was preventable. You just needed to boil or chlorinate water and wash your hands. During the epidemic, villagers followed our advice and thanked Allah that they didn't get sick. But once the epidemic abated, they reverted to drinking unpurified river water because it tasted better and because their ancestors had consumed it for centuries.

At the clinic, Momo Rahim was my right-hand man. With his salt and pepper hair and long beard, he was a *riche safet*, which literally means "white beard" and signifies that a man is no longer a threat to other men's wives and daughters. The concept made me smile. Momo Rahim's riche safet status was a godsend for me because I had no female interpreters. When we interviewed women, he followed a strict code. He would sit in the same room as married women with children, who were considered old, but if they were younger than twenty-five, he would translate through a curtain or a doorway, his deep voice projected to us as if from a loudspeaker. Out of sight, he could even ask questions about their fertility and menstruation. As I became more skilled in Dari, he only asked questions periodically to ensure that I hadn't missed anything important. Sometimes, during our walks home, he would tell me that he had peeked at a young woman, his words uttered with nostalgia, as if he wished he could rewind time to a freer era.

At times, I found him staring at nothing and he would smile bashfully. "I am sorry, Khonum Murreen. It is my memories. Nothing good comes from speaking about them." Only once or twice did he share them. "Dr. Murreen, Kabul University used to be so beautiful. Pretty roses and so many beautiful girls. Yes, in miniskirts!" For a brief moment, his sad eyes sparkled with a zest for life.

In the clinic, the Taliban had insisted that we construct barricades between the male and female sides. A fence made of white oil drums full of red geraniums served this purpose but also became a magnet for voyeurs of both sexes. Under the guise of enjoying the beautiful flowers, they could peek across at the opposite sex, yearning for what couldn't be. The Taliban threatened to close the clinic, so we employed a guard to shoo men and women away from temptation. Momo Rahim and I used to joke about that conundrum.

On the male side of the clinic, Nazim, an experienced medic, saw most patients. At times, he enlisted help from Dr. Saachi or me. One day, he hurried toward Momo Rahim and me. His jaw was tense and a torrent of words rushed out of his mouth. I understood "sick,"

Villagers from near and far travelled by foot or by animal to the Bala Morghab clinic. I often caught myself wondering if I had been transported several centuries back in time.

which sounded like *malaise* in French, except that "l" was replaced with "r." I also recognized the names of two drugs, ketamine and midazolam, that are used to rapidly sedate patients before medical procedures. While he spoke, I scrolled through my mental formulary of the drugs' uses and warnings.

"Doktar Murreen, we need midazolam! The boy has—" and the rest was unintelligible. Momo Rahim's forehead scrunched into a leathery frown and he said nothing. Medics couldn't order sedatives that might cause a respiratory arrest, but I could.

"What sickness does the boy have?" I addressed Nazim, but my eyes again sought out Momo Rahim, who scratched his brow, a puzzled look on his face.

"Come and see. You know it. I am sure." Nazim turned around and scurried back toward the clinic room, beckoning to us.

As Momo Rahim bustled beside me, he whispered softly, "That word in English, I can't recall."

At the entrance to the men's clinic, Nazim screeched to a halt. Placing his right hand on his heart, he motioned to me with his left hand. "Bafarmin." After you.

Momo Rahim stood behind him, a palm outstretched.

Doorway etiquette in Afghanistan is important. Everyone must feel respected. To a foreigner, it is a confusing process. The first person to arrive at the door offers passage to the person with the highest status in the group. This time, that was me. That person is supposed to refuse to proceed and insist that others enter first. A negotiation ensues to determine the appropriate hierarchy. Ideally, everyone wins. The person who loses the negotiation passes through first, so they are held in high regard. The person who wins the argument passes through last because they won. In the past, my attempts to play this game had slowed us down, so I hid behind my ignorance and complied with whatever they told me to do. When worried about a patient, who had time for such details? I just hoped that they didn't think that I was rude or self-important.

As I walked through the doorway, Nazim spoke in English mixed with Dari. "The pharmacist says expiration for midazolam is soon. We must use it before expiration. Last year Dr. Saachi used it for this problem. She showed me."

Midazolam, a rapidly acting benzodiazepine, was the kind of drug that I wanted solid justification for before administering. Using it up because of an expiry date just didn't cut it.

Up ahead, a boy about five years old leaned against the outer wall of a clinic room and calmly watched us approach. He was pushing a Tetra Pak juice container around with a stick. The sunlight highlighted red and golden hues in his ash brown hair. His father calmly conversed with another man.

Momo Rahim stopped so abruptly that I nearly bumped into him, two of his fingers touching his eyebrow, as if an idea was forming. "A worm that swells up and when you kill it, it bleeds."

"A leech?" Why would Nazim want to sedate a kid with a leech? Rural Afghans were colossally independent, do-it-yourself people who reminded me of the hearty Newfoundland fishermen I had met. Afghans repaired their own lacerations, extracted abscessed teeth and tried all sorts of manoeuvres to "help" women give birth, so why hadn't the father removed the leech?

Momo Rahim's eyes brightened. "Yes, a leech. That is the worm that sticks to the skin and sucks the blood. Sometimes we use them to treat too thick blood." His cousin and uncle had received phlebotomy treatments with leeches for a familial condition known as hemochromatosis.

"Yes, it sticks onto the skin and when it falls off, it leaves a sore that bleeds. In Canada, we don't use leeches anymore for treatment of thick blood. But many years ago, we did." Medical textbooks describe the historical method of bloodletting as a way of removing toxic humours that, prior to the nineteenth century, were believed to cause a multitude of diseases. I had only ever experienced leeches while on a week-long trek in Laos. Upon removing my hiking shoes at the end of a long day, my soggy, grey socks had developed crimson polka dots. In my shoes lay squished corpses. Sores on my feet bled.

"I thought Afghanistan was too dry for leeches," I said with a shudder.

"We have only a few kinds." Momo Rahim smiled at the boy and ruffled his hair.

I turned to Nazim. "Tell me why you need midazolam?" The boy looked so healthy, and his father seemed unconcerned.

"Be gulu hast! Mushgil dorat." He opened his mouth and pointed down his throat.

"How does a leech get into the throat?" Had he swallowed one on a dare from an older brother?

"Children drink water from the buckets in open wells." Momo Rahim watched as I thought about how frequently I recommended well water even when I knew they used buckets hanging from ropes. Not everyone had access to the enclosed kinds that protect water from microbes and other beasties.

Momo Rahim continued: "Leeches hide under the lip at the edge of buckets that are not cleaned regularly. Next time, look closely and you will see them. Children never check. This problem happens often."

"Leeches fall off when they have eaten enough blood. This one will let go soon. Are you worried that the child will stop breathing?" As I counted, I watched the boy's chest rise and fall in an easy rhythm. No wheezy sounds suggested a blocked airway. He seemed content to play his made-up game.

"Yes, soon the leech becomes very fat." Nazim shot a worried look toward the happy child.

"Do leeches often block children's airways?" I asked Nazim, then turned to the boy. "As salaam alaikum."

"Wa alaikum e salaam." The miniature man placed a hand on his heart, his feet in a sturdy stance. My heart melted. He enunciated well, even the glottal stop. There was no hot potato voice, cough or gag. My preliminary assessment suggested a patent airway. Would it stay that way?

"I am Dr. Maureen. Open your mouth." I had learned that if doctors in Afghanistan didn't get down to business quickly, patients thought we didn't know what we were doing. Afghan doctors waded through a hundred or more patients per day.

The boy hesitated. Was he ashamed of what wiggled in his throat or had I mangled the words? Imagining a leech in my own throat, I almost retched. Few things in medicine get under my skin. Slimy, airway mucous was one of them. Momo Rahim repeated my command. Both of us opened our mouths. The boy started to comply, then ran into his dad's arms. With his son in front of him, the boy's father wrapped an arm around the child's limbs and torso, his other hand pushing the boy's head backward into the father's chest. "Waz ko!" he commanded gently. By then all four of us had our tongues sticking out, but the boy's mouth was clamped shut, as if he knew what was coming.

As we waited, the father described how his son had complained that he couldn't swallow, that something was stuck in his throat.

When the mouth opened, Nazim and I moved in, wooden tongue depressor sneaking in quickly to hold the tongue out of the way. Momo Rahim peered in too. The brownish-grey worm looked like a minute sausage dangling in front of the uvula, the pendulous part of the soft palate that you often see depicted in cartoons. Six more of them could fit in the back of this kid's throat before obliterating his airway. I couldn't imagine a leech becoming big enough to block his breathing.

"What is the biggest leech you have seen in Afghanistan?" I asked.

Momo Rahim brought his little finger up to his chin. "Like this." So about as big as this one. The risk of a bad outcome was very small. Nevertheless, I preferred to remove it.

"Get him to gargle with salty tea. That should kill the leech." I told him how much salt to mix with a cup of tea. Nazim looked disappointed. I mimed gargling. I had chosen tea rather than water because tea had fewer microbes in it. Afghan kids were used to it and every office in the clinic had a tea thermos. Tea in an Afghan workplace was akin to purified water in Canada.

Nazim, Momo Rahim and the father bowed together in conversation. I waited on the sidelines, anticipating a backlash against my simple solution.

Momo Rahim interpreted. "Nazim did not try this before. He thinks maybe midazolam is a good idea. Once he is sleepy, we grab the leech with forceps. Nazim already tried to remove the leech but the boy vomited."

"Midazolam is more risky than salty tea. Encourage the child to gargle. It will taste awful, but it will kill the leech. It is a simple solution that the man can repeat at home if he has this problem again. If gargling doesn't work, we will use a topical anaesthetic and remove the leech with forceps." In remote parts of Canada, I had learned to appreciate simple forms of treatment. "Try it. I will come back in a few minutes. Do not use anaesthetic before he gargles. If you do, he may swallow the tea into his lung and then get pneumonia."

Momo Rahim and I left Nazim and the father with their mouths open, demonstrating the art of gargling to a five-year-old.

Ten minutes later, we returned to check their handiwork. Bowing slightly, hand on his heart, the father thanked all three of us, his eyes lingering for a split second longer on mine. The boy had retched. The leech was gone. The child proudly opened his mouth. A trickle of blood oozed from a tiny sore, the only remaining evidence of the critter.

"He did not spit the leech out. Maybe he swallowed it?" Nazim spoke quickly in a high-pitched tone. "What is the possibility that the leech causes bleeding inside? Will he need an operation?"

It was a good question. "If the leech was alive, it would no longer be hungry. The salt should have killed it. If it didn't, stomach acid would. The boy is safe." His young body would rapidly seal the tiny wound.

"Tashakoor. Be man e khuda." Hands on their hearts, the little man and his father thanked us for a job well done.

CHAPTER SIX

TRUST

"When we try to pick out anything by itself, we find it hitched to every-thing else in the Universe."

—*John Muir*

Inside the barricaded MSF compound, the only place where I could see any of the outside world was at the top of a steep slope in our backyard orchard. A small adobe mosque's minaret poked skyward above mulberry trees that shaded the neighbourhood *madrassa*, the religious school where boys studied the Holy Koran as they strove to learn reading and writing. Five times a day an innocent, prepu-bescent voice floated in the silence and cracked on the high notes as it called everyone to pray. It was a naturally amplified and innocent song that crescendoed to a climax, then faded into the sweet sounds of animals and birds.

For too many days, the only expat I had lived with was Martin. During the daytime, the compound brimmed with the Afghan men he directed, but at night, once the generator was switched off, it was a silent place. I felt alone. Twice a day Momo Rahim walked with me to and from the clinic, even though MSF guidance stated that I was supposed to be driven there with an expat man. This escape was of-ten the highlight of my day, when I got to observe the sprouting rice and wheat in the nearby fields, or saw how people transported their possessions on donkeys and camels or watched men in fields share what looked like relaxed but earnest conversation.

Like a tour guide, Momo Rahim answered any question that I asked. One day, two minutes from our compound, we passed a large adobe building with no signage.

"In here are the baths. Most villagers bathe once a week. Every-one bathes together in a big pool. I never go there. The water that flows out of the lower pool is black! I am lucky. My lovely wife pre-pares hot water for me at home." His warm smile was accompanied by a glint in his eye. "The best days to go to the baths are yak-sham-bé or du-shambé."

I stayed calm and centred by walking the paths of Bala Morghab with Momo Rahim, who introduced me to everyone we met.

Having started to learn the language, I translated the Dari words. *Shambé* was Saturday. *Yak* was one. Saturday plus one was Sunday. *Du* was two, so *du-shambé* was Monday.

"Those are the quietest days. Most people bathe on chor-shambé or panj-shambé so they are ready to be together with their wives on juma." He had placed two index fingers side by side and rubbed them together, his eyes shining, as if he was daring to share a secret that I had no business knowing. I confirmed what he was insinuating: that everyone in Afghanistan made love on Friday night. So Afghans did rock 'n' roll!

"Do women go to the baths? Or do they bathe at home?" Maybe I could go in one day, he suggested. My stomach clenched. Perhaps women in the village were cleaner than men. A tour was out of the question, and I wasn't prepared to bare myself as a way of joining in. He told me that one day each week was reserved for women, and I imagined him wishing that he could be a fly on the wall on those days.

Over the previous weeks, I had amused myself by studying Dari. At the night guards' insistence, I had continued John's tradition of drinking tea with them while practising Dari words and teaching them English ones. It was a nice diversion of lighthearted human contact with two people who didn't seem to want anything from me but my company. I had planned on perfecting my Spanish skills and had even brought a Spanish study guide. To me, it was a more useful language, but I quickly realized that being able to say and understand a few words in Dari was a fast ticket to be able to enter people's homes—and that's where women were. By the end of the first week, I knew how to say the days of the week and how to count to twenty, and I had memorized a set of nouns and verbs that was expanding by ten words each day. Every night, I repeated them before falling asleep, and I reviewed them again in the morning as I got ready for the day. Then I practised them at the clinic at every opportunity. Hundreds of people waited impatiently to see one of the four health care workers I supported: Dr. Saachi, who was a medical doctor from Kabul; the midwife from Maza'ar-I-Shirif; and the two male medics from Bala Morghab. To strengthen their diagnostic and treatment skills, I backed them up whenever my medical opinion was needed. This approach led to a more sustainable outcome than if I was to provide direct patient care. Each time I uttered a few words in Dari, the room became friendly, as if I'd stepped off my foreigner pedestal and joined locals in some meaningful way.

And yet, my world felt like it had shrunk. I felt suffocated. Once again, I schemed of ways to climb over the back wall so I could walk freely along the riverbank, or run along the dikes in the fields, or even sit in the shade under an apricot tree. Villagers' daily routines were fascinating to me. I had never lived such a simple life. Time in Bala Morghab moved at a snail's pace—which gave someone like me, who had always been so busy, an opportunity to slow down, and to appreciate simple pleasures such as the many colours of the sky, the golden hues in the wheat or a kindly conversation.

As the days passed, my urge to escape the compound escalated. I tried yoga routines, dance steps and even shadowboxing with myself or imagined opponents, all of it done in the privacy of my yellow bedroom with the curtains drawn. Although movement diminished my angst, there was still a gnawing sense in my gut. How many months could I tolerate this?

The day John's replacement, Jim, arrived, I crossed my fingers and voiced a quick prayer in hopes that Jim would be another John. Please, please, please, make him want to explore the villages with me. Why would you come to Afghanistan if you weren't interested in learning about the place? From his bio, I knew that he was an overland truck driver from England who had ferried tourists all over Africa on flatbeds. What an adventurer!

The day Jim was slated to arrive, a lanky man in jeans and a T-shirt jumped out of the Land Cruiser. He rolled a cigarette, lit it, then pushed his curly locks away from stark blue eyes. A bluish-brown cloud billowed from his shy smile as he made his way down the reception line. That first day his eyes shone as soon as he saw the automobile pit. He shared ideas about how to improve the compound. He seemed nice enough. But he couldn't understand why anyone would want to go for a walk in the village.

Within days of his arrival, Mary Anne, a Swiss midwife, joined us. She was personable and kind but, after spending the day teaching illiterate women how to assist at deliveries, all she wanted to do was hole up in her room or watch movies on DVD. How was I going to understand the villagers if I didn't have a maharam or, at the very least, a female co-conspirator? I simply wasn't interested in delving into the make-believe of Western-made movies as an escape from such a fascinating place.

Several times, Momo Rahim had saved my sanity. We found reasons to go on house calls and village visits so, as he put it, I wouldn't become sad. At my insistence, we walked whenever the opportunity arose, and he always found an old relic or a bit of history to show me. Neither he nor I thought that walking to these places was dangerous, even though MSF's rules made it clear that driving was the preferred option. In my opinion, walking was the best way to learn as much as possible about villagers' perspectives because Momo Rahim introduced me to everyone.

I didn't blame Jim for wanting to spend his free time tinkering. He had quickly improved the ambiance in our compound. A set of batteries, charged from the generator during the day, created silence from 4 p.m. onward, rather than 9 p.m., which gave us the opportunity to hear the cries of owls, hyenas, jackals and the occasional wolf in the evenings. But it just wasn't enough for me.

One evening as I shadowboxed against an imaginary enemy, I felt particularly frustrated at being confined. I punched an unknown face that could have been anyone's. I was determined to find an acceptable solution and I had an idea.

Using a chador to hide my sweaty shalwar kameez, I walked to the office, where Jim was cleaning a rusty metal pipe. The pungent odour of solvent overpowered the rose scent from the garden. As I spoke, his steely blue eyes peered through unruly locks.

"Jim, for me it is important to get out of the compound and go for a walk. Just twenty minutes would make a big difference. I know you are busy. What if I asked one of the guards to be my maharam? As the person responsible for the team's security, would you agree to that?" Martin had returned to Quebec, and Jim had taken over some of his duties. I watched Jim's dirt-encrusted fingernail pick a rusty flake off the pipe.

His response was quick enough that he didn't seem to think about it. "I don't see why not." He turned back to rubbing steel wool against the pipe.

I had fretted for an entire hour, even planned arguments like I used to do for my dad, because I sensed that Jim had a similar temperament. None of it had been necessary. I couldn't believe that I was free! I skipped to my room, fetched my Nikon camera, then walked directly to Asif and Kareem, who were already sitting on the mat in front of the guard hut, their English cahiers and pencils poised for action.

When they offered me a cushion, I shook my head. "Today we speak English when walking." My index and third finger of one hand stepped across the palm of the other one. Pointing to Asif, Kareem and then myself, I mimed the action again. "You walking. Me walking. One guard here." I pointed to the ground.

"Walking?" Asif's eyebrows lifted and his forehead crinkled. He drew back.

"Outside." I pointed to the large metal door, the barrier between me and where I wanted to go. "Walking outside. It is beautiful to go walking now." I held up my camera, a well-loved gift from a Japanese friend in university I had visited once in Tokyo. "Taking photos." Although the Taliban forbade photographs of people, Momo Rahim had shown me that villagers were often very willing subjects if we had a short conversation before seeking their permission.

Asif, arms folded across his chest, frowned and shot a glance at Kareem. "Walking inside good!" He smiled, but today he looked like a weasel trying to get out of something that he didn't want to do. Who would want to walk inside the compound?

"Jim says: one guard and Doktar Maureen walking now, only twenty minutes. A little like a maharam but not. Which one, Asif or Kareem?" Neither could truly be my maharam since we weren't related or married. I was simply asking them to do what Momo Rahim often did. They were our employees, and I believed that I could trust them. At the time, my brain registered Asif's aversion to my proposal, but I really had no idea how strange my request might appear to two conservative villagers who had never travelled outside of Badghis Province. I was imagining that I could be unobtrusive, formal and respectful even though everyone knew me as the foreign female doctor and they watched everything that I did. There wasn't much other local entertainment. What could go wrong in twenty minutes?

Stepping toward the metal gate, the toe of my shoe drew figures in the dirt as I waited for their decision. The sun was rapidly descending in the pale blue sky. The golden hour of photography was upon us and it was time to shoot film. I tapped my foot.

"One guard come with me." Hand on the latch, I feigned unlocking it. Asif's left eyebrow arched upward and he pointed his chin at Kareem.

I sighed. Why was going for a short walk such a big deal?

Finally, Kareem shrugged, adjusted his turban and stood up. Placing his *patu* over a shoulder and smoothing it with both hands, he watched me position my chador over my hair and tuck in the stray strands, cinching it tight. A patu looked like a man's chador, only it was more versatile. For warmth or sun protection, a patu could be worn over the head, or as a shawl. It also served as a shopping bag, a small suitcase, a pillow, a towel and a bathing suit. Not once that year did I see a villager carry a suitcase. The nicest ones were made of the finest wool and were perfect for any temperature.

The metal gate creaked open. Kareem stood aside, his right arm extending toward the doorway. "Bafarmin." He followed me out while Asif sipped his tea and looked in the opposite direction.

In the deep shade of a large mulberry tree, I walked along a narrow, hard-packed dirt path, then jumped over the irrigation ditch. The pressure in my head and chest abated. We followed a well-trodden, sun-dappled dike to the mosque and madrassa that I could see from our orchard.

A white and grey horse, hitched to a large mulberry tree, nibbled grass. Behind it a red wooden door in an earthen wall was the entrance to someone's compound. I pressed the shutter release and snapped a photograph of the horse in the warm, golden light. Kareem made rapid clicking sounds with his tongue. The horse flicked its mane. Flies rose up from it. Kareem rubbed its neck. The horse nuzzled his hand. It raised a hoof and Kareem turned it over. A shoe was missing.

"Your horse?" The ease with which he interacted with the animal was remarkable.

"No, my cousin's." Rubbing its flank, he gently replaced the hoof. We continued onward. Just beyond the madrassa, a teenage boy I'd seen at the clinic was milking a brown and white cow. An irregular splotch of violet ink covered a bald spot at the top of his head where it periodically brushed against the cow's belly. Fungal infections from cows were common and treated with a medication called gentian violet.

"As salaam alaikum." He smiled at me as I recognized the first words that Asif had taught me.

"Wa alaikum e salaam. Aks mekonam?" I pulled my camera from its bag to illustrate that I was asking for his agreement to be in a photograph.

Before nodding, he furtively looked both ways, as if ensuring that no Taliban were nearby. As the camera approached my eye, his body stiffened. His shy, self-conscious grin turned into a serious, tight-lipped scowl reminiscent of my great-grandparents' expressions in ancient black and white photos. I pretended to take the image, clearing my throat to cover the absent click of the shutter just in case he noticed. Then I mimed milking a cow. He looked puzzled, kept his hands by his sides and his lips glued in that stern expression. Squatting next to the cow's udder, I pretended to rhythmically pull the teats. He and Kareem stared, not comprehending. I stood up and arranged my face to look impassive and I shook my head. Squatting again, I smiled and nodded while miming with my hands.

Finally, I stepped away, ready to give up, but my camera was primed in the event that he had understood my theatrics. He squatted, grasped the teats and a jet of milk sprayed into the bucket. I pressed the shutter release. His grin widened so that his cheeks reached his ears. I snapped another one, my face beaming too, at the joy of connecting with him for a shared moment.

I disliked posed portraits. Even as a kid, I had been the troublesome family member who made faces. I wanted these photographs to replicate the fun and enjoyment that I witnessed in Afghanistan, which was so different from what I had expected, and from anything I had read. Every news report depicted Afghans facing sorrow and strife, as if none of them ever had any fun. Wasn't that perspective rather one-sided?

Kareem chuckled as he patted the cow's neck. When he inhaled, his tongue clicked a rhythm distinct from what he had used with the horse. The cow's ears twitched. Then he turned to me and said, "My son." He touched the boy's shoulder and glanced into the bucket, as if assessing the quality of the boy's work. Then, without another word, he walked off down the path.

"Khud offez." Go with God. I waved to his son and scurried along.

"Be man e khuda." The boy turned back to the cow and the bucket. He squatted, his grin wide.

I caught up to Kareem. "You talk to cows. What do you say?"

Kareem chuckled. "All people talk to cows. Talking to them makes good milk."

After passing the mosque, we crossed the canal on a bridge

that consisted of large pre-formed metal tracks designed for army tanks that had been recovered from a defunct vehicle then embedded deep into the canal's earthen walls. I stopped and stared. Tufts of grass sprouted from the mud that reinforced the structure. While framing an image of the scene, I noticed that the sides of the bridge were fashioned from empty bandoliers linked together, and that farther downstream another canal crossing was made from the hood of an armoured car. Afghans were experts in reusing everything! The environmentalist in me liked the fact that such destructive items could be transformed into community assets for everyone's use.

A few hundred metres down the path, rice stalks grew in a flooded field. "Berenj," Kareem said as he pointed toward the pond. "Mohr hast." His arm wove snake-like in the air and his other finger pointed to a long, irregular, serpentine shape cutting the water.

"Khaternogh?" I had just learned the Dari word for dangerous. The graceful, green body twitched sharply, breaking the expanding ripple pattern.

"Ne, niste. Saps." He shook his head, confirming Momo Rahim's opinion that Afghanistan's green snakes were harmless. I had limited data on which to base any medical opinion. We had no field guide to reptiles in the region, and the project's copy of the textbook *Harrison's Principles of Internal Medicine* only described North American species. I knew that Dr. Saachi never took any chances. She administered antivenom and steroids to all snake bite victims.

Pointing to several plant species in sequence, Kareem slowly pronounced the Dari words and waited patiently after each one for my mangled version of it. He then corrected my diction a few times until it resembled his. I scribbled the phonetics in a notebook that I balanced in the crook of my arm. My new words included: eggplant, zucchini, tomato and sesame seed.

A little farther on, a group of older men, adorned with white turbans that glowed like beacons in the golden light, squatted in a field. Long, crisp shadows mimicked their every action. One man crouched beside a pile of weeds that he was placing by the armful onto his patu, likely dinner for a cow or a goat. His calloused fingers with deep, dirt-encrusted fissures and torn fingernails raked more straw into a pile. Another man used a hoe for the same purpose. A stooped figure, whose face resembled a wizened apple, smoked a cigarette. His chocolate-coloured eyes gazed peacefully at his world.

A lazy plume of smoke twisted upwards in the still air, backlit to perfection by the low angle of the sun.

Hand on his heart, Kareem greeted each farmer. Glancing at me, they nodded at him. They knew who I was. And I recognized Momo Rahim among them.

"Where are you going?"

I missed whose lips had moved.

Shaking hands and touching the farmer's shoulder, Kareem spoke quickly, saying something about walking that he combined with *digh*, a word that meant sad or lonely. The sentence ended with "Doktar Murreen is not Afghan," as if that explained everything.

Sitting beside the others, Momo Rahim contemplated the crops at his feet while inhaling deeply from a cigarette. "Khonum Murreen, don't be sad. You are walking with my nephew. The evening is beautiful. Walking makes the sadness better, doesn't it?" The long ash of his cigarette pointed to Kareem.

"I feel happy when walking outside." I smiled and raised my camera, then asked if I could photograph him. He agreed and assumed the serious posture and expression that Kareem's son had. I pretended to take a photograph.

"Now I want a photo of you smiling or laughing like you are having fun. You are too serious. Momo Rahim, smile for me like you always do!" I raised the camera to my eye.

"Dr. Murreen, you did not take the photo." He didn't budge, and his disappointed expression triggered my guilty conscience. Was the price of the image I wanted taking a serious picture that I would throw away? Since so many villagers wanted copies of their photographs, I had bought several rolls of print film that could be developed in Pakistan. I wouldn't see images from the slide film brought from Canada until I returned home. I loved witnessing our employees' gleeful expressions when I doled out sealed envelopes containing images of their wives and daughters. They had no idea that the Pakistanis who had developed the film had ogled them.

Rolling my eyes, I twisted my face into something that I hoped looked comical but not offensive. "Momo Rahim, a photo of you smiling is much nicer." As I continued my antics, the corner of his mouth began to twitch. A giggle escaped, and then another. Finally, his face exploded with laughter and I released the shutter.

"Khonum Murreen, you are too much!" He flicked the ash into

the field. From that moment on, both Kareem and Momo Rahim encouraged my subjects to continue their activity and relax instead of assuming stern postures.

Once I'd taken enough photos, Kareem and I offered the usual farewell: "Khud offez." Then we turned and walked toward the Morghab River. A few minutes later, we approached the remnants of the Hippie Hotel, its exotic flare still evident in the domed earthen ceiling, intricate latticework and a crumbling patio right on the bank of the river. Momo Rahim had told me that, in the 1960s, beautiful women in bikinis used to sunbathe there and smoke local marijuana.

Under the shade of a tree at the hotel entrance lay a snoozing wolf-like dog chained to a metal stake. Kareem passed and the dog showed no interest. Swallowing my childhood fear of being bitten, I placed my feet right in Kareem's footprints. All of a sudden, the animal lunged, its bared teeth snapping at me. I jumped into a cornfield. Reaching the end of its tether, the dog rebounded and fell on its rump, its teeth clenched on a piece of orange material the same colour as my kameez.

"Good?" Kareem's eyes looked worried, but he laughed thinly, the tinny sound of concern rather than humour. Only months later did I realize that in agreeing to accompany me, he had assumed responsibility for my safety. I had made the request to comply with MSF rules, but if I was truthful, in such a patriarchal place, I did feel safer with a man by my side.

With a thudding heart, I swallowed my tears and nodded. Like that of a soldier, my medical brain switched on and squashed my emotions. Afghan dogs weren't vaccinated against rabies and when chained outside could be exposed to rabid animals like hyenas. I was thankful for having received my primary series against rabies in Canada, although if I was bitten I would need another set.

"Do you know this dog?" I watched Kareem raise a pointy stick.

"Bad man. Dog very bad." Like a jouster, Kareem crouched low and held the sharp end of a stick toward the dog. He periodically rapped it on the ground while holding the other arm wide to give the impression of an imposing hulk. "Never drop the stick. If I do, the dog attacks."

I shuddered. No other sticks lay nearby. I made a note to ask Momo Rahim if he could request that the man move his dog to a place far away from where people walked.

In the evening stillness, the call to prayer sounded even more exotic than usual. Kareem's brow furrowed, the wrinkle in his forehead deepening. He sped up. It would take us at least ten minutes to get back to the compound. Every evening, Kareem prayed right when the call occurred. Did that make him a more devout Muslim? He looked so uncomfortable that I felt guilty for having insisted on him accompanying me.

At a heavily laden apricot tree, he stopped and fiddled with an end of his patu, which he had twisted into a tight roll.

"Khonum Murreen, I pray?" The slight inflection in his voice suggested that he was asking me for permission. In the background, two meadowlarks sang. A donkey brayed.

"Yes please, you pray. I wait here." Trying to make myself less conspicuous, I moved toward the trunk of the tree. Above me, seated on a branch, a boy swung his legs, his face smeared with apricot juice. We both nodded, hands on our hearts. He was my next-door neighbour.

Kareem unfurled his patu and spread it on the bare ground. Facing west, hands clasped in front of his relaxed body, his lips formed voiceless words. It was like he had journeyed far away. I sensed peace. I wanted to be respectful but I felt compelled to peek. I was fascinated by his ability to transform angst into tranquility as he knelt, then prostrated himself, his head touching the rosy gold soil. The prayer movements reminded me of a sun salutation in yoga.

At the end of the ritual, Kareem was standing, head bowed, hands clasped in prayer, chains of pink mountains and a rainbow-coloured sky surrounding him. Part of me still regrets not snapping the photograph, but doing so would have felt wrong. Even twenty years later, I vividly recall the details of that scene.

That walk seemed to shift our evening conversations—they became more personal. His life had been so different from mine. At twenty-seven, he had already experienced more losses than anyone I knew. Almost everyone in his family had been killed during the war. His mother, who was still living, had been the youngest of his father's four wives. Each wife, along with her children, had occupied a house inside a shared compound. As a child, Kareem had been raised as a semi-nomad. For half of the year, he had shepherded goats, sheep and camels. His eyes shone when he described the care he had given to his horse, brushing it daily and feeding it eggs

Young shepherds, one wearing a discarded army coat, herded goats along dusty paths near Bala Morghab. I stumbled across remarkable scenes like this every time I went for a walk.

until its coat glistened. He loved the natural beauty of the land, and he loved to learn, especially by pondering big questions.

When he was eight years old, Kareem used to walk half an hour to school. One day, he arrived to find it on fire. Crouching behind a bush, he watched it burn. Afterward, he walked home. His father, a village elder, told him that the mujahedeen were responsible. From that moment on, he became his father's apprentice, learning to read, write and calculate. He also developed skills to resolve conflicts between villagers. Kareem did mental sums, subtraction, division and multiplication quicker than I did, and not once did I identify a mistake. Yet he had never touched a telephone, a television, or a computer, nor had he seen a movie. He had never even travelled to Herat.

Every day he listened to BBC's shortwave news bulletins in Pashto, his first language and, like Dari, an official language of Afghanistan. I tuned in to BBC or Voice of America in English. Those were our only news sources. The internet and phones had yet to arrive in Bala Morghab. In the evening over tea, we compared notes. One time, I began to wonder how fair the recent US election was. The Pashto station said it wasn't. But English BBC was neutral, and Voice of America minimized any concerns about it. No matter what happened in the world, life in Bala Morghab changed little.

CHAPTER SEVEN

PEACE

"Peace begins with a smile."

— *Mother Teresa*

On most evenings during that first six months in Bala Morghab, I talked with Kareem and Asif, their friendly dark eyes and wide welcoming smiles lifting my spirit as we lounged on pillows on a mat under the stars when the night was warm, or in the guard hut when it was cool. By lantern light, we wrote Dari and English words in three notebooks lined up side by side like a barrier between me and them. In the flickering light, we frequently enlisted the help of a Persian–English dictionary, which was only useful about 60 percent of the time because idioms in Iran were often different from the ones spoken in Bala Morghab.

Kareem pumped the handle of the tea thermos. It belched several times as it built up enough pressure to force hot, straw-coloured liquid to gurgle into our glass teacups, the sort that even Afghan nomads owned. He served me first, the steam momentarily obscuring his face like a veil hanging between us.

"Khonum Murreen, Musulman hastid?" Religion was so much a part of Afghan life that asking if I was Muslim hadn't seemed odd. The fact that he hadn't brought it up before then was a bigger surprise. I was glad that he hadn't because discussing an emotionally charged topic before I had developed conversational Dari would have been risky. Our first few conversations had involved pointing and miming while parroting the names of whatever it was in our own tongue, then waiting for the other person to name the same item in theirs.

"No, I am not Musulman. I am, uh…" I scratched my hairline. Most of the time, I spoke Dari to him, adding an English word whenever I didn't know the Dari one. "Ker-is-tchan." I made the word up. In Bala Morghab, everyone was Muslim. Meeting someone of another religion must have been novel for him, although I suspected that the previous expats were not Muslim either.

"Isawi?" The word sounded unfamiliar to me. He cocked his head to the side, repeating it again.

Religion permeated daily life, even in the smallest villages. This rural mosque would be crowded on Fridays.

Shaking my head, I struggled to recall the context in which I had previously heard that term. Momo Rahim had used it once or twice, but he hadn't translated the meaning of it. To remember Dari words, I had to write them immediately or the confusing muddle of phonetics evaporated like a puff of smoke on a windy day.

Kareem flipped through pages of the Persian-English dictionary and pointed to *Isawi* in Arabic script and Roman characters. Beside it, "Christian" was also typed in both scripts.

"Yes, I am Isawi." I pushed my shoulders down. I didn't feel very Christian since I rarely practised the rituals. Every few years I attended church, most commonly at Christmas. As a child I had gone to Sunday school and, as an adolescent, I had been confirmed in the Anglican Church. But I prayed only when I felt lost, fearful or particularly grateful. The last time had been on the plane heading out of the world's consciousness en route to Afghanistan, when I had wondered if my decision to go in had been wise.

Kareem gazed into his teacup, as if in it he would find answers to questions that he hadn't yet worked up the courage to ask me. "Isawi. Isa."

If *Isawi* meant "Christian," *Isa* probably meant "Jesus." I leafed through the dictionary and tried to recall the fundamental dispute between Christianity and Islam that had led to such a monumental rift between their followers. MSF's introductory materials had described a disagreement about the roles of Jesus and Mohammed. There was something else too, but I couldn't remember it. Every day, Kareem and Asif mentioned Mohammed. Jesus never came up, and yet he was foundational to Christianity. In the dictionary, Jesus was translated into *Hazrate Isa*. Close enough.

As I sipped tea from my cup, I considered how inappropriate my sitting every night with two Afghan men must be to the Taliban. For more than an hour each evening, we shared ideas while slowly familiarizing ourselves with the other's language. Had I been a guy, the Taliban wouldn't have cared. John had been Vicky's chaperone and she had reassured me that I could trust these two men so I had simply decided to do that unless something caused me to re-evaluate. To date, they had been courteous and helpful. Was I taking stupid risks?

MSF documents briefly described how foreign men and women should behave in the presence of Afghans. Foreign women were supposed to sit in the back seat of vehicles. Men and women should arrange themselves so only one gender shared the same seat. If that was impossible, foreign men and women should sit together. Foreign women were to stay metres away from men when drinking tea or sharing a meal. Romantic relationships were discouraged. A foreign man was not even allowed to be in the same room as an Afghan woman.

When I considered bending rules, I asked Kareem, Asif and Momo Rahim what the consequences might be. But I was cautious about discussing religion with someone as conservative and religious as Kareem because I feared that our perspectives might be so different that the relationship we had built might disintegrate—or, if word got out, my religious views might jeopardize the project. The Taliban would never sympathize with an infidel who didn't believe in their version of God. To date, I had only solicited information. I hadn't shared much.

Asif chimed in, shifting his stocky torso to the other hip. "Good. Christians believe in Allah." The finality in his tone intimated that the issue was resolved and it was time to switch topics. A knot in my neck released a smidgen. That was my preference too.

"Yes, Christians believe in Allah, only one Allah." I parroted the phrase that I knew would satisfy them. "Allah" rolled off my tongue, the phonetics gentler than those of God.

Although I did believe in a God-like presence of some sort, my ideas about Him or Her were in constant flux. Dad had been an atheist, attending church begrudgingly when I was very young because Mum found the community comforting and she wanted to introduce her kids to the concepts. Each Sunday, Dunkin' Donuts had been our reward. By the time I was twelve, I had wanted proof of His/Her existence. Later on, I had been enchanted by Buddhism in Thailand. I had learned a few things about Judaism from fellow medical students in Montreal. And I had been fascinated by animist beliefs taught to me by Inuit elders. I was still working on synthesizing these ideas into a unified vision that made sense to me.

In medical school, my roommate had been a devout Catholic. In her family, Catholicism was an everyday touchstone and a pillar of strength for difficult times. One evening I had been keen to explore what proof she had that God existed. She described "a knowing." She had felt His presence ever since she could remember. I asked what that was like. She tried to describe the sentiments, but they meant nothing to me. How did she know that the Bible wasn't just an embellished story written by a group of guys? She had pressed her lips together and sighed, her eyes rolling back just a bit. "You either believe or you don't. It's inside your heart. No analysis will convince you of God's presence. You choose to have faith or not. It is simple." Was it?

In Bala Morghab, for the first time since childhood, I had the gift of time. I sensed some kind of unity that was hard to name. In the village, I connected with strangers through a shared smile or laugh. We stopped to smell roses. I felt at peace with the land and with the people I met. There I considered Allah to be God, Mother Nature and Buddha wrapped into one.

"Mohammed, peace be upon Him, is Allah's prophet." Kareem's voice brought me back onto the mat under the stars. His slender fingers, which might have played piano in another life, rolled his empty teacup back and forth as he seemed to consider what to say next. "What do Christians believe about the prophet Mohammed, peace be upon Him?"

"Christians believe that Mohammed, peace be upon Him, was a prophet. In Christianity, other prophets are important too." That was true, wasn't it? I wrestled to knit together my shredded memories from Sunday school and confirmation lessons from so long ago. "For Christians, Allah and Isa are most important." I omitted the Holy Spirit because describing it would complicate the story and I had never really understood its significance anyway. Wasn't it just Jesus after death?

Asif sat bolt upright, his chin jutting out and his finger stabbing the air. His mouth formed a thin crease and his eyes flashed. He was usually the jovial one.

Like a slender Buddha, Kareem raised his hand, his outstretched palm stopping his friend's voice. He spoke to me. "To Muslims, Isa was a prophet. Mohammed, peace be upon Him, is Allah's prophet. He is most important. Is this what Christians believe?"

Cold armpit sweat dribbled down my torso. I shivered, but my thoughts were clear. I didn't believe literal interpretations of any scriptures. What was the Christian view of Mohammed? Was he a prophet of no particular importance? I had heard him described as aggressive and unforgiving, the opposite of Jesus. I hesitated. What to say? What to hold back?

"Christians believe that Isa is Allah's son." My tone was matter-of-fact. I assumed that they already knew this about Christianity.

With a dull *thunk*, Asif's teacup landed on the mat as a flood of English and Dari erupted from his tongue. His index finger seemed to battle against an invisible enemy right in front of his nose. "Khonum Murreen, Isa not son of Allah! Allah no son! Mary not good woman. Not possible, Allah have son!" On he went half in English and half in Dari, his eyes narrowed to a squint.

The chasm between me and them had just widened by several metres. How could I narrow it again?

Kareem spoke slowly. "Christians make a mistake. Isa is not Allah's son. Isa is a prophet. Mohammed, peace be upon Him, is Allah's prophet. He is most important. Isawi do not know this?" He cocked his head to the side, an eyebrow arched.

Leaning forward, I placed my empty teacup on the mat and willed my hand to steady the tremor that threatened to become obvious. Butterflies in my belly had rapidly spread to my whole body. Even my toes vibrated. I felt chilled, and the hair follicles on my head rose up as if ready to fight. I collected my thoughts. Son or prophet, did details really matter when the stories were supposed to promote connection and a sense of oneness that inspired humans to respect each other and get along? I held my breath and thought about the many wars that had wreaked destruction in the name of religion.

"What do you believe?" Kareem peered at me as if attempting to unpack my hesitance. One day, he would step into his uncle's shoes and become Momo Kareem. He was thirteen years my junior, but he nudged my thoughts in a fatherly way that astonished me. How could he be so mature? The two of us were so different, yet a bond of trust had formed that puzzled me. He had grown up fast in a tight-knit extended family that had survived the havoc of war for many years. Constantly moving, I had straddled many cultures, languages, locations and perspectives. Safety for me had been a given. Where he saw black and white, I saw grey tones and colours.

"To me, Jesus was a leader, like a prophet. The Bible says that Isa is Allah's son, but I have difficulty believing this is really true." Pausing to grapple with what next to say, I realized that I didn't believe that God had a flesh and blood son, but the idea that Jesus had been deputized in some way was palatable.

"Khonum Murreen, to a Muslim, never say Jesus is Allah's son. It is impossible. He is only a prophet." Kareem spoke softly, but his tone had an edge.

Sipping tea, I was buying seconds to ponder what he really meant and scout for any quicksand into which I might sink.

The next question he murmured softly, like my conscience might. "Do you pray?"

I breathed in the night sky. I didn't want to lie.

I exhaled. "Each night, Christians pray before sleeping and eating." I had done so as a child. Leafing through the dictionary, I pointed to the word "church." "One or two times each week, Christians pray in a *kalisa*."

"What is kalisa?" Kareem studied the dictionary and shook his head. He had no reason to hear anything about churches except possibly when listening to international news in Pashto on shortwave radio. Maybe he knew the Pashto word. Was there one?

"It is like a mosque for Christians, a house where Christians pray together one or two times each week. Some Christians pray at a kalisa every day." While bicycling through Italian villages, I had seen people praying at all hours, and Mass was said every day. "Christians pray at home too."

I added a church to the list of photographs that I planned to ask Peter to bring from Canada for our two-week rendezvous in the Pakistani Himalayas. Without internet or a digital camera, I relied on the generosity of visitors to transport photographs, books and magazines.

"Christians pray to Allah. Very good." The creases in Kareem's leathery forehead had softened, as if he was grateful to have one less thing to worry about.

The muezzen sang in the still of the evening. The naturally amplified prepubescent boy's voice slipped off the high note. To me, the singing was magical because it signalled a pause for spiritual communion.

Kareem turned to me. "Khonum Murreen, I pray here. Good?" Raising a brow, he pointed to the ground between us. "Evening prayer, only one minute, then finished. Then talking again." He had previously told me that the duration of prayers varied depending upon the time of day and the amount of time available. Omissions in one prayer could be made up in a later one. He was saying this one would be quick.

Kareem sucked in his breath and stood up, not waiting for my reply. Heat rose from my belly all the way to my cheeks. I nodded. Had I just gained more of his trust?

Ignoring the conversation, Asif continued to write in his cahier. I had seen him pray only once as I walked by the guard hut. Maybe to him, it was a private activity. Or perhaps he was angry with God because he had no sons. Sons were important because males inherited everything in Afghanistan, and parents relied on them for housing and support in their old age.

As graceful as a dancer, Kareem pulled his shoulders back, adjusted his turban and spread out his patu. Standing at one end of it, he began the ritual: kneeling, hand to ears, head to mat. Peeking several times, I felt like a voyeur, but I couldn't help myself. His arms hung loosely by his torso. His eyes closed and his mouth moved soundlessly. His breath was deep, like someone in a heartfelt meditation who had travelled to a faraway place. He looked so peaceful. But didn't praying inches away from a female infidel with my depth of doubt somehow invalidate the good deed?

Surrounded as Kareem was by uncertainty and death, religion was a beacon of strength for him. His peacefulness and acceptance of what was soothed me. How would life and work be different if I cultivated that within myself? Would I deal with challenges more peacefully? Telling a father that his only son would die could be an act of kindness. All I needed was the inner peace, trust and courage to make it so every time.

Kareem sat cross-legged once again. Asif trundled along the stone path toward the cubbyhole room where he slept. Kareem described the Day of Judgment, when everything would stop and our destinies would be determined. His vision of heaven included rivers of milk and honey, abundant everything and many young virgins. He planned to get there. He asked me to repeat some phrases. Allah was mentioned in all of them. His tone was urgent. He wanted me to get to heaven too.

When I left a short time later, I almost skipped down the path. Jackals barked. A donkey hee-hawed. A rooster cried out. A star zipped across an ebony sky full of others that almost whispered. I made a wish. In my bedroom, I knelt on the miniature carpet beside my bed, brought my hands together and prayed peacefully like I had as child.

I felt a sense of peace when Afghans prayed.

CHAPTER EIGHT

A Scar

"Our greatest glory is not in never falling, but in rising every time we fall."

— *Oliver Goldsmith*

In the distance, the sudden, strangled shriek of a woman crescendoed, then sounded over and over again like an eerie echo. Through the scratched window of the pharmacy, I scanned the nearby area, trying to identify the source of the howling that had pierced my brain and precluded meaningful thought. I had been listening to the pharmacist complain yet again that he had too much work to do even though, to me, he never seemed busy enough and his tasks were rarely finished on time.

That day Momo Rahim moved faster than I did. The midmorning breeze seemed to guzzle my saliva, and I craved an ice cold drink as we scurried toward the screams that reverberated off the unadorned clinic walls.

En route to the women's entrance of the minor surgery chamber, my brain listed possible patient scenarios. Afghan girls married just after puberty, so perhaps a young mother's labour had failed because the baby's head was too big for the girl's pelvis and it demanded to be let through anyway. Maybe someone had fallen and the pain from the broken bone or cracked skull was unbearable. It could be a mine victim who had lost part of a limb and required amputation of the rest of it. Or possibly someone with a psychosis whose grip on reality had weakened when the pain of life became too arduous to endure. I could have thought through a hundred other potential causes, but there was no point. I needed facts.

We entered the surgery room to find five Afghan men standing around a form completely encased in burlap. Not even the face was visible—but it was a woman. I could tell by her curves. The pale knuckles of their meaty hands pressed her arms and legs onto a polished, steel table. The force they used struck me as harsh, even cruel. Were they Taliban? They had the right turbans, but their eyes weren't made up. Even after a few months, I had trouble recognizing who was who.

Most Afghan men I met wanted peace and harmony. They told me how ashamed they felt of maiming and killing in the name of honour.

The usually jolly dresser methodically laid out bandages, forceps and cleaning solutions with a jerky precision that seemed forced. Even though he had lived through more gore than anyone I knew, on most days his stories warmed a bare room and provided words of encouragement to others. But I knew that underneath his gentle soul was a solid core of steel.

"As salaam alaikum." My greeting was terse and matter-of-fact. I didn't trust them.

The silence that greeted me was interrupted only by the dresser's clink of metal on metal. Pressing my shoulders back and puffing my chest out, I strode toward the woman, walking as near to them as I dared. With shifting, downcast eyes, the whole group tensed. I felt like a tarantula or a snake. I knew that they would never touch a foreign, female infidel, and I had the distinct impression that they preferred to keep this story, and whatever grim event had precipitated it, under wraps and far from my eyes. Of course, this piqued my curiosity. I also took it as a warning to tread carefully.

We needed to focus on the woman while appeasing them enough to keep everyone safe. Part of being an MSF volunteer was to bear witness to human rights violations, atrocities and gender-based violence. MSF shared these stories with the world in hopes of generating awareness of under-reported issues. Bringing medical services into unstable locations was our ticket of entry for this work. In the room, their hands continued to pin her down, as if they were afraid that she might rise like a ghost and flee at any moment. If she did, I hoped that she cursed them!

The dresser's white hair was dishevelled. His face sagged, as if he hadn't slept enough recently, and his forehead was creased into a frown. He wheeled a steel table with surgical instruments, bowls of brown iodine solution and sterile gauzes nearer to her. He seemed to force his hands to slow down, as if preventing them from slamming steel on steel or throwing something at the men. Under his breath, he cursed. His thick lips were puckered in concentration as he grasped a corner of the rough brown cloth with a pair of forceps. He folded the fabric back on itself. Beneath it, a bloody blue burka framed a face that gazed vacantly at the dresser's belly, as if attempting to avoid being seen. Eyes closed, she breathed raggedly.

Tap, tap, tap. The used iodine from the table hit a small metal bowl on the cement floor. Each drop spattered the concrete like blood does after an artery is severed.

"What happened to her?" I spoke Dari so everyone would understand. Could I earn one tiny speck of their trust? Momo Rahim remained silent, his eyes glued to the floor, his head nodding to the beat of the iodine droplets. His creased lips refused to let any words out. What did he know? What power did these men hold in the village?

"Jang…fusil…" The dresser spat out the words—war and gun— swear words to me and yet so much a part of everyday life in this corner of the world, where every house sported one or more Kalashnikovs, which most boys learned to shoot at the same age that Canadian kids learned to ride bicycles. Raised in such a hostile environment, how on earth had the dresser maintained his gentle spirit?

He tore off a blood-soaked layer of emerald green fabric that had once been a dress and was now tattered and singed. He tugged where it clung to her chest, glued with her own blood. She flinched once and the vice-like grip of the men tightened. Where was she going to run? Her unseeing eyes fluttered, as if she were resigned to whatever happened next.

Removing every fleck of fabric so infection could be avoided, his forceps probed into the rounded mound of fat that had once been a breast. It had no skin. Even the nipple was gone. How did this happen? With each of the girl's shallow breaths, the amorphous lump oozed yellow and red fluid. I had assisted at countless breast surgeries. The nipple was always preserved and a flap of skin always covered the adipose tissue. For this woman, these were impossible luxuries.

Observing his work and ready to help if needed, I inhaled deeply, only to gag on the taste of charred fat, like from a barbecue but different. Bile rose into my throat. I swallowed hard. Deep in my gut, a knife blade was twisting. Inhaling slowly, my hand on my abdomen, I willed it to stop. My breath steadied. I covered my mouth and nose with the tail of my chador, in hopes of diminishing the acrid taste and cloying odour. Turning my face away, I panted shallowly and pushed back my tears. I tried to swallow and couldn't.

"What caused the burn?" I spoke softly to Momo Rahim in English so the others wouldn't understand. I didn't want to make the situation any worse. The men were already seething. Had she done this to herself as an attempt to avoid an unwanted marriage? Was it a failed suicide? The breast tissue, the skin surrounding it and half of the other breast were scorched like a steak cooked rare. Had someone knocked the gun so the ammunition burned her chest instead of hitting her heart? Or had she simply been in the wrong place at the wrong time and wound up in someone else's line of sight?

Having worked in several emergency rooms, I had treated a fair number of suicide attempts, mainly overdoses and hangings. The few that had involved bullets had taken place in tiny villages in Northern Canada. They were more like cries for help, not attempts to die. Searching for clues, I scanned the woman's body, my eyes straining to notice details, my jaw clenched. My brain constructed a scene. Angry man raises the barrel to kill and decides instead that maiming her for life was a better lesson. Every day, she would see that scar, feel the rough skin and remember this day that ended her life as she knew it.

Momo Rahim remained mute. Slowly, his head shook back and forth as if seeking comfort in the movement. In his eyes I saw dry-eyed despair and shame.

My brain continued its investigation of the situation. No one could hold a Kalashnikov and inflict this kind of injury on themselves. The barrel of the weapon was simply too long, unless it had been cut. I was sure that someone had punished her. Families sometimes gained back their honour by injuring or even killing wives and daughters. I had heard heart-wrenching stories but never witnessed any. A slow form of torture was to bury a woman to the waist, then invite villagers to throw stones at her. After days of starvation and dehydration, she eventually shrivelled up. What a horrendous way to leave this life, being scorned by those she had once trusted. I would pray for a direct hit to the head and a quick death.

My chest felt like it was on fire. I wanted to throw stones at these men! How heartless, to wreck someone's life like this in the name of honour. What in the world was honourable about it? Her family was probably punishing her for adultery, which could have been as innocuous as her insistence on marrying a man that she chose. Wounds of the heart could be so complicated.

My eyes probed the right side of her face, the side I could see. I felt her shut me out. She responded to nothing. Had her life always been this tragic? Would she ever feel worthy of a better one?

Right then, my medical brain took control. With relief, I felt it smother my emotions like it always did. It began estimating the extent of the burned surface area and concluded that she would survive without intravenous fluids as long as she continued to drink. The breast was beyond saving, plastic surgery being a far-fetched dream in a place like Bala Morghab. The nearest plastic surgeon was in Pakistan. She would never get there.

Would she drink enough to save herself? Would I in her situation? Wouldn't I prefer to hole up somewhere, take some painkillers and hope for death? All we could offer her was simple, straightforward wound care that felt woefully inadequate for such a monstrous wound. More than bandages and ibuprofen tablets were needed to deal with this kind of injury. The overstretched, fibrous scar that would barely cover the destroyed breast would greet her every day, whether she observed herself in the mirror or made love to someone. It would limit her movement, and she would feel it tearing every time she lifted her kids. It would shield her heart when she hugged someone. If ever she became pregnant, breast engorgement would literally tear her scars apart. Milk in the confused mess of ruptured ducts would never find its way through the nipple that no longer was, its exit sealed off by a proud man with a gun.

I winced. What could we do?

The woman's jet black hair was peppered with fat globules and matted with blood. Her plump face was wrinkle-free. She looked about nineteen. Numbness would harden her tattered heart, trust only a memory. If she was single, who would marry her now? And if she was already married, would her husband provide the support that she needed or would he shut her in a dark room to toil alone? What would it take to bear the shame, to find the resolve each day to get out of bed and strive to be her best?

I had never experienced anything remotely so horrendous. Having lived through the usual childhood injuries of skinned knees, fractured bones and stitched-up wounds, my physical scars were hard to find. And my other scars were invisible, buried deep for so long that I no longer felt them. In fact, I no longer felt much of anything. Craving to feel was what had lured me to Afghanistan. I felt so much anger that I wanted to pummel these men, but I wouldn't dare. Uncontrolled anger wouldn't help anyone.

My invisible scars had accumulated so gradually that I had no idea when they first began. According to family stories, I had clung to Mum as a baby, terrified that she would disappear. So I imagine they went way back.

They might have started at the age of four when Daddy let me drive the car. My little butt had been perched on his thighs, my legs lying alongside his. Sitting up straight, I had been barely able to peer through the bottom of the windscreen. Heart thumping, my hands had turned the steering wheel as I concentrated intensely, trying to prevent the car from veering into the ditch. Every so often, his hand gently nudged the steering wheel.

"No, Daddy! I can do it." I tapped his hand off the wheel. I so wanted him to be proud of me. Often, he wasn't happy. He never told me anything, but I was pretty sure that I could make him feel better if only he would let me.

"Okay." His voice sounded distant. He patted my shoulder. "How about if I tell you a secret?" He spoke gently, as if to a confidant.

"Okay." My flat chest puffed up like a songbird's in spring. I didn't want to say too much for fear of breaking the magic of the moment. A secret meant that I was special!

"You know, you are going to like school a lot. You're going to learn so much." His voice had sounded wistful.

"Uh-huh." I frowned. It was hard not to feel disappointed. What kind of secret was that? Mummy had already told me that.

"I liked school a lot. I was good at learning things, but I wish that I had learned more at school." He was sad again.

He already knew everything. Why would a grown up want that? They don't go to school.

"I wasn't done learning when I left school. I wanted to be smarter. I wanted to be a doctor." That's what my four-year-old brain heard as it concentrated hard on the action at hand, which was to keep the car out of the ditch. Later on, as a teenager, I realized that he had longed to complete a Ph.D., not a medical degree. He loved chemistry. His mouth formed a line when he spoke again: "But you and Janet came along and we became a family. I have to work so we have money to spend and a house to live in. There is no time for me to study." His voice had trailed away.

The car stopped. My short legs couldn't reach the gas pedal. Why had he stopped? I let the wheel go, folded my legs under my rump and stood up, my saddle shoes carving deeply into his thighs. Then I wrapped my chubby arms around his head, my hands rubbing his neck like Mum sometimes did to me. He didn't have to feel sad. A seed of a thought began to germinate. Was it my fault that he was unhappy? After all, he had to make money for us. My little kid's brain told me there was no other explanation.

I held him, and in my head I told him, *Daddy, you are so big, you can do anything!* After all, he was my hero. If he wanted to, why didn't he just go back to school?

Later, in the kitchen with Mum, I asked the question that had been bugging me. "Mummy, did you want kids?"

Her frown lines got deeper. They disappeared when she wrapped her arms around me and pushed my face into her bosom. It was always warm and safe in there. "Yes, of course I wanted kids. I love you."

Mostly, I believed her, but I knew deep down there was something she wasn't saying, something that I couldn't read. I could tell that she was mostly happy, just not always.

"Did Daddy want kids?" I watched her face—trying to detect a fib, just like she did to me.

"Yes, your father wanted kids. He had some other plans, but when you and Janet came along, he was very happy! He loves you just like I do." Her face looked truthful, but there was that sadness again that didn't quite jive with what she said.

Had he wanted school more than he wanted me? I never asked, because it might have been true. I decided then and there to make Daddy proud. I did well at school, winning prizes and scholarships. I succeeded no matter what. I even started saving my nickels and dimes in a piggy bank so I could go to university without asking Daddy to pay for it. I was strong and independent. Marriage and kids were for other people. And in keeping with my childhood intention, I had known almost limitless freedom in my pursuit of learning and life experiences.

In the bare clinic room, iodine still dripped. I touched the woman's shoulder. It felt dead. Had she given up? Self-inflicted, done by another or caught in crossfire, the effect was the same.

The dresser removed the last fleck of fabric from the weeping flesh. He spread ointment on it that looked like cream cheese. I watched her face for any signs of life. Did the ointment soothe the ache a bit? It was impossible to tell. The dresser had this. I wasn't needed or wanted. Maybe one day I would share this story.

Momo Rahim's eye caught mine. He tipped his head toward the door. Our farewell hung in the air like a cobweb. No one answered. In his office, we drank chai saps. I blew my nose, but the pungent odour of charred breast remained.

"Murreen-jan, sometimes our culture is shameful. It can be dangerous to ask too many questions. This is a private problem, a family matter. They will solve it in their own way, behind compound walls. It is the Afghan habit." His sad mouth swallowed a swig of tea.

I went home early that day and headed straight to my bedroom. I closed the drapes, and in the darkness I shadow boxed against those men, "(I Can't Get No) Satisfaction" by the Rolling Stones blaring in my ears. With each punch, I let out a bit more anger and judgment. The gap between my right and wrong and theirs felt enormous. But if I wanted to change anything here in a meaningful way, I had to meet people where they were. Only then could we move toward a better reality, whatever that was.

CHAPTER NINE

SCIENCE

"Mystery creates wonder and wonder is the basis of man's desire to understand."

— *Neil Armstrong*

As the sun sank below the horizon and a rejuvenating coolness rose from the land, I pushed "send" to dispatch my short, text-only emails to friends and family as far as the Outbox, where they waited. To launch them into cyberspace and receive emails, Jim connected our one satellite phone to the rest of the world each evening for a minute or two. Apart from emails, news broadcasts on shortwave radio and old-fashioned letters in the mailbag, we received virtually no information about the world outside of Afghanistan. The Taliban had outlawed televisions and cellphones. Longer emails saved on floppy discs and handwritten letters left Bala Morghab once a week,

Wealthy inhabitants of Bala Morghab travelled by animal or horse-drawn cart. Most villagers had no exposure to the rest of the world.

eventually reaching Peshawar, where an MSF employee copied and pasted our emails into a generic account before sending them to the named recipient. She even placed stamps on our letters since we couldn't buy any in Afghanistan. Often, floppy discs were returned because they were unreadable, and we had to repeat the process again. I was learning to be patient.

The satellite phone was used in secret, its antenna hidden on the roof behind a chimney because the Taliban sometimes seized them. At least once a month it didn't work because the neighbour's chickens had kicked it over. Once, I phoned my boyfriend, Peter. Anticipating a heartfelt conversation, I had carefully chosen a private place in our compound. The call failed twice before he answered.

"Hi Peter, it's Maureen." An echo loudly repeated my words. Pause. Nothing. I started over: "Peter, it's Maureen." Again, the echo, then silence, like I was having a conversation with myself. I was timing the call, and only five minutes remained before each subsequent minute would cost me $7.50 US!

When I was about to give up, a faint voice spoke. "Hello! Hello! Hello?"

"How are you?" The parrot-like voice repeated my question.

"It's good to ####I won##### what #####?" Every second or third word that Peter said hissed with static.

In the Canadian Arctic, I had often begun phone calls by introducing the delay to the other person and asking them to count to five before they answered me. By doing that we avoided interrupting each other.

We interrupted each other several times before establishing that there was a twelve-second delay at both ends. I told him about the clinic, then counted to twelve. He answered. I counted again. I described the mud compound and counted. I mentioned the guards and learning to speak Dari, then counted. As I talked, I sought better reception, and by the end of the call I had covered the entire compound. I had even climbed halfway up the ladder. Five minutes disappeared just like that. I ended by saying how much I missed him.

In truth, I missed his support but not the compromises, or the cage that routine life together had represented. That cage had been a repeating pattern in all of my serious relationships. Afghanistan had been my ticket out.

At the end of our conversation, I felt frustrated. I had had to explain everything, and still I felt unheard. In five minutes, you can only touch the surface of such a different world. I felt utterly alone.

Exiting the office, I joined Kareem on the cushions in the court-yard. Asif was already sleeping. Sitting cross-legged, Kareem twirled a pencil across the back of his hand, his index finger keeping his place in the cahier. His serene expression suggested that he was still communing with God after having prayed. He filled my cup with chai saps as we exchanged greetings.

"In Vancouver, i-i-it is early morning now," I pushed the words out with some effort. I missed my life in Canada and yearned for the ease of the familiar. I wanted to take simple comforts for granted, like ceramic bathroom tiles and gleaming faucets. I wished to share my exploits with friends and family so they might savour the odd moments and humorous conversations too. But few of them would ever truly *get* this experience. How could they, with such precon-ceived ideas about Afghans?

As a medical student, I had worked for three months in Thai-land. After my return, people had asked to hear my stories. Some-how they expected me to be unchanged by my adventures, to still care about the same old things and speak the same language. But my world had expanded enormously, and the propensity to consume, to complain about luxuries, to plan every moment and to minimize the importance of meaningful connection had irked me. At the time I had wanted to take the next plane back to Thailand—but instead of doing that, I finished medical school, then dove head first into residency, burying these concerns beneath an avalanche of medical facts.

After spending nine months in an Afghan time warp, where life revolved around prayer and survival, how could I fit into my old life?

"Khonum Murreen, you are sad for home." Kareem smiled as he read my thoughts like they were words on a page. His capacity to know my mind was both disturbing and heartwarming. Looking down at my teacup, I tried to hide my feelings. Tears threatened to spill down my cheeks.

Kareem refilled my cup. After I sipped some tea, he spoke ten-derly: "The way to Vancouver is how long?"

If I counted all stopovers and delays, travelling to Bala Morghab had taken two weeks—but that wasn't the answer to his question. "It took eighteen hours by plane. Travelling to Herat involves four planes. I do not count the waiting time for planes. With waiting time, maybe it takes three days."

His upper lip glistened wetly in the lamplight. "It is so far!" Didn't I know it! By the clock, Afghanistan was twelve and a half hours ahead of Vancouver—halfway around the world—yet Afghans, by almost any measure, still lived centuries ago.

How could I describe to a man who had never seen a map of the world where Canada was relative to Afghanistan? The only map in the office was a National Geographic version of Afghanistan's provinces and major cities, not the rest of the world. We used this map to identify the locations of the latest violence so we could modify our travels. We had four escape routes.

"When it is night in Afghanistan, it is day in Vancouver." In such a simple place, the concept did sound weird.

The glow of the lantern accentuated the deep wrinkles between his furrowed eyebrows as he silently waited for me to continue my story.

"Now, in Vancouver, it is eight o'clock in the morning. Here, in Afghanistan, it is eight and a half hours in the evening on the same day." I studied his face to gauge if the idea had landed. The flickering of the light on rich skin tones had softened his angular features and reminded me of campfires in the woods.

He planted his teacup between us with an uncharacteristic finality and spoke quickly. "No, Khonum Murreen, Allah makes day and night. How is it day, when it is night?"

I felt both amused and jarred by his response. He knew nothing about science, a topic that I had spent so many years studying. Religion was his life. What might resonate for him? How might I think if I hadn't travelled, had never seen a map of the world and had never studied science?

"Yes, Allah makes night and Allah makes day. But right now it is not night everywhere. In Vancouver, Allah makes night when, at the same time, Allah makes day in Bala Morghab." I paused for him to catch up. "Vancouver to Afghanistan is very far, eighteen hours in a plane. Vancouver is on the other side of zamin." In my limited vocabulary, zamin meant "soil," "earth," "land" and "field." How do I specify that I meant earth as opposed to field?

I patted the ground with my left hand. "Bala Morghab." Then mimed drilling with my right index finger into the ground. With my arms stretched as far apart as possible, I wiggled my right hand. "This is Vancouver."

He sat calmly, as if waiting for a punchline. Well, that hadn't worked! Miming a sphere, I pointed to the two opposing sides. "Vancouver. Bala Morghab." A vacant expression greeted me. Did he even know that the earth was round? The imam probably considered such topics superfluous for herders and farmers.

His thin lips curved upward into a smirk. Oops, a grown woman mimicking something round was a little too suggestive of topics that I preferred to avoid. It was time to switch tacks.

"If we make a hole in the ground..." I flipped through the dictionary and pointed to the Arabic script for tunnel. "Right here, we dig and dig and dig..." I mimed the action. "And we make a deep tunnel, very deep...." I spread my arms wide. "...through the earth to the end of it. There is Vancouver." I smiled expectantly, willing his puzzled expression to metamorphose into an exuberant tribute of recognition and gratitude. It didn't.

His brow remained furrowed. He sipped tea and shook his head. "Namefamam." He didn't understand, so I scanned the area for props that I could use in a demonstration.

Extensive systems of gravity-fed irrigation canals are used throughout Afghanistan.

"Khobe." I meant okay. Good and okay were the same word. Reaching toward him to pick up the lantern, I placed it on the mat between us. "Let's think that the lantern is the sun. It is not true, but let's think that it is, like a game." Sitting back, I scanned the other objects on the mat. What else could I use? "The sun, make it strong." I pointed to the lantern.

With a turn of the key, the kerosene-soaked wick glowed and the lantern rumbled. A crisp shadow of me glided across the stones. "Let's think the tea thermos is the earth." Its tubular shape was imperfect, but lantern light illuminated one side while the opposing side was in darkness.

"Here is Vancouver." My index finger pointed to the bright side of the thermos, and I drew a tiny circle with Kareem's pencil. I drew another circle on the shaded side. "Here is Bala Morghab, khobe?"

He nodded.

"Look. At the same time, it is dark in Bala Morghab and it is light in Vancouver." I pointed at the two pencil marks on the thermos, then paused to search for a glimmer of comprehension in his eyes.

"When the earth moves, watch what happens." I turned the thermos slowly one full turn, then continued to rotate it at a slower speed so he could notice how changes occurred gradually. "You see? In Bala Morghab it is light and now in Bala Morghab it is dark. Like day and night." I spun the thermos again. "Now in Vancouver it is dark and now in Vancouver it is light. Night, then day." He nodded, the intensity of his concentration urging me to continue.

"Pretend that I am here at this spot." I pointed to the pencil marking for Bala Morghab. "The sun that I see from here moves from the eastern sky to the western sky. See?" I rotated the thermos again. "Watch. The lantern, the sun, is staying in one place while the earth turns."

He studied the rudimentary model, his grin so wide that it pushed his cheeks toward his eyes. "Yes! When there is sun in Bala Morghab, there is no sun in Vancouver. When there is sun in Vancouver, in Bala Morghab it is dark! Like day and night." In the lantern light his eyes radiated pride, reminding me of a boy who had just solved a puzzle.

I twirled the thermos so Bala Morghab was in shadow. "Now is night in Bala Morghab. Watch. When the earth moves, a small light begins just here in Bala Morghab. See? Very little light. When the light is so little, the sun is very low in the sky. When is this?" I glanced at him.

"Maybe it is now. Sunset." He shifted forward, and his excitement was almost palpable.

As a child, I had found science magical. Dad used to bring home powders and liquids in little vials that he would combine to demonstrate them changing from a liquid to a solid or from red to colourless. He had once made Styrofoam, which was like baking a cake but on steroids. I liked mercury best of all because it was silver. He let us chase it around a table but never touch it. He told us it was poisonous.

"Yes! And maybe it is sunrise. At both sunrise and sunset, the sun is low in the sky, right?"

"No, Khonum Murreen, the night is following it. It is sunset." He was right.

"Yes, if day follows the low light, it is sunrise. Now, here in Bala Morghab, which one is it?" I turned the thermos so Bala Morghab changed from darkness into light.

"It is sunrise." He laughed with glee, his eyes twinkling.

"Now, you take it." I gave him the thermos with the two pencil marks, and he recreated the experiment with all the details. Then he handed it back to me, as if anticipating lesson two. What was next?

"Always, the earth is moving. In one day—twenty-four hours—the earth returns to the same place. We know that the earth is not straight. It is tipped like this." I tilted both the thermos and my torso at an angle of about 20 degrees. Then I picked up the thermos and walked in an ellipse around the lantern, my crooked shadow bouncing off the stones and the mud walls. "In one year, the earth travels around the sun like I just did. One year later, the earth is back in the same place again. Now right here, in Vancouver is it summer or winter?" The thermos was tilted toward the lantern as I spun it around the north-south axis.

He shrugged. "I don't know." The light in his eyes had fizzled. Fearful that it would extinguish, I launched into teaching mode.

"When the earth is like this, it is summer in Bala Morghab and in Vancouver too. See. Both places are on the top half of the earth, and that is where the sun is brightest." My hand sliced the thermos in half. "In summer, the sun is brightest and days are long on the top half of earth. Watch." I spun the thermos a couple of times and we compared the amount of light in the southern hemisphere with that in the north. Then we discussed while I demonstrated the difference between sunrise and sunset in winter and in summer.

After he understood that concept, I carried the thermos, still tipped, to the far side of the lantern. The northern half of the thermos was now away from the lantern glow. "Now in Bala Morghab it is winter. It is also winter in Vancouver. In winter there is little sun and days are short. Do you understand?" He nodded. I handed him the thermos. "Here, now you show me."

He replicated summer and winter, then all by himself he figured out how to model spring and fall. I lounged back on a pillow, feeling like a science missionary in a religious land. Had I brought food to a starving man?

To rural Afghan farmers, roads impeded much-needed irrigation. On irrigation day, they often dug a canal through the road. It was narrow enough to step over but just wide enough to trap a car tire.

CHAPTER TEN

A LOSS

"Spying among friends is not at all acceptable."

— *Angela Merkel*

In Bala Morghab, days began at sunrise. That summer, I awakened between 4 and 5 a.m., my alarm clock a mud swallow that chirped a bright song every day while perched on the same wire outside of my bedroom window. It was a pleasing melody for which my tired brain made up lyrics: "It's time to wake up. Get up. Get up. Get up." Repeated over and over, the vibrant tune was hard to ignore, the singer's air bladder paradoxically continuing to make music even when it took a breath, like what happens with bagpipes. Craving more sleep, I snuggled deeper under the blankets and wrapped my arms over the pillow that covered my head.

Inevitably, the swallow won, its happy tune eventually luring me out of my warm cocoon and into the blinding sunshine. Towel over my shoulder, toiletries in hand, I would stop briefly in the ventilated pit latrine, a ceramic squatter that thankfully had few flies because of the sawdust and lime that we used several times each day. Then I would head next door into the dark, cave-like bathing room. Inside it, the lone twenty-watt light bulb barely illuminated the darkness, so I often flipped back the yellow nylon curtain that covered the postcard-sized window in the cockeyed wooden door. For a moment a ray of sunshine would highlight the large drainage hole that snakes sometimes slithered up. Vicky had screamed once when she'd found an asp at her feet. Asif and Karim had sliced its head off with a shovel. After hearing that story, I shut and locked the door only after cautiously scanning the room for critters.

Twisting a metal valve on the vertical pipe, I scrutinized the lopsided L-shaped steel tubes that sourced the shower head. The sickly ducts shuddered as a dribble of cool water burped twice, about the same amount that an infant might spit up after nursing. So much for the shower. Much more reliable was a red plastic ladle and cold water from the cistern.

I removed my chador, the long, cotton veil that sat on my shoulders like a scarf when I was inside our compound and that I raised to cover my hair before joining village life. Next, I slipped the calf-length kameez over my head, removing the long-sleeved, loose-fitting dress that was bereft of zippers and buttons. Then came my shalwar, the drawstring-waisted pair of the widest pants ever, complete with cuffs at the ankles. They were so gigantic that three of me could fit into one pair. They hid every curve from prying eyes, for sure. The only sexy aspect of them was the triple-stitched cuffs that gave them the appearance of a genie's pantaloons. I needed only ankle bracelets to complete the costume. Stepping out of a shalwar without dunking the cuffs in puddles on the floor was tricky. About half of the times I exited the shower, the wet fabric felt like a dead fish slapping my ankles.

Bending forward, I stepped out of a lacy, black thong—underwear being the only erotic clothing that I had brought with me, a token of the sexuality that I had left behind, along with the jeans, short-sleeved tops and shorts that now sat in a cardboard box in Peshawar. I had no intention of having an affair while in Afghanistan. I had simply brought pretty lingerie because I felt feminine and desirable when wearing it, even when being ignored by most men. Apart from the cleaner and his mother, who hand-washed our clothes in her own home, only I saw them. At least, that's what I had thought. Each day the cleaner placed my provocative panties on top of the pile of laundry that he returned to my bedroom. Why didn't he cover them with a kameez or a shalwar? Maybe he had paraded them around the village amid lewd conversations and guffaws. Maybe the entire village knew what my underclothes looked like.

I reached for the ladle that floated in the cistern. Squinting in the darkness, I inspected the water for leeches. I was a tad paranoid because of that young boy at the clinic. Gritting my teeth, I exhaled as cold water drizzled over my head and shoulders, snatching heat from wherever it landed as it quickly evaporated in the thirsty air. The tepid water caused my nipples to point. Romance would come again one day. Lathering soap, my fingers followed each curve of my body.

The last time I'd made love had been in a tent under the stars in the Arizona desert. Peter and I had bought Hopi rings as a symbol of our commitment to each other, and to ward off any unwanted attention that I might receive in Afghanistan. At the time, the BBC had reported that an unmarried couple had been shot along the Karakorum Highway, an area that we were planning to visit. No reason had been given for the murders.

Since arriving in Afghanistan, my day-to-day activities had been in the company of men, with the exception of Dr. Saachi and a few other ladies who worked on the female side of the clinic, and at mealtimes in the compound with the reclusive Mary Anne. A rare treat when I visited families at home was a real hug from another woman, the kind that lingers for a few seconds. Although most Afghan men greeted me with a hand on their heart, several insisted on handshakes that sometimes lasted as long as fifteen seconds. Some even caressed my palm with their middle finger, as if that was a turn on! Disgusted, I would jerk my hand away.

Although my body ached for tenderness, proximity and connection, I was loyal to Peter. He was a good man, and I still had hope for us as a couple, even though my heart felt distant from him. Perhaps I expected too much?

In Bala Morghab we led quiet lives. I wasn't attracted to Jim or Martin, and Afghans were simply off limits. Other foreigners were a two-day drive away. Bala Morghab had no restaurants, bars or other social diversions. Liquor was outlawed, and we never tried to smuggle it in because the Taliban were strict about confiscating it and then targeting us. Although Mary Anne and Jim often spent time together in the evenings watching movies on DVD, I didn't join in because I preferred to learn about Afghan society through my conversations with Kareem and Asif.

In the bathing room, I shuddered as I poured several cups of cold water over my head, torso and limbs and watched the suds disappear down the drain. Within a minute my damp skin was dry.

The items that I missed most in that Bala Morghab bathroom were shaving cream, bright light, warm water and white-tiled bathroom floors. Shaving by feel left me with irregular patches of stubble and a multitude of nicks that I covered with bits of pink toilet paper.

This time, I smeared fruit-scented hair conditioner mixed with cold water onto my legs, then noticed a discarded bobby pin on the shelf by the sink. Folding a corner of the yellow curtain back onto itself, I secured it with the hairpin. A beam of sunlight highlighted my pale legs. Suddenly shaving became a whole lot easier. I hummed "You Can't Always Get What You Want" by the Rolling

Stones as my razor sliced another long, straight line through the glistening conditioner.

As I finished the stroke, the subtle, high-pitched sound of a smooth stone scraping against another one caused me to stop and listen. Was it close to the bathroom door? I waited and listened. The world outside was silent. Had I imagined the sound? I made another stroke, and the sound repeated three more times. Quickly, I tossed the razor onto the rickety countertop and tore cat-like toward the wooden door, flattening my naked form against it as I crouched beneath the tiny window. Outside the door, footsteps quickly approached. Mary Anne was usually the only person who was up at this hour. She would have called out. Jim always slept in and Martin had returned to Canada. The staff wouldn't come close to the bathroom door, would they? Panting, I extinguished the anemic light bulb and waited, my body far enough away from the door to avoid splinters.

The opening in the curtain covering the window was so small, it was hard to believe that anyone had noticed it. Someone must have been spying. The bathroom and women's bedrooms were off limits to the staff. Everywhere else in the compound, Afghan men milled about cleaning, guarding, fixing cars, cooking or doing administrative work. The Taliban had expressly forbidden us to hire women in the office. Only the eighteen-year-old cleaner was allowed in the back orchard during office hours, and he started work later. Once, I had caught him with his nose buried in Mary Anne's panties. Grossed out but thinking the behaviour was harmless, I had let it pass. Asif and Kareem had been so respectful and honest. The cook? No, he seemed pretty genuine. Who else could it be?

Men went to great lengths to protect the honour of women in their families.

The window in the door, mostly covered by the scrappy curtain, was also so scratched that a voyeur, if he was to see anything, would have to jam an eyeball right up to the glass. And if he did that, the light source would be blocked. What would he see? I crouched below the window and waited. A shadow closed in. Like a jack-in-the-box, I sprang up, flinging the wee curtain upward and placing my eyeball squarely in the middle of the postage-stamp window. I glared at what I couldn't see. My anger, not my nakedness, would be his reward. A dilated iris almost kissed mine through the window pane. The furtive eye scanned. I hurled silent insults at it. The pupil suddenly constricted. I waited like a statue. Who would be that disrespectful? As he drew back, Asif's round face appeared. The guard that I had trusted backed away, turned around, then scuttled away like a tortoise pursued by an eagle, stones clattering with every step.

I trembled. The cheat! How could he? It felt like he had stolen something, even though he had seen nothing. I wanted to scream at him and tell him how worthless he was. You might think that I was naive or that my reaction was overblown. Didn't I expect an Afghan man to do something like this, given the stringent restrictions between genders? The fact was, I didn't. The consequences for breaking their rules were pretty awful. A violated woman's family might retaliate with guns. Honour had to be maintained, so I simply thought that people adhered to the rules. I was used to having lots of male friends when travelling, competing in sports, working and socializing. I had thought that friendship with Afghan men was possible, even when uncommon. I had even visited his family and provided fertility advice to his wife. What signal had I overlooked? Without an Afghan family to defend me, I was a target.

As I dried myself, I brainstormed what to do. Our organization could fire him, but that didn't seem fair. Like most Afghan men in the village, he wasn't used to being close to women who weren't family members. I wasn't going to distance myself from Afghan men since my working world was replete with them, and I was too independent to have an expat chaperone at all times. Besides, no male expat would want that job. Yet I refused to ignore the issue, because Bala Morghab was inhabited by conservative Afghans, some of whom were Taliban. My safety depended upon local people valuing our work. If I let Asif get away with this, would he or others do it again, or something worse? Afghan laws offered me no protection whatsoever.

I pulled my kameez over my head. With temperatures as high as 45°C, I never wore a bra. A chador draped over a kameez provided sufficient coverage for my small breasts. At least that's what I thought. Bra-less, I felt avenged in some way for the many misogynous restrictions that I had little choice but to follow.

Twice I had been proved wrong, however. It was the Afghan matrons who had demonstrated their displeasure with strong, claw-like fingers that had darted out so quickly that I had failed to protect myself, and pain had radiated to my armpit as a vice-like grip clamped onto my nipple. The first time had been at a wedding during my first month in Bala Morghab. A woman with voluminous hips and pendulous breasts had zeroed in for the strike. The second time had been while bathing fully clothed with Afghan women in a creek where water flowed only ten centimetres deep. No men were nearby. I had rolled in the water to cool off, and when I stood up, my kameez had clung to me like plastic wrap. As I was repositioning my drenched chador, a pincer-like squeeze had caused me to jerk away. Why was she so nasty?

Fully dressed, I stood in front of the mirror in my bedroom, mascara wand in hand. Defiantly, I stroked the black tint the lengths of my eyelashes. If I had lived a life like Asif's, I certainly would have been a different person. Nevertheless, if he wanted to work for MSF, he had to control himself. I outlined my lips with a burgundy shade and smiled at the saucy woman who stared back at me.

At breakfast, the crusty flatbread was tasteless and the sour cherry jam was too sweet. I didn't want to give up my evening conversations with the night guards. I was learning so much. What punishment would be fair?

Mid-morning I approached Jim, a guy's guy whose unflappable judgment had struck me as both fair and gruff. Jim and I worked well together as long as we had lots of space. I respected his ingenuity when it came to car maintenance, any kind of travel, security issues and anything related to compound upkeep and improvements. But his unpredictable temper awakened a whole family of emotions inside me. One word or expression could set him off. When he was angry, I avoided him and buried my fury. Just like Dad, he seemed to see my pain and instinctively identify where I was most vulnerable. I would wager that Jim and I probably struggled with similar childhood demons.

We met in the back garden where no one but the cleaner might interrupt us. Cigarette in one hand and coffee cup in the other, he silently inspected my face. I'd never before requested a private conversation with him. Words rolled off my tongue faster than I had intended, as if they needed to escape before I changed my mind and decided to withhold them.

"Jim, Asif peeked at me through the window in the bathroom door while I was showering. I know without a doubt that it was him. When he backed away, I clearly saw his face." I paused to wipe a bead of sweat from my forehead, noting as I did, that my finger shook. Tears pricked at my eyes and I willed them away. I wanted him to put his arms around me, to comfort something deep inside, but I would never ask. I was strong. I could handle this. "I can't live and work here if that happens again. I don't trust him anymore. I wish I could, but I can't".

I watched a bird pecking a hard green peach in one of the spindly trees, then dragged my eyes back to meet Jim's. I read concern, which caused the knot between my shoulder blades to loosen. He kept silent.

"I don't think he should be fired. He needs the job, but he made a mistake that MSF can't accept because it will make life difficult for other expat women. If we do nothing, other Afghans may think that they can behave similarly." We all knew that word travelled fast in Bala Morghab.

He exhaled smoke and watched it billow outward before responding. "How did he see you?"

"The shower is so dark, it is difficult to shave my legs." It was such a weird conversation to have with a truck driver. "I folded back a small corner of the curtain to allow in some light. The staff aren't supposed to go there, and in the early morning, very few people are around."

Jim's head rolled back and his jaw snapped in a jarring rhythm as ring after ring of smoke swirled from his lips into a serpent-like chain stretching skyward.

I continued: "If there is no consequence for his behaviour, I am afraid that he'll do it again. He knows it's bad behaviour. For Pete's sake, it's wrong in Afghan culture! An Afghan man never peeks at another man's wife. Respecting women is a necessary part of his job. You have already warned him about his habit of sleeping during the night when he should be working. It hasn't made a difference. I caught him sleeping the other night."

He sighed. "You're probably right. What do you want to do with him?" His thumb picked a torn yellow cuticle.

"He's a good person. I think it's best to transfer him to the clinic for the night shift." No women will be there then. I twirled the two ends of my chador into tight spirals.

He ground out the stub of his hand-rolled cigarette on an adobe wall. "Okay, tonight he'll work at the clinic. Which guard do you prefer to replace him?"

"Salim." I had attended a wedding at Salim's house and had noted how much he respected his mother, though it probably didn't mean much. Asif had seemed to respect his wife. "Thanks, Jim. I feel bad for Asif, but I think this is best."

A few minutes later, I lifted my chador to cover my hair and cinched the cloth around my face. The daytime guard opened the gate, and I walked for eight solitary minutes to the clinic while contemplating what I would say later on to Kareem. Jim, Momo Rahim and I had decided that an eight-minute walk by myself to the clinic every day was safe enough.

That evening, after sending an email to Peter in which I described the escapade, then exaggerated my confidence in our solution, I stood up and stretched, noting how late it was. I was procrastinating. I reminded myself that Kareem wasn't Asif, but a niggling voice asked whether I had misjudged Kareem too. How well did I really know him? As I exited the office, I veered toward the living room. With papers in hand and a preoccupied expression painted on my face, I feigned being too busy for our evening chat. I just didn't feel like rehashing the event.

"Khonum Murreen, bio. Chai bokho." From his mat near the guard house, Kareem called out, asking if I would drink tea with him. He patted the straw mat. The new guard had already retired to the cubbyhole bedroom near the kitchen. I summoned my courage. Better to get this over with. As my stomach flip-flopped, I folded my legs beneath me. Steam from the cup of tea in front of me swirled upward.

"Drink tea." Kareem gulped the pale liquid. "Khonum Murreen, what happened? Now Salim is here and Asif is at the clinic." His voice was soft and kind, but his eyes were sifting through my thoughts like an octopus's tentacle explores the seabed. He swallowed again. Was his mouth as dry as mine?

Letting my vision go out of focus for a second, I slowed my breath and quieted my pounding heart. I donned the professional mask that I wore when giving patients bad news and steadied my voice. "This morning, when I was in the bathing room, Asif peeked at me through the window." My voice rattled on with a life of its own, the Dari words coming together more easily than I would have expected. "To do that is very bad. It is a big problem. Now I do not trust Asif, so he cannot work in this compound. From today, he only works in the clinic at night." I watched Kareem's eyes, trying to read what he wouldn't say.

He looked down at his cahier. "Khonum Murreen, is peeking very bad?" I sensed his guilt. Had our friendship screwed him up too?

"Yes, peeking is very bad! Peeking means that a man does not respect a woman. In Canada, men never do this!" I was blatantly exaggerating. Men peek at women everywhere. But at the time, I had convinced myself that male friends who respected me would never do such a thing. At least, I had never caught them in the act. "Never! If a man in Canada peeks at a woman like Asif did, he can lose his job." I clapped my hands and Kareem withdrew, as if I had just slapped his cheek. "In Afghanistan, peeking at an Afghan woman is a big problem, isn't it? For example, let's pretend Asif peeks at your sister when she is bathing. What do you do?" I paused to scrutinize his eyes.

Frustrated with his lack of response, I upped the stakes. "Or maybe it is your wife? What happens if Asif peeks at your wife when she is bathing?" I sat back. Kareem cared deeply for his wives and his mother, and he was very private.

"If my wife is bathing, Asif is never in my house. It is impossible." He flung words full of disdain at me.

"Suppose Asif comes over to discuss something and your wife is bathing. What then?" Some scenario would make sense to him.

"I don't let him inside, Khonum Murreen." Poised to take another drink, he peered at me like I was an opponent. "In the bathroom, why was the curtain open?" If we had been playing chess, he would have curtly muttered, "Check."

Did he think that Asif's actions were acceptable? I stretched my neck to relieve the tension that had built up. "The bathing room is dark. With light from the little window, it is easier to see. Guards do not go into the back garden. You know this. Good men never peek at a woman in the bathing room. It is a sin." If he was going to continue to work with expats, he needed to know this.

He said nothing but his eyes softened.

"Pretend Asif or another man is a guest in your house. Pretend there is a hole in the curtain and he peeks at your wife. Maybe she is changing her dress." Kareem's wives stayed in the family compound most of the time. His family forbade photographs of women. To him, this was normal.

He refilled my teacup, anger flashing briefly across his eyes before he snuffed it out. "It's not possible. Asif cannot do this."

The muezzen's voice beckoned him to pray. Tilting his head, Kareem stood up and spread out his patu. Facing Mecca, he prayed for the standard time. I breathed in the soothing rhythm. Afterward, he sat cross-legged, looking peaceful and content. His patu, once again, was neatly draped over one shoulder. How different the world might be if everyone meditated for a minute or two, five times a day. Would we live more peacefully and connected? Would there be fewer wars?

Peeking was ubiquitous in Afghan villages.

After taking a sip of tea, Kareem spoke. "Khonum Murreen, sometimes, I am peeking too when you do sports in your room." He paused, and as he did, he tumbled face first from the pedestal on which I had placed him. I recoiled. Him too? It was so hot and stuffy in my room that I did calisthenics in my lingerie, which was the closest thing that I had to gym gear. While exercising, I clipped back a small triangle of curtain to let in light, thinking that because my room was at the very end of the back orchard, no one would ever notice. I suppressed an urge to throw my tea in his face.

"Never leave a curtain open if you do not want an Afghan to peek, Khonum Murreen. Afghans always peek. Always." His lips twisted into a rueful grin.

I nodded. Kareem was bright. He was motivated to learn. I decided to teach him. "Never peek at expat women. It is very bad, like a sin. If you peek, I cannot trust you, and maybe you lose your job." My frown deepened.

Bowing his head, Kareem looked relieved. I examined his eyes for some kind of remorse. He looked genuinely sorry that I was upset by this, but I wasn't convinced that he agreed with my point of view. He did, however, respect what it meant to me. He would probably think twice before doing it again. And I would never again allow him, or anyone, the opportunity.

CHAPTER ELEVEN

WOMEN

"A woman with a voice is by definition a strong woman. But the search to find that voice can be remarkably difficult."

— *Melinda Gates*

Alone in a dusty street, I knocked for the third time on the wooden door that seemed to swallow every sound created by my fist. No one answered. There was no metal knocker, and I didn't dare try the latch. Afghan compounds were private places and, like most villagers, Kareem probably had a gun. Surprising an armed man was a bad idea.

Looking both ways, I verified that no Taliban police were nearby, ready to charge me for one of their ridiculous misdemeanours that mattered to no one else. Apart from me, the street was empty. After five months of being chaperoned by men almost every time I left the compound, standing alone in the street felt risqué. My heart pounded, even though I could still see our compound gate. It was Friday, the Afghan holy day. I rehashed Kareem's invitation. I counted the doorways again. This one was the fourth on the right. Like a disheartened kid, I whacked the door again. My hand hurt.

Earlier that week during one of our evening conversations, Kareem had seemed distracted. He had rolled an empty teacup from hand to hand, like it alleviated nervous energy. Silently, as if acknowledging what I'd noticed, he placed the cup between us with a sheepish grimace. Immediately, he started spinning a pen over the web linking index to thumb, something he did when struggling to answer a tricky question. His finger trembled. Finally, he blurted out what was eating him up.

"Murreen-jan, I invite you to my home this Friday for lunch. Will you come?" His earnest eyes had drilled into mine. This was a big deal for him. Invitations by most others had been off the cuff, simply an offering. Kareem wanted me to accept.

Feeling as giddy as a schoolgirl being asked out on her first date, I had said yes and my whole body had smiled. I was dying to meet his two wives and to discover the real story behind this remarkable man

I loved visiting families on my days off. This young woman posed for me with her infant in the doorway to a room, inside her family's compound.

who had become my confidant and key source of Afghan informa-tion. After waiting months for an offer to meet his family, I had given up on the idea, assuming that his reasons for holding back were im-portant to him. Entertaining an independent woman like me might be difficult for him. Perhaps he didn't want his wives to hear ideas that didn't fit with Afghan norms. Or maybe he was ashamed of his two-room rental property. The large land parcel that he owned in a village farther north was mined, which is why he had moved south to find work.

In the distance, the friendly figure of Salim turned into the street.

"As salaam alaikum, Doktar Murreen! How are you? Are you well? Where are you going?" he called out loudly, his elf-like body swaying jauntily. He lived two doors away from the MSF compound.

"Wa alaikum e salaam, Salim. I am well. How are you? And your family?" The greeting went on like it usually did.

"You are at Kareem's house. Khobe!" His eyebrow rose as he turned to face the door, raised an arm like he was going to pitch a baseball and, using his entire body, he slammed his fist against the wood. A deadened sound reverberated through the door. We stared ahead at the deeply fissured grey wood that was flecked with crim-son paint. His eyes asked what I was doing at Kareem's door on a Friday, but he didn't voice the question, and it was none of his busi-ness anyway. Everyone in town eventually found out where I went. Later, Momo Rahim or another employee would ask me for details that I rarely provided.

Kareem appeared in the doorway, his cheeks sucking inward. He scanned the street, then stepped forward. Their greeting was lengthy. Ours was short. Behind him, the fluttering of a curtain her-alded the arrival of Kareem's eldest son, Abdulkhak. He was the shy boy with the scalp infection whose picture I had taken with the cow. Lifting his bangs, he pointed to the bald patch, where short, dark hairs were sprouting.

I grinned. "Kheli khobe! You are better."

He smiled self-consciously.

"Chai mekhorid?" Kareem offered tea to Salim. He refused. No second invitation materialized. Momo Rahim proclaimed that Afghan offers for tea or for meals were genuine only if repeated three times. Any Afghan worth his salt refused the first two offers.

"Thank you. I go home to my wife." Hand on his heart, Salim turned in the direction he had come from.

After closing the door, Kareem wedged a thick wooden beam against it, slipping both ends securely into supports on the door frame. He drew the curtain aside and we entered the inner sanctum. The brown and white cow, flanked by two sheep, nibbled grass stacked against the house. Abdulkhak silently squatted near her, tugging at her teats. Milk jetted into the bucket.

"The milk looks rich. Do you sell it?" I spoke Dari to him. He was too shy to use any English words, if he knew any. The relationship between Kareem and him felt stiff. Abdulkhak's mother had died when he was born. A kid could believe that he was responsible for such things.

"It is for the children." His tone was condescending, as if he no longer considered himself one. He was almost the age Kareem had been at his first wedding. Hefting the weight of the milk bucket with one hand, his body curved into a C as he shuffled across the courtyard, past the open-air kitchen, through an archway, then out of sight.

In the kitchen, naan, wrapped in checkered cotton, steamed at the top of a tandoor oven. A hand-stitched hat that hung on the adobe wall. Rural women wore such hats to provide structure for draping

A young child swung gently in a hammock-like cradle as I spoke with his mother.

a *chaderie*, a full-length, head-to-toe covering used instead of a bur-ka. It glinted silver in the sunshine. Below it, a large tin spoon hung from a hook. A young woman used a gigantic aluminum ladle to stir a burbling pot over a fire. Her eyes were outlined with kohl. Her kelly green dress ended just above her ankles, which were covered by lacy white pantaloons. Squatting next to a pile of sheep scat, she added a shovelful of it into the fire, all the while cooing to an infant wrapped in a shawl tied around her waist and across a shoulder. A magenta chador slipped off her hip-length dark hair. Grasping an edge, she pulled it back up. She stood up on sturdy bare feet and a delicious, meaty aroma saturated my nostrils. Then, in a silent swirl of green and fuchsia, she disappeared down the hallway where Abdulkhak had gone. I stifled an urge to call out. Why had she disappeared before we met?

"Let's drink tea!" Kareem said with a grin. Patting the cow, he offered it stems of dried grass from the stash. "The cow pastures in Momo Rahim's nearby field. In my home village, we had much land for animals and for houses, but here the cow must spend the night in our home." He spoke as if wishing for past comforts, like Momo Rahim often did.

His son returned with the empty pail.

"Son, take the cow to the pasture."

Abdulkhak picked up the rope and led the sauntering animal through the curtain, pulling it shut behind them. Only then did I hear the front door open.

A powerful hand on my elbow gently steered me toward the door of a room at the opposite end of the compound from the hallway where the young woman had vanished. Looking down, I noticed a wizened face near my shoulder. A white chaderie printed with tiny blue and purple flowers cascaded over her head and ended at her ankles. Women in Bala Morghab used the term "chaderie" for two types of coverings: a thin chador-like robe when at home, and a thick, heavily embroidered garment like a medieval mantle for going outside. When necessary, the face could be hidden by wrapping the two front edges around the head.

The woman's body curved forward like a parenthesis, probably a result of osteoporosis. Using Kareem's age, I calculated how old this matriarch must have been. We were a similar age, yet she looked two decades my senior! Although her life had been infinitely more difficult than mine, her grey eyes beamed a warm welcome. This tiny woman seemed fortified in some way. I instantly liked her. At the same time, I felt lucky.

"Bio, chai bokho." Her calloused hand grasped mine. Together, we walked through the sun-dappled shade beneath a mulberry tree toward the guest room doorway.

"My mother, Doktar Murreen." Kareem mumbled self-consciously, his pride mixed with boyhood self-consciousness. I imagined the intensity of their discussion about whether he should invite me into their home. Was her vote the reason why his invitation had taken so long?

Glancing over my shoulder toward the archway on the far side of the courtyard, I saw two young women standing side by side and whispering, each one bouncing a baby in her arms. A two-year-old and a four-year-old hid amid the folds of their mothers' skirts, peeking out to smile coyly before quickly ducking behind the drapery. My first impression of Kareem's wives was that they were healthy and of a similar age. The one who had been stirring the pot was bigger and looked jovial.

"Kalakashak konand," Kareem said with a smile. I loved that phrase, which meant "they peek." In Bala Morghab, where so many activities were forbidden, we all peeked. I beamed.

Extending a hand toward his older son, he spoke softly. "Doktar Murreen, hast. Give her your hand."

The stocky four-year-old clung to his father's fingers and peeked doe-like at me. His eyes darted here and there, as if paralyzed by an internal argument, before abruptly releasing his dad's fingers and strutting toward me, his right hand extended, his eyes glued to my fingers. As soon as he was close enough, he slapped a pudgy palm onto mine, then yanked my index and third fingers with surprising strength.

His big brown eyes met mine. "Khosh amadid!" he yelled, welcoming me. For a split second he stood tall and stiff like a miniature soldier, then he bent down, pumped his arms up and down like a goose preparing to fly, and torpedoed back to the dark-haired beauty from the kitchen. Diving beneath her skirt, he plowed between her legs. Struggling to maintain her balance, she rubbed his back and whispered what a brave boy he had been.

Just then, the younger son closed in, his kohl-outlined eyes locked onto my hand. Sticky fingers grabbed mine for a moment, then threw them away as he arced his body in a pirouette that enabled him to barrel back to his mother's protective skirt. The elder boy shoved him. The smaller one slapped his big brother's shoulder, then both of them scampered to their mothers' skirts and a scolding. The stout wife approached with an infant in her arms, the four-year-old trailing behind her.

"This is Bibi-gul." Kareem introduced his senior wife. Bibi meant grandmother and gul meant flower. Laying a hand on her heart, she nodded, smiled, then extended her palm. As we shook hands, the many callouses on her powerful fingers stimulated images of the heavy pots that she had lifted, the mountains of laundry done by hand, and the loads of water and other things that she had carried.

"I am so happy to meet you, Bibi-gul." I was conscious of my soft pianist's fingers, my decades of higher education and my barren uterus. She looked content with her mapped out life. If she fit into Afghan norms, she would have nine pregnancies, possibly each spaced by a couple of years. With luck, she would survive them all. Several of her children would die in childhood, and when she reached my age, she would be a stooped grandma.

My life hadn't come with such a road map. I chose a direction, took a step, and a path unfolded. In moments of loneliness, I envied her place in the family, and the clear expectations that provided her with structure. But I would never be happy with a life like hers.

The smaller wife approached, her youngest suckling a bulging breast. Her elder son grabbed her thigh. She stumbled, then smacked him with an outstretched palm.

"Fadheela, hast." Kareem pronounced her name. It meant virtue. She reminded me of Rapunzel, her thick mane caressing her waist.

They looked like sisters, both of them cousins from different arms of his large extended family. His wives' world was made up of household tasks, family, the rare visit to a clinic, and on occasion chores outside the home when accompanied by a maharam—usually Abdulkhak. They had lived in a small village north of Bala Morghab until they were forced to escape after Kareem's family was butchered. Kareem probably told them stories of life beyond compound walls.

At such a young age, he was fortunate to have four sons. The boys that made it past childhood would take care of him and his wives until they died. A man's mother became the matriarch of his family, the boss of her daughters-in-law, which was probably the zenith of a village woman's career. Did that somehow pit women against their own gender and disempower them all, or did it strengthen them?

Most of my visits to other households with more than one wife had been pleasant. Rich elders housed each wife in a different compound where the man visited them individually. However, one visit to an employee had broken my heart. After having eaten dinner with the men, I had met the well-dressed and confident wife, as well as several other ladies who were busy washing dishes, eating and minding children. Noticing a woman squatting alone in a corner, her eyes downcast, her dress dirty and patched, I started to approach her, a hand on my heart.

"She is my senior sister-wife. She bore him no sons. Now she is too much sad." The employee's younger wife had spoken impatiently, tugging at my arm, as if she felt ashamed by this woman.

The ghostly form's tattered chador covered her straggly hair, and draped itself across cracked, calloused feet. As our employee, the husband could have provided better care for her. Chances were that she was depressed—but in Afghan village society, mental illness was taboo. I thanked his younger wife for the lovely meal, despite its bitter aftertaste, and vowed that I would watch this man.

During our nightly conversations, Kareem often extolled how peaceful his existence was at home. His father had taught him the importance of creating equity to maintain tranquility. He told me that he divided everything equally between his wives and among his sons. Was he truly as just as he professed to be? His mother did appear to be the gentle soul that he had described. I tried to think like his wives but failed. How could I? What would life be like if I spent day after day inside these walls? As a Westerner used to so much freedom, I shook my head. I would go nuts. But if I had never known this liberty, would I feel satisfied with such a secure existence? Were his wives simply better at accepting rules than I was? Or were the potential consequences of breaking them just too dire?

"Let's drink tea. Welcome." Pulling aside a curtain made of fabric identical to her chaderie, Kareem's mom stretched a hand toward the door. A puff of cool air caressed my cheek, remnants of night air safeguarded by thick adobe walls.

What if I told her that I preferred to stay outside with the boys building towers with rocks and sticks and other household refuse instead of enduring another stilted conversation about my marital status? What convinced me to duck into the room was my curiosity about her and how she had molded Kareem into the man he had become.

She indicated the place of honour, a cushion near a shuttered bay window overlooking the courtyard. When she folded the wooden shutters back on themselves, a warm breeze blew in.

"Bishinid." She asked me to sit, smiled and pointed at the cushion. As soon as I sat down, the two-year-old and four-year-old appeared in the doorway, hauling pillows about the same size as they were. They looked like they were dancing clumsily in a zigzag trajectory that caused them to bump against each other. When the cushions landed with a thump, clouds of dust rose from the carpet.

Abdulkhak brought in a thermos of tea and a tray of glass cups. A flowery plastic tablecloth was tucked under an arm. The younger boys opened the tablecloth and spread it on the floor, finishing the job with their bare feet. The feat having been accomplished, they somersaulted, one landing spread eagle and the other toppling sideways, a foot landing on his brother's head. Kareem's mom waved them aside and smoothed out the kinks. Bibi-gul set down trays of sun-dried green raisins and roasted pine nuts and sunflower seeds encased in shells. I plucked a few raisins and savoured their flavour, which was so much more pungent than that of varieties bought in Canada.

Kareem sat at the end of the room near the door, as if eavesdropping. His mom perched on a pillow near me. Bibi-gul and Fadheela sat together, each cradling an infant.

"Welcome! You are our guest." His mother pumped tea into glasses, serving mine first. "Eat!" She nudged the snack trays closer to me and away from the boys' frisky fingers, which had already snagged a few morsels.

"Let's eat together." I plucked a few more raisins and sunflower seeds, then pushed the trays toward Kareem's wives.

"How many children do you have?" His mother's expressive grey-blue eyes reminded me of Nancy Dupree.

"I have no children." Hadn't Kareem told them anything about me? Or had they not believed his stories?

Fadheela dug an engorged breast out of her neckline. Milk dripped into her infant's mouth just before he gobbled the nipple and sucked hard enough to cause her to wince, his fists grabbing at her soft flesh. Her older son snuggled in, his fingers struggling to release the other breast. She pushed his hand away. He pinched her. She swatted him. Kareem sat the boy down.

Bibi-gul's eldest was using sunflower seeds to draw in the dirt. Every so often, one of them went into his mouth. She tapped his hand and spoke in Pashto. He spat the seed out and wailed. Pouting, he threw a handful of them on the ground. She smacked his head, then stood up, and while cradling the infant in her arm, she tugged the naughty boy toward the door.

In the silence, the infant slurped wetly. Gosh, I wouldn't have the patience for kids like these! How did his wives maintain their sanity? Fadheela's baby mewed, then burped, the spit-up milk dribbling down his chin. She wiped a string of mucous off with an edge of her dress.

"Your husband, where is he?" His mother asked the tiresome question that I answered as usual. "Why do you have no husband?" She peered at me with a look of sympathy while picking at a knotted thread in her chaderie. Any respectable village woman my age would have married long ago. "Children are too important! Without children, what is life?" She probably wondered if I was sick or if my family was ashamed of me. I usually said that I hadn't met the right person. In truth, I was afraid of losing myself in a marriage like Mum had. When I was a teenager, I had seen and felt her sorrow at having lost an independent part of herself.

"If I have a husband and children, I cannot do the kind of work that makes me happy." Although I didn't want kids, I was content to borrow them periodically.

"But you must want children!" Her eyes probed mine just like her son's sometimes did.

"I never wanted children," I replied and sipped some tea. I didn't usually say it so bluntly. "I love travelling too much. If I have children, I must stay home. If I stay home all the time, I feel unhappy. In Canada, a single woman can own a house, earn money and buy things. When I am old, I won't need children to take care of me." A caring daughter would be nice if I became feeble, but so many children, preoccupied with their own lives, shelved their parents in retirement homes. Given my drive and impatience, that's how my kids would have turned out. At menopause I would have made a fine mother!

"You are happy...?" The slight inflection suggested that she didn't understand how that could be.

"Yes, my life is good." I burrowed straight into those grey-blue eyes, trying my hand at reading her mind. Had she wanted more from life? Probably. I imagined that religion had helped her deal with disappointment and contain her adventurous spirit so she could do what was expected.

"You are not lonely?" Her face looked curious, possibly fascinated.

I glanced at Kareem, who knew my answers to these questions by heart. He watched quietly, his face a mask. "Sometimes I am lonely, but mostly I am happy. I read a lot. I write. I work. I have friends and a family."

"Friends?" Her forehead crinkled, and her head tipped to the left. Her eyes asked many questions. Given cultural restrictions, her only friends had probably been during childhood. Perhaps her many brothers and sisters compensated for that.

Kareem interjected. "Friends, like two sisters drinking tea and eating sweets." His description sounded Victorian.

Bibi-gul and her elder son reappeared in the doorway. He wiped a dribble of snot with the back of his hand. Maybe they had snuggled in the back room.

On the carpet, I placed photos of my family, skyscrapers in Vancouver, a church and people on the seawall in Stanley Park. Bibi-gul, Fadheela and the kids closed in. Bibi-gul pointed to the family photographs. "Who are these people?"

Filling the room with stories, I introduced my father, mother, three sisters, nieces and nephews. My parents had been married for forty-one years. I told them who fit with whom as I filled the blank spaces with pieces of a puzzle. I was no longer a solitary question mark. I was a part of a sentence. A wise Thai woman once told me that in Asia a person without a family simply did not exist since there was no context to support who they were. She went on to say that in North America, we believe we are free, but she thought we were lost.

I didn't feel lost. I loved change and the possibility of growing from every experience. Armed with new perspectives, I could improve systems and organizations. I could also help people transform their lives into new versions that served them better than previous ones had.

"Do you live with your parents?" Bibi-gul stared at the family portrait, then glanced up. Any woman she knew would.

"No, I live by myself. My home is far from their village. My sisters and I live in different cities." My parents had moved to the USA just after my little sisters finished high school. A couple of decades later, when my parents returned to Canada, moving to Quebec, my sisters had stayed in New England. Mum had Canada in her bones, and Dad was a capitalist at heart. Our family story was too complex to explain with my limited linguistic skills.

"But you see them often." Kareem's mother stated the obvious—which, in my case, was untrue.

"I live far away. One week it takes to drive to my parents' house." She looked disappointed so I changed topics. "Here is the city where I live." I pointed to a photograph of glass skyscrapers that looked like giant mirrors and to two women and two men on the seawall in Stanley Park. They were random people whom I'd met while cycling.

"Are they your family?" Fadheela's Pashto question was translated by Kareem as her infant tooted and the sweet odour of poop filled the room.

"No, they are friends. We are walking on a path that follows the ocean." My finger traced the seawall in the image.

"Why do you have a photo of them?" Bibi-gul grabbed the image to peer at it more closely. Her son stole it from her and ran away but was caught by Kareem, who forced him to give the picture back.

"Because it is a pretty place. They agreed that I take the photo. This is a forest in the middle of the city." I pointed to the big trees and the waves that crashed into the shore. "This is the ocean. It is like the Bamian Lakes only much bigger."

"This is a woman or a man?" Ignoring the wonders of nature, Bibi-gul pointed to the twenty-year-old dressed in slacks and a shirt.

"A woman."

"Women do not wear chaderie?" Bibi-gul brought the photo close to her face.

"No. Before I came to Afghanistan, I did not wear a chador or a chaderie. It is not common in my country. My country is Kaa-naa-daa."

"Kaa-naa-daa." Bibi-gul parroted the word. Her eldest mimicked her like an echo.

"Is this your mosque?" Kareem's mother touched the photograph of a Quebec church enshrouded by autumn leaves.

"It is like a mosque but for Christians. It is where Christians pray." Churches didn't exist in their world.

"You pray every day?" Bibi-gul asked.

"Every week, maybe one or two days, Christians pray in a church. The other days, Christians pray at home." I thought about gratitude expressed before meals and prayers children often recited before sleep.

"Is your father sad that he has only daughters? Is he lonely?" Bibi-gul gave voice to the burning question that they all had.

"My father says that he is happy with only daughters. In Canada, it is fine to have only daughters because daughters take care of their parents, even when they work like me." Secretly, I believed that Dad would have liked a son, but he never did admit it. Instead, he had decided that girls could do anything, whether it was playing golf, curling, cycling, woodworking, painting, photography, gardening, polishing rocks, stamp collecting or anything else that he might have dreamed of doing with a boy.

Fadheela's older son stole the baby's soother, so she pressed her nipple into the whimpering mouth as she chased the boy around the room. When she slapped him, the infant cried.

The two toddlers tumbled into the tea, and Kareem spoke sternly: "Go outside!"

Both wives exited. Suddenly, it was peaceful. How could adults in this house have any grown-up time together? No wonder Kareem enjoyed studying English at the MSF compound!

His mother spit out bits of pine nut shell and wiped a dark fleck from her lower lip. "I married when I was fourteen years old. As I left my family I felt very afraid. His father already had three wives." She pointed to Kareem. "I didn't know how to be a wife but I learned. It was a good life. I never saw my family again. They are all dead except for Kareem. Now I teach the children." She smiled. It looked genuine. What had she done with all of that grief? She went on to explain how she liked wearing a heavy, embroidered chaderie when she left the security of the compound. The first time she saw a man who didn't belong to her family, her heart had raced. Closing the front of the chaderie had made her feel safe. Covered up, she could peek out without being seen.

She glanced at the top shelf attached to the wall. On it lay something wrapped in embroidered white cotton.

"My husband and my other boys died in the fighting. Thanks to Allah that Kareem is a wonderful son." She smiled at him, her eyes momentarily melancholy.

Reaching up, Kareem lifted the bound bundle, raised it to his forehead, kissed it, then lay it on a wooden stand that he placed beside his mother. Beneath the fabric was a beautifully-bound leather book with golden Arabic script. The Koran was a regal object in their simple compound. Reverently, she flipped its pages.

"I am sad that I cannot read the Holy Koran." From the middle of the book, she extracted a black and white photo of a man, raised it to her forehead, kissed it, then handed it to me. It was a formal portrait of a good-looking man wearing a turban and shalwar kameez just like Kareem wore. "My husband, his father." She kissed him again, then replaced him between the pages of the sacred book and dressed it once again in its cloth. Raising it to her forehead, she recited a prayer.

Kareem replaced it on the shelf. At the time, it was illegal to have photos of people. And although no one hung them on walls, many families stashed a few cherished ones in secret cubbyholes just in case the Taliban came knocking at their door.

After a time his mother left, and Kareem and I were face to face again. But the energy between us was different in his house, more formal and less comfortable. I wanted to make him laugh but couldn't think of anything to say that would change his thin-lipped smile.

Abdulkhak appeared in front of me with a tin flask of water and a fresh bar of Lux soap. I washed my hands. Kareem did the same. Abdulkhak brought in a tray with two steaming bowls of soup, two Uzbeki naan and a bottle of water with two cups. He set them down on the tablecloth and disappeared.

Where were the others? Two bowls was a little awkward for his entire family to share even if they were used to communal dining. I shifted my weight to the other hip.

"This is lovely! And bottled water, what a treat!" Why had he wasted money on expensive, bottled water when he knew that I drank tea? He shrugged a little too disinterestedly.

Smoothing out his patu beside me, he began whispering a prayer. Why was he praying beside the only infidel in his home? Wasn't it better if Muslims prayed together? Or did he simply relish the peace and quiet? Were the others praying in the other room?

Once finished, he began ripping apart a round loaf of flatbread and tossing the pieces into the broth like I used to do as a child. I followed his lead. He tasted a spoonful. I pressed my tongue against the roof of my mouth, the friable mutton and potatoes falling apart with the pressure.

"The soup is delicious." Rich broth spiced with paprika and cumin.

Kareem nodded. Continuing to eat, his face remained inscrutable. His soup was disappearing rapidly. Why was I dining alone with their husband? Usually I ate with the entire family unless male guests were present. In those situations, I dined with the men. Was this a test of some kind? A niggling voice deep inside my head spoke. What if this was a date to assess me as a contender for his third wife? I wouldn't want to offend him, yet... yikes!

I forced myself to eat slowly, leaving about half of the food because I worried that someone in the back room might need my leftovers more than I did. What if they didn't have enough food and that was why we were eating apart?! Recalling the large pot, I reassured myself that they weren't anticipating my dregs. Kareem was too equitable for that.

"Kareem, your wives and children, where did they go?" I watched him spoon broth into his mouth without spilling a drop onto his beard. Eating with utensils wasn't common for villagers.

"They are eating." He contemplated his soup. His face twitched. Did Kareem never eat with his wives?

"Why are they not eating with us?" I tried to read the answer that he wouldn't share, while shifting my kameez so it absorbed the beads of sweat rolling down my ribcage.

"They think that you like eating in peace, without my noisy sons. That is why they eat in the other room." He grinned sheepishly. That was his preference, not mine!

"I would be happy to eat with your children and your wives," I said as I swallowed another mouthful of broth.

"They are noisy. You do not think this is true?" His crow's feet crinkled, as if he was laughing.

"Of course they are noisy. They are children." I put down my spoon.

"I told them to join us, but they said you would not want to eat near children. If it makes you happy, go to the next room and tell them to come back. They do not believe me." His eyes twinkled as he used his last scrap of bread to wipe the bowl. What had given his wives the idea that I didn't like kids? Rolling onto my knees, I was standing up when Abdulkhak reappeared.

"Son, if they have finished eating, tell them we drink tea here." Kareem smiled at me. Suddenly, I felt lighter.

"Which wife cooks the bread?"

"Sometimes they cook together, and other times one chooses to do the cooking by herself. It is their decision." His muttering made it sound like these issues didn't concern him.

"Which one cooks best?"

He shrugged. "Different things they do well. One makes delicious pilau and the other makes tastier bread. They teach each other." He looked uncomfortable. I was simply wanting to know if they got to do what they liked.

"Do they share childcare?" I wished to be a fly on their wall for a few days so I could see what really went on without my presence causing their interactions to change. How did they decide who did which chore? Did they fight like my older sister and I had done? Or did they have some kind of system that made everything fair? Heck, having a sister-wife would provide instant childcare!

"Mostly, they look after their own children. If needed, they take care of each other's kids, like if one of them is giving birth. My mother helps them too." His eyes were closing, as if he would soon doze off.

"Your mother is kind." Like mother, like son. Both of them had been forced to mature rapidly.

Abdulkhak cleared the dishes as everyone else piled in with an eruption of yelps, imitation motor sounds and comments.

"You eat so little. You must have more soup!" His mother was really asking whether I found the food tasty. I flooded her with compliments. Again she insisted that I eat more.

At last, Kareem came to my rescue. "She always eats little. See? She is too skinny!"

I would have liked having a brother like him. The first time I heard myself described by Afghans as too skinny had been a shock.

Inside compounds, I shared many stories with Afghan women. Burkas made chance encounters with women in the street difficult because they obscured facial cues. These mothers and their children were travelling in a donkey-drawn cart led by their maharam.

My athletic build was a weakness! To them, *choc* meant well-nourished enough to withstand bouts of food scarcity, but it was simply translated into "fat." The idea certainly made sense in a place where starvation occurred every few years.

Kareem inhaled a cup of tea, then slung his patu over a shoulder. "I go to the mosque. It is time to pray." It was a Friday ritual.

His mother patted the air, inviting me to stay longer. She rose to pray. The boys chased each other, jumped over the teapot, then wrestled until the younger one cried out. Throughout their entire escapade, she quietly prayed. Once finished, she shooed them outside. At that moment, I heard several women laugh. More of them giggled. Suddenly, burkas and chaderies entered in bunches, all of them chattering, their babies attached to their sides while older children ran and played together. Within moments, the room was full of women perching wherever there was space, their children crawling, playing peek-a-boo and cooing.

Bibi-gul fired questions at me in Dari, interpreting everything I said into Pashto. Tell us what life is like in Canada? Why do you come here? Do you like it here? Why aren't you married? With no children and no husband, aren't you lonely? The fact that I was content mystified them. Without a husband, you must work. Doesn't working make you tired? Gosh, their lives would tucker me out far more than my worst days would!

My photos travelled from hand to hand while Bibi-gul and Fadheela highlighted memorized details. "Here is a church. It is like a mosque. It is where she prays. She prays at home too. In her country, women don't wear burkas or chaderies. See, the clothing is different. This is her family, her sisters. She has no brothers but her father is not sad." The conversation roamed over known territory, then onto novel ground.

Bibi-gul's eldest was perfectly illuminated by a ray of sunshine. I asked permission to take his picture. Bibi-gul agreed, and both wives wound chadors over their faces. I had promised Kareem that I would never photograph them. In his family, images of women from the family were sinful. Photos of me were accepted since I wasn't Afghan.

We then amused ourselves by arranging their children in different poses: with the tea kettle, draped in colourful cloth, with more kohl outlining their eyes and always with a cute expression. Kareem's wives would pester him for weeks before the photos completed the round trip to Pakistan. I made sure to give equal film to each son. Underneath his wives' camaraderie, I sensed competition.

An hour later, a faint cough that I barely noticed caused a flurry of whispers.

"He's back!" Bibi-gul spoke urgently.

From ledges and hooks flew burkas and chaderies. The ladies rapidly finished their sentences as coverings fluttered overtop of their heads. They scampered and giggled through the arch to a hidden back door. The party was over. The man of the house had returned.

A WEAKNESS

"The great art of learning is to understand but a little at a time."

—*John Locke*

"My wife is weak from too many pregnancies. Can you help me?" Kareem looked exasperated. "She must become choc again." He sighed, his shoulders hunching forward and his angular face lengthening as if stretched by a humongous weight. To him, if a woman was choc, she conceived healthy babies and made rich milk. Maybe she was more energetic too.

"Which medicines must I buy for her?" He showed me a long list of vitamins and other tablets that he had already purchased from the bazaar. As we discussed each one, I crossed several of them off his list. They caused no harm, but none of them would solve her underlying problem. Basic blood tests and x-rays were available in the regional hospital, a two-day drive away, but there was little point in recommending any of them.

A trial of birth spacing was much more practical, and yet it was such a controversial topic in a village where most people believed that Allah controlled fertility. According to Momo Rahim, a few progressive mullahs secretly supported birth spacing when it helped moms stay healthy, but most held steadfastly to literal interpretations of the Koran. The topic was broached only in secret among a trusted group.

"Your wife can become strong if she is pregnant every three years, not each year. Her body must recover after making a baby or she stays weak." I knew that he spoke of Fadheela, his thin wife who looked like she needed a break.

"How many babies do you want?" I did a quick calculation to factor in the expected loss of life that was common in Afghanistan. At the time, a quarter of Afghan children died before their fifth birthday. Young men's lives were lost in accidents or armed conflict, while young women perished in childbirth. By the time he was old enough to require help from his children, he might have lost half of them. So he would want at least eight. To date, he had five.

A young girl watched me as she stood among domed compounds. Birth spacing could give her the opportunity for education.

"Khonum Murreen, it is Allah's will. Only Allah knows that I accept His decision." His smile beamed with the certainty of the fervently religious.

If I could make even one method of birth control palatable to him, I might be able to help her.

"Do you know how to space her pregnancies?" I fiddled with my teacup. The topic was a potential minefield. Where was solid, common ground? Healthy mothers made healthy babies. Most people could rally behind that. But different families interpreted this in different ways, with husbands and their mothers determining what was permissible. Allah's will was followed by most, but Kareem had very much enjoyed and accepted our conversations on science. I needed to shift his mother's stance too.

The leathery skin of his forehead furrowed deeply. "When she breastfeeds, I am thinking she does not become pregnant, but she does!" He flung a pencil onto his cahier.

"There are other ways to space births. Do you know them?" As I spoke, my cheeks felt hot. I felt flattered that he trusted me enough to ask for help with such a sensitive issue, but what could I present that he hadn't already heard?

He shook his head.

The midwife in the MSF clinic provided several methods, but she never broached the topic. It was safer for her to wait for patients to name it first. Only then would she provide guidance or procedures. After discussing birth spacing options with their husbands and choosing one, they returned to the clinic. Rarely, a woman decided her husband's wishes. For those few, the midwife inserted IUDs, cutting the strings so short that a husband wouldn't notice them.

I watched Kareem as I outlined how the birth control pill worked, explaining that it contained hormones made by women's bodies that fooled their ovaries and womb so a pregnancy did not occur. His wife would take a pill every day. If she forgot more than two of them, the method would fail.

He listened intently. I felt hopeful, but the tone of his response sounded final. "You said there are hormones in it. Pregnancy is Allah's will. Allah does not agree with hormones. Hormones are not good for a woman's body. Tell me other methods."

I could have argued with him about the relative risks of hormones in pills versus those in pregnancy, but his expression suggested that little would be gained. Next up was Depo-Provera, an injectable progesterone given every three months. Because it contained only one hormone, would it be more acceptable than the pill? It was less likely to be forgotten, so it might be more reliable. The weight gain that often happened would benefit her. The loss of menstruation was never popular with Afghan women, however, because a non-pregnant woman without a period meant infertility, which was an Afghan woman's archenemy. In this case, losing her period would likely cure the anemia, so she would feel better quicker.

He shook his head. It was against Allah. I felt annoyed. Of course these solutions went against Allah's will! That was the point!

I began drawing a schematic of a uterus, a vagina and ovaries. I placed a T inside the uterus to represent an IUD. "The midwife, puts the IUD inside the womb. The IUD is a very good method. One IUD can last nine years. When your wife wants to become pregnant, it is easy to remove an IUD. It takes only two seconds and is so simple. She does not need to remember to take tablets and there are no hormones." Up to that point, it was a win-win. Then, I drew a thick arrow up the vagina all the way into the uterus. "The midwife puts it inside your wife here, the same place where the baby comes out."

His lips curved upwards into a tight smile that might have been a smirk. Did he understand? With red hot cheeks, I suppressed my wandering thoughts. Talking about sex while alone with an Afghan man felt weird. He knew that, as a doctor, I had to know about intercourse, but he probably had difficulty reconciling that knowledge with his assumption about my virginity.

"Difficult is it to put..." He grimaced as he pointed an index finger at my bold arrow. "...in there?"

"No, not difficult. She already had two babies come through there. A baby's head is very large. The IUD is this small." I held my thumb and index finger about three centimetres apart. "Maybe she feels a small pinch for a minute but very little pain." If he showed any interest in it, I would discuss the risks.

"Before nine years we have another baby!" His reproachful tone was accompanied by a mischievous smile.

"Taking it out is very easy and so fast." I watched his face. Should I push a bit more?

"Hmm... maybe another way is better." His eyes danced with a kind of merriment, or was it delight? I tried to imagine what it was like for him to receive this information from me but gave up. It was novel and forbidden, which probably made it tantalizing.

Next up were condoms. I breathed in slowly, trying to quell my discomfort with describing what he would do with one. When teaching adolescents and refugees, I had used bananas, zucchinis, even my fist as props. I was hoping that he already knew how to put one on. Our relationship had been strictly platonic, and I wanted it to remain that way even though, at times, my love-starved imagination flirted with other options.

Unfamiliar with the Dari word for condoms, I drew a picture of the package. "The man wears this."

Recognition flooded his face as he shrank backward into the shadow. Wearing a distasteful expression, he drew a big X through the image. If a black marker had been on the mat, he probably would have used it. So much for that idea! At least I didn't have to explain the how-to part.

I sighed.

"This last method, I call the counting method. You count the number of days from the start of your wife's monthly bleeding to the start of the next monthly bleeding. From that number you subtract fourteen, which is the number of days it takes her body to become ready for pregnancy. Let's pretend that every thirty days, your wife's monthly bleeding happens." I continued explaining the simple addition and subtraction and giving examples.

"Then we calculate the days when your wife is most likely to make a baby if you are together with her." We calculated a range of days because of the uncertainty.

"In this example, from day thirteen to day nineteen after the start of the monthly bleeding is when your wife is most fertile. If you are trying to space births, this is the time that you must *not* be together. If you want to make a baby, this is the time that you must be together." I drew a line in his cahier and put Xs and arrows for each calculation.

As he listened, his eyes blazed. Was he intrigued by the fact that he could use simple math to space pregnancies? We spent the next half-hour reviewing the calculations and estimating how to correct them for different menstrual cycles. He calculated in his head quicker than I did.

Concentrating hard, he flipped back and forth between examples and the current problem. With some prompting he got the first calculation right. I gave him a second one and a third, which he aced. I loved teaching students like him.

"Think that your wife's monthly bleeding is thirty-two days from start of bleeding to next start of bleeding. If you want no pregnancy, which days should you not be together? You tell me." I handed him the pencil and the cahier with the diagrams and sample calculations.

"Here is the time when we make babies. It is best if we are not together on these days." He pointed to the period of highest fertility, then grinned like a schoolboy who had just won a math quiz. "This is the method I use."

I sat back, gratified by his exhilaration. I was continually in awe of his ability to grasp new concepts. Had he been blessed with my opportunities, what would he have become?

"Compared to other ways, this one is less good. Maybe your wife becomes pregnant because we do not always know when her body is ready to make babies. In this method, we are guessing, so it is possible that she gets pregnant, but it is better than relying on breastfeeding alone." My mum had used the rhythm method successfully for nine years!

"If we use this technique, for two years she does not become pregnant. This way has no hormones, so it is pleasing to Allah. It is the right way." His eyes radiated confidence—and something else. Was he proud of having solved a puzzle? Would this solution for one wife cause inequities?

"You have two wives. Sometimes this method is difficult when there is only one wife because she forgets the time of her last bleeding. If you are counting the time, will you remember the time of monthly bleeding for both wives?" I watched as his jubilation turned thoughtful.

Momentarily stumped, he paused. "Yes, it is easy. I will remember this." His eyes glittered with determination. I crossed my fingers.

Three nights later, we were again chatting under the stars.

"Khonum Murreen, with two wives, the counting way is difficult. Maybe another way is better." His voice sounded uncertain.

"You do not want a way with hormones. They are the best." In the silence, I considered how to present the remaining options.

"Using hormones is against Allah."

We were almost back to square one—but not quite, because I had done some homework. I had reread passages from the Koran and discussed them again with Momo Rahim. He told me that the Koran did emphasize the importance of keeping women healthy, and we had created new scripts for health care workers at the clinic.

"In the Holy Koran, I did not see any words that forbid hormones. The Koran says that your wife must be healthy. Which method is best for your wife's health and for your children's health?" We reviewed the options again. In his opinion, the IUD still looked unhealthy and condoms were repulsive. I saw no opening to discuss either of them.

Half an hour later, he made a choice. "The injection is best. She becomes stronger most quickly. Maybe her monthly bleeding is lost for some time, even nine or twelve months, but it comes back and she will birth again. This method makes her stronger because she has no bleeding. This is the best way to make healthy babies. I will speak with my family tomorrow." His eyes had recouped some fire.

Would he speak with his wives individually, or would all the women in his family be involved? Would they decide by consensus or just follow his direction?

As I watched him, a question that I had pondered for months burst out of my mouth: "Kareem, in Canada, one man has only one wife, so they spend Friday night together. Here, if a man with two wives works every night but one, how does he spend equal time with both wives? Is he very busy on Friday nights? Maybe not sleeping at all?" Lifting my eyebrows and puffing out my cheeks, I tried for a baffled, goofy expression.

Did he alternate by week? Or did they sleep as a threesome? Did he split the night in two, switching mattresses and wives partway through the night? Wasn't paying such close attention to equity exhausting? Was the hassle worth the benefits?

Raising an eyebrow, he cocked his head sideways, as if mocking me, and a chuckle escaped his lips. "Maybe half the night he spends with one wife and the other half with the other one. He makes it the same for both. Always, he makes it fair. If it is not fair, his wives become grumpy and his life is difficult."

Was it that simple? Sometimes normal life events could be perceived of as unfair. He confirmed this with a story. One wife had become upset because he had given something to the other's son. Talking had failed to resolve the tension, so he had laughed and told her that he would be waiting for her when she was finished brooding. Her bad moods never lasted more than a day or two.

That night, I left him bathed in golden lantern light, his nose in his cahier as he rehashed new English words. As I walked along the stone path toward my bedroom, other questions rumbled in my brain, ones that I would never have the courage to ask. Did the children stay in the same room when he and a wife were making love or did they sleep with their grandma? Did each woman have her own room, or did he roll from one mattress to another? Did one wife enjoy watching when he was with the other one? Did the wives enjoy each other?

The next evening, as soon as Salim left, Kareem asked for a prescription for the injection. He preferred not to go to the clinic because he was worried about Taliban spies. He would take the prescription in secret to the bazaar.

I had no prescription pads in the office because everyone in Bala Morghab asked if I could write one for them, as if believing that expats could cure the incurable. When I told him that I had none, he wasn't fazed.

"No problem. Write it here in my cahier. I will tear it out." He wrote his wife's name and the date, then handed me his cahier.

I broke my own rule that night when I wrote the prescription for one year and signed at the bottom. In Afghanistan, anyone could sell drugs, and pretty much anyone could prescribe them. He pressed a thumbnail along the folded edge and carefully tore out the newly minted prescription.

"She wants more children. This is not forever, right?" His eyes dug into mine.

"After her body becomes strong, she will have many more children. Every two or three years she can become pregnant. To make sure that she gets stronger, give her one injection every three months." I didn't blame him for doubting me. Imams had probably told him that Christians sterilized Muslims. Westerners spin just as many half-truths, emphasizing whatever slant is important to us.

"Will you go to my home to give the injection to my wife?" He watched me as I realized that our talks might have shifted his perspective on a few issues.

I nodded. "When she begins her monthly bleeding, you tell me and I will give her the needle." If I didn't do it, she would wind up pregnant again.

Two or three weeks later, he handed me a brown paper bag with syringes, needles, gauze, alcohol swabs and a glass vial of medication. "I work at the clinic today. You go to my home? Bibi-gul interprets."

I nodded. Fadheela spoke only Pashto, and Bibi-gul knew Dari as well. "You already told her everything and she understands?" Although I trusted him, I doubted that he had emphasized the same points that I would have.

He nodded. "Yes."

Shortly before lunch, I walked down the street and pounded on their door just like Salim had taught me. Abdulkhak answered. "As salaam alaikum."

"Wa alaikum e salaam." We finished the greeting as he showed me in. Then he disappeared. He knew why I was there and showed no curiosity whatsoever.

In the courtyard, Bibi-gul and Fadheela whispered and giggled. The boys were nowhere to be seen. Grandma probably held onto them in the back room. I tried out my Pashto greeting. A tittering

Wherever I travelled in Afghanistan, I tried to highlight that women were capable of many things.

Fadheela put her hand on my shoulder while the two of them corrected almost every word. Pashto was way harder than Dari.

Slowly, I asked Fadheela questions to ascertain her comprehension of what Depo-Provera would do to her body. After each one, I waited for Bibi-gul's translation and Fadheela's answer with the corresponding translation. She told me she understood each point. She had no questions. She skipped around excitedly and said that she wanted to get stronger. I pulled out the brown paper bag of supplies and showed her everything. I demonstrated how to stand so the side that I would poke was relaxed. I cleaned the area with alcohol and let it dry, then pulled back the plunger of the syringe to draw in the viscous medication. Expelling air bubbles, I asked if she was ready. Then I sunk the needle deep into the muscle of her buttock. She didn't flinch.

They both smiled. She was safe for a while. I said a short prayer asking Allah if he would ensure that she received the doses for the following two years, as I would return to Canada before the next one was due.

CHAPTER THIRTEEN

A Friendship

"The privilege of a lifetime is being who you are."

— *Joseph Campbell*

In early November, the mercury in the thermometer outside the little guard hut descended to -10°C, normally a minor inconvenience for a hearty Canadian who had spent years in the Arctic. The challenge was that the windowless hut was heated solely by our two bodies and the kerosene lamp. A kerosene heater sat unused in the corner because we didn't like the carbon monoxide or the smell that it emitted. To conserve warmth, Kareem had closed the wooden door that hung loosely in its frame, the cracks wide enough for a cold wind to sneak through them. Shivering, I willed my body to jack up heat production.

Through foam mattresses that buffered our backsides, the bone-chilling cold of the earth still seeped through my cocoon of long johns, two shalwars, two kameezes, a worn-out winter fleece, two chadors over my head, winter socks, mitts and two blankets, one dyed with a giant blue tiger and the other one decorated with pink hyacinths. While hefting two fuzzy acrylic bed covers over my shoulder, I had felt like a kid heading to a friend's house for a sleepover.

Compared to Kareem, I was massively overdressed. His one wool shalwar kameez was covered by a round-necked sweater, a wool patu that he had wound over his head and torso and one thick blanket similar to mine but with red water lilies flowing across it. He also boasted a pair of gloves and a turban. His tolerance for cold temperatures reminded me of Inuit I'd met who were hearty enough to dip their hands into water just prior to smoothing snow sculptures.

The glow of the lantern danced across our notebooks, their dust-tinged, dog-eared pages lying side by side on the mat between us. Opened to a fresh page, they sat poised to receive new words offered by the other. Every few minutes our conversation was interrupted by one of us checking the pronunciation of a new word in the other's tongue, then penning it and the corresponding translation on the page. Two halves of a dictionary were in the making.

In Afghan villages, friendship between genders was easy until sometime before puberty. I found no word to characterize friendship between men and women.

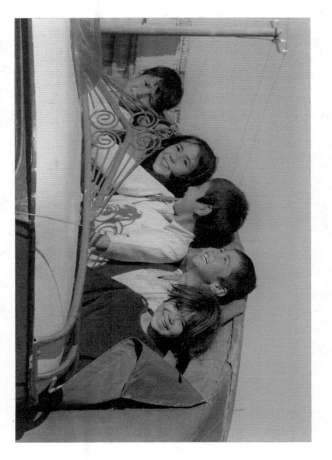

Seven months before, neither of us had known many words in the other's tongue. With remarkable speed, our tea time conversations had developed a late night, innocent trust, like what exists between adolescents when a voice in the dark seems more honest and the heart somehow freer. Rarely did I have a specific topic in mind. I simply wanted to share a moment, exchange ideas and learn something new. Strikingly content for someone who had lost so much, Kareem seemed privy to a wisdom that I had yet to acquire.

No Dari word accurately described our friendship, at least none that we devised. Dari terms for "friend" pertained only to males, or at least that seemed to be true in this village setting. Some Afghans called me sister, repeating it over and over, as if convincing themselves that the relationship was real. Kareem never called me sister. He simply used my name, adding -jan at the end to signify a level of trust.

"You will return to Kaa-naa-daa too soon!" A deep sigh and a faraway expression tainted his contentment like a shadow.

"Yes, in two months I go back to Kaa-naa-daa." I wasn't ready to leave yet, but I would be when the time came. I watched his index finger tap the woven fibres of the plastic mat. Having lived a life of travel, I was used to leaving people. He wasn't. People left him when they died. With such limited options for communicating, would our friendship survive? Or would we have been two passing ships over nine months? As long as MSF remained in Bala Morghab, we could write old-fashioned letters that would be delivered in the mailbag.

"In Kaa-naa-daa, I live in a little house too, but it is smaller than yours and closer to other homes." I went on to explain that an apartment was a large building that housed many small compounds in which people lived separately beside, above and below their neighbours. He marvelled about why families would choose to live in such close proximity. There was no advantage as far as he could fathom.

"Do you own this little house?" His perplexed expression conveyed distaste.

"When I return to Kaa-naa-daa, I will rent one." In Vancouver, houses of any kind were so expensive that buying one with the nest egg that I had accumulated seemed wasteful, especially given my plan to work with MSF.

"Murreen-jan, if you rent a home, the owner can take it away. It is better that you buy a house and some land." He spoke like a father teaching an adolescent.

"In Vancouver, buying a house is very expensive." The housing market in Vancouver was hard for anyone who didn't live there to fathom. Heck, my parents had difficulty accepting the fact that their house outside of Montreal, if located in Vancouver, would cost a few million dollars!

"If it is too expensive, perhaps you could live with your parents." He emphasized the last word, hinting at his own bias.

"No, I like my life in Vancouver. It takes me many days to drive to my parents in their village. I don't see moving in with them." My throat felt constricted as I struggled to find words to express what I felt. Although I loved my parents, I would never live with them again. Feeling stifled at seventeen, I had moved away to university so I could grow in ways that I couldn't in their house. Each time I returned home, I would cross my fingers in hopes that I had matured enough to show them the powerful, intelligent woman that I had become. Each visit, conflict arose and I slipped into powerlessness.

"You are a doktar. Doktars make good money. How much does a house in Vancouver cost?" His tone was controlled, but his chocolate brown eyes flashed momentarily in the darkness.

I sipped tea. How best to respond?

"You make a salary. How much is it?" His shoulders relaxed a bit and his voice became affable once again.

Discussing money with Afghan villagers was tricky. I often told them how many months it took to pay for something. His living expenses were minuscule by comparison. In Bala Morghab, a loaf of fresh bread set you back 10 cents and you could buy a generous portion of kebabs for less than $1. I had paid $10 for a tailor-made shalwar kameez, and Momo Rahim had told me that a mud house in a compound would cost about $1,000.

What made discussing finances even more challenging was my discomfort with the topic. My family had never discussed money except to emphasize the importance of saving it. People who didn't conserve their pennies were frivolous and irresponsible. Even as a seven-year-old who had received birthday money from my grandparents, I agonized for weeks before purchasing anything for myself. I had ogled a white plastic horse with a plush leather saddle several times before finally handing over the cash. I still remember it cost $8, which seemed so expensive at the time. At around the same age, I began saving money to go to university since Dad had told me that it was up to me to pay for it. No way was I going to let that stop me! Years later, after completing two university degrees, I began saving for retirement because I sensed that the repetitive, fast-paced world of medicine was unsustainable for me.

"MSF pays me $800 per month." In Bala Morghab that bought a lot, but memberships, licences, insurance and storage back in Canada ate it all up. For years, I had wanted to be an MSF volunteer, to step away from the daily grind of exchanging time and knowledge for money, which had become so pervasive and so mind-numbing.

In Afghanistan, for the first time in my life, money had become irrelevant. I felt joyful and free—despite living in a war zone where strict gender restrictions were practised. Over there, I never carried a wallet, a phone or even a passport. MSF covered all local expenses. I only paid for vacations and the rare memento that I bought in Herat at the carpet bazaar or in the glass shop where ancient techniques for making blue glassware were routinely used. Filled with a sense of freedom, I realized that I had bought into the same scarcity story as Dad. How much money does someone really need?

"And you have been working for how long?" Kareem's voice sounded strained, as if he was worried about me.

"Fifteen years." I watched as he turned into a human calculator. I could almost hear the click of the keys and the whir of the gears.

"One hundred forty-four thousand dollars. This is enough to buy a good house!" He tapped a finger on his teacup and examined the standing waves in the liquid.

"In Vancouver, a house costs maybe five hundred thousand Canadian dollars." I multiplied in my cahier. "Billions of afghanis."

His breath crystallized, and the momentary cloud obscured his chocolate brown eyes before it rose upward.

"This is expensive, but Murreen-jan, I do not understand. You are a doctor. Doctors make good money. You are forty years old and you own nothing, not even a house! What do you do with your money?" He shook his head. I felt like a delinquent youngster. "With that money, you must own something!" His eyes flashed. Was he annoyed, concerned or judgmental?

I studied the rough notebook page with a fingerprint smudge, then began doodling a series of expansive swirls. How could I make my situation seem logical to him? What part of my world could he understand?

I exhaled a misty cloud. "I own furniture, a computer, clothes, a bicycle and many other things. I keep them safe in a ... um... hm-mmm." How do I explain a storage locker to a man with so few possessions? For more than half his life, he had lived as a semi-nomad. When pasturing animals, his home was a goat-hair tent. When his family planted crops, he stayed in a mud compound with four separate houses, one for each of his father's wives and their many children. What was a storage locker to someone with those experiences?

His hawk-like eyes watched me as he sought to stitch my partially formed thoughts into something sensible before I did. Closing my eyes to help me focus, I inhaled long and deep.

"I own many things. I am not like a refugee who has lost their belongings and moves from place to place with only their clothing." I thought back to my childhood dream of becoming a wise hobo, the storybook kind that walked everywhere with their belongings wrapped in a checkered handkerchief strung up on a stick that they balanced on a shoulder. Compared to other Canadians I owned very little, but it was many times more than what Kareem's family of nine possessed. "Before leaving Canada, I put all of my things into a room, this big." I pointed out about two thirds of the guard hut.

"I pay money every month like rent so I can put my things in the room. When I want my things back, I take them out and stop paying rent." I glanced at his face to ascertain his interest in the topic, then turned my attention back to the intricacies of my notebook so my words could percolate undisturbed. "This room is beside other rooms in a large building like an apartment. Each traveller rents a room just big enough for objects that they do not need when travelling. For example, on this trip I don't bring my mattress or chair. I left those in the room. Only the travellers have keys to open their rooms. A guard at the main door of the building makes sure that thieves stay out of it so the stuff is safe."

Warmth from my teacup permeated my frigid fingers, then travelled up my wrists. I searched his face for a sign of comprehension: a raised eyebrow, a slight nod or a tip of the head. I spoke like an eight-year-old so I frequently probed for feedback.

He swilled a mouthful of tea, sighing as he set down the cup beside his notebook.

"You rent a room." His jaw muscle clenched twice. His forehead glistened in the lamplight, and the shadows accentuated the cleft of his rumpled brow. "This room is like a house. Can you sleep in it?" His voice sounded like an overly tight guitar string.

My jaw dropped. I had never considered that.

"No, I cannot live in this room. It is not possible. I rent it to store things that I don't need while I am here in Afghanistan. When I return to Canada, I will move those items into a house."

"If you pay rent, you can sleep there. That is only fair." He relaxed back on his cushion and the tension between us began to fall away.

"I signed a contract where it is written that I leave only things in the room, I don't sleep in there." In the guard hut the rules sounded overly harsh and lacking in compassion, but when I had signed the document, it had seemed quite fair.

An emotion I couldn't read played across his features, morphing into a frown.

"Murreen-jan, this contract is a bad idea. Why do you agree to it?!" He spun a pen over his thumb. "It is smart if you ask them to change the agreement. This one is not fair for you."

I shook my head and pretended to consider his advice, which of course wasn't possible.

"How much does the room cost?"

I often scaled back prices because they were so absurdly high compared to Afghan equivalents, but this time, I told the truth. "Each month, $100."

The call to prayer floated over. Kareem stood up, dropped the blanket, smoothed his patu on the ground and faced Mecca. A minute later he continued our conversation, as if there had been no interruption.

"So each year, you pay $1,200 for a room to store things you do not use and where you cannot sleep! This is not wise, Murreen-jan. It is better for you to own a house. No matter what happens, you can always live in a house. It is important."

Well, it was important for him but not for me. Finding an adequate place to live had rarely been a problem.

Once, years before, my six-year-old niece, who had just finished watching a program on homelessness, had asked me if I was homeless, her wide eyes trying to figure out if I was like the storytellers on the television. I told her that I'd had many homes, and that I selected each one of them. Early on in my travels, I had simply decided that I would feel at home everywhere. I wanted to be one of those rare individuals who really understood the people they met. I wanted to have the capacity to see from so many perspectives that I could visualize the whole. Buying a house, raking leaves, fixing fences and repairing appliances just weren't part of my plan.

Ludicrous as it might seem, I worried that Kareem might feel compelled to offer me financial help because he thought I was destitute. I wanted him to understand that my lack of home ownership stemmed from my fears about overspending as I stepped off the work treadmill and chose to travel the world instead.

Seeking inspiration, I sucked in the night air, letting it out with an audible sigh. Words began to flow. "I never bought a house because I travel a lot. I have no husband or children, so I do not need one. In Canada, people like me put their money in a hmm... uh... a money house." How do you say "bank" in Dari? I thumbed through pages of the dictionary. Beside bank was *baank*, the same word with different intonation. "A baank." I pronounced it with a long "a," like the "en" in encore.

He hesitated, then looked bewildered. "Baank?" I nodded.

He shook his head, picked up the dictionary, tilting it so the lantern light played across its pages. My finger still identified the dubious word. He read the Arabic script.

"Baank, I do not know it." Slowly, he shook his head, as if disappointed with himself. Was he unfamiliar with the concept because so few Afghans had extra cash to stow away in such institutions? Most villagers invested in tangible items like land, houses, jewels, carpets, antiques and businesses. Or they gave it to family members. Saving money in a bank was a foreign idea. Or perhaps he simply did not know the Dari word since Pashto was his first language.

"It is a house where money is kept."

"Tell me more about this money house." His eyes began to dance once again.

"A money house is where you can store afghanis that you don't need right away. The owner of the money house borrows cash from someone like me so he can lend it to other people who need it right away. For example, someone may want to make their business bigger, like a baker buying a second bakery. Or maybe the baker wants to create a new business, like repairing tires. As he makes money from the second business, he returns the funds little by little each month." His intrigued expression spurred me on.

"The baker might ask his family for money first because he has too little to buy the second bakery. If they can't give him money, he goes to the bank and requests the funds to build the bakery. At the bank, when he receives the money, he signs an agreement where it is written how much rent he pays to use the money. Each month, he pays back some of the borrowed money plus the fee." I paused and waited for his agile mind to catch up.

Sitting completely still, he seemed enraptured by the notion.

I continued: "Sometimes I buy part of a business from someone, and they pay me each year because their business does well. If their business does less well, they pay me less." I took his fist as a sign of comprehension.

"So Mureen-jan, you help people. You give them money and, in return, people pay you. It is a good business for you, and it gives people an opportunity to grow their business and provide for their families." He shifted his turban and scratched his temple. "But how do you get the money back after you lend it?" His quirky smile said "gotcha"!

"When I need the money, I sell my part of the company to someone else and receive cash." Of course in real life it didn't always happen exactly like this, but I hadn't figured out how to portray risk or other complexities.

"It is very good." The grin on his face stretched to both ears. No longer did he think of me as destitute and irresponsible. I had just become a resourceful businesswoman.

Wrapped in my cocoon, I padded to the doorway in sock feet. He sat in the lamplight, coal eyes peering out of a golden face.

"Shab-e-khosh! Khop khobe bibinid!" I wished him goodnight and happy dreams as I slipped on my weather-beaten leather shoes with the crushed heels. Wishing someone sweet dreams wasn't customary. The first time I had tried out the phrase, he had looked completely baffled, only warming to the concept after understanding that I was wishing away his nightmares. After that, it became a nightly ritual.

"Khoshal khastam. Shab-e-khosh. Be man e khuda." Laying a hand on his heart, he said he felt happy and wished me good night.

"Khud offez." Hand on my heart, I said goodbye.

His voice followed me out the door. "Murreen-jan, promise me that when you return to Canada, you will buy a house. A house is a place where you can always return after travelling. This is a very important idea. A home is where you belong."

His face looked so solemn that I promised, but I didn't specify when. The door closed behind me. In the frosty night, I felt a warm glow expand across my chest.

About two months later, I would return to Canada. In my busy life there, I often looked back on these peaceful evening conversations with fondness. I cherished the memories of awkwardness and ease that nourished our friendship. Learning Dari had become my portal of entry into the local culture, a gift that I would use over and over again to bring a grounded approach to my later work in the country.

CHAPTER FOURTEEN

A TEAM

"Earth laughs in flowers, to see her boastful boys earth-proud, proud of the earth which is not theirs."

— *Ralph Waldo Emerson*

In Canada, Peter and I moved in together. We painted a new apartment in exchange for six weeks of rent. He had been granted unpaid leave from his work as an engineer and, within a couple of months of my arrival in Canada, left for Cambodia on a year-long MSF mission. I busied myself working in Vancouver's Downtown Eastside, serving disenfranchised groups, and in Nunavik, Quebec, where I had previously lived for several years. In various presentations and interviews on my experiences in Afghanistan, I did my best to shift clichéd perceptions and prejudices. After taking a journalism course, I tried my hand at writing human interest stories for periodicals and managed to have some of them published. My fortieth birthday present to myself was a two-week course on street photography in Florence, Italy.

In June 2001, I fell in love with a French man and realized that my relationship with Peter was doomed. I broke things off by email before we began a four-week vacation in Cambodia, Thailand and Laos. Travelling together but no longer committed to each other, we were once again able to have honest and open conversations.

The tragedy on September 11, 2001, occurred while I was participating in a mock plane crash in Nunavik, Quebec. Every news report that I read supported the invasion of Afghanistan. Afghans were the new enemy. How could these gentle souls with whom I had dined, swam, walked and spent hours in conversation with be the devils that were now to be hunted?

Determined to learn what was really going on, I contacted MSF, and in early December 2001, I flew to Ashgabad, Turkmenistan. On a freezing cold night, I boarded a steaming train with three other MSF volunteers. Sixteen hours later, we walked the final kilometre into Afghanistan, the muzzles of border guards' machine guns aimed at our heads.

The United Nations High Commissioner for Refugees was closing migrant camps in Iran, claiming that Afghans could safely return home. Jim, my old teammate from Bala Morghab, and I were to lead a new mission: setting up remote clinics for the returning refugees.

Several of our previous MSF staff joined us, including Zia, our head driver, and Reza, an interpreter. We set up a base in Qala-I-Nau, the halfway point between Herat and Bala Morghab. From there, we visited potential clinic sites farther afield. On the map, the remote market village of Char Taq in Jawand District seemed like a promising first site. It was isolated enough that none of the hordes of new international organizations brought in on a tsunami of funding were willing to go there. None of our staff had visited Jawand, so Zia sought advice from fellow truckers in the bazaar. They described the terrain as challenging. The drive would take twelve hours and, as was the case in most of Afghanistan, road signs didn't exist, so Zia came back with a mental list of landmarks to guide us.

Through a static-laden radio connection, the Oxfam team in Char Taq offered to house us for a few nights. We loaded two vehicles with enough food and equipment to camp for a week, just in case our plans fell through. The next day, before sunrise, eight of us departed in a two-vehicle convoy.

On savannah reminiscent of Utah, we followed the undulating dirt tracks left by transport trucks. We zigzagged up and over a mountain pass, managing to avoid slipping off cliffs on the way down. Zia kept an eye peeled for telltale navigation landmarks. On the rare occasion he asked for directions in a bazaar, always careful to conceal our real destination.

At the four-hour mark, we bought ten naan, then turned into a canyon, the second Land Cruiser following right behind. On either side, steep cliffs covered in zigzag animal paths rose higher and higher. In the front passenger seat, Jim peered through the dusty windshield, pointing out obstacles that might blow a tire or hang up the undercarriage. With each directive, Zia threw his weight against the steering wheel as loose rocks pulled us off course. In the back seat, we swayed like spring-loaded puppets. Tires slipped. My head hit the roof. Each jolt caused my lower back to feel like a wrung-out towel. I cinched my seatbelt, hooked my arm over the bench and gripped the handle above the window so tightly that my knuckles turned white. My hand felt like it would never open again.

"Zia, the r-r-road is v-very d-d-difficult. We are j-just at-t the b-beginning. H-h-how is the r-road later on?" I spoke Dari in ragged fragments. A glance at my watch implied six more hours of this. Farther in, it would be worse! Should we abort the trip?

"Khonum M-murreen, too much water from rain in the mountains moved too many rocks." Speaking in Dari like he always did, Zia gunned the engine and the vehicle shot forward, then slammed over a rock. I felt a sting in my finger, noticed a bruise forming and wrapped my chador around it to apply pressure to the ruptured blood vessel. Zia understood a little English but rarely spoke any, even though he, like all of our staff, had taken English lessons.

"Did b-big s-stones roll d-downriver from too m-much r-rain?" I saw him grimace in the rear-view mirror as the vehicle jolted yet again.

"Yes, water moves stones, some as big as this one." He pointed out the window at a boulder, then swung the wheel hard to the left. Great, we were driving into a narrow canyon known for flash floods and had no exit plan!

To the left, a skinny cow strained against a plow. The plowman yelled, waving his arms in wide arcs. Zia signalled back. Pointing ahead of us, the farmer flapped his arms like a vulture. Frowning, Zia stopped the car. I heard a torrent of Pashto and understood nothing. Reza, the interpreter, leaned forward. The man yelled. The Land Cruiser torpedoed ahead. We bounced over a rock, landed heavily and stayed on course, bobbing up and down like a yo-yo.

"It is a mine, a mine!" Zia croaked, his eyes glued to the uneven terrain. Who would place an explosive along a road to a market village? We never mentioned our destination to anyone because kidnapping expats was a business, albeit unsanctioned. How I hated mines! I thought of Kareem's unused land and his family's poverty. What a waste!

Minutes later, Zia stopped the car and Jaafar, the other driver, braked right behind us. "A break is good?" Zia noticed me nod in the rearview mirror. From a kameez pocket, he fished out a crushed pack of Lucky Strikes and a booklet of matches. Jim began the meticulous ritual of rolling a cigarette. I never complained about their habit. The breaks gave me photo opportunities.

Where we stopped, the canyon walls were nearly vertical, and the cliffs on the plateau above them were covered in a dusting of

Driving up the Jawand Canyon was challenging for many reasons, including the possibility of flash floods. Arriving on time was a rare event.

fine snow. The farmer had apologized for his use of dynamite in an attempt to remove a boulder from his field. None of us had heard an explosion. Did that mean the dynamite was faulty, or would it become yet another unexploded ordnance primed to maim innocent people?

After tapping his cigarette against a rock, Zia inserted it between pursed lips. Cupping the flame, he inhaled long and deep, the tremor in his index finger abating. "Maybe in one hour, where we join the Morghab River, the road becomes better." His voice was shrill. The Morghab River flowed all the way to Bala Morghab and into Turkmenistan—we had swum in it the previous year.

I snapped photographs of the stunning scenery until Jim and Zia flicked away their spent butts. The last few hours of the drive were as smooth as taking a defunct logging road in British Columbia: on one side a roaring river raged, while on the other a vertical cliff rose to the base of mountains above.

In the sleepy village of Char Taq, the local commander and governor promised to protect us. The governor also told us that the village name was in fact Jawand, the same name as the district. Why did we call it Char Taq? I pencilled in the correction on the map, which by then looked like a spider's web of amendments.

When we measured the upper-arm circumference of children, we discovered that most of them were malnourished. We counted about a hundred houses in the village. At least double that probably lived beyond the end of the road. Adding those from nearby villages that we had passed en route and a thousand semi-nomads who exchanged goods on market days, a clinic in Jawand might serve a few thousand people.

Oxfam's quarters in Jawand were bare-bones basic, its four rooms used for work and sleep. Yet because of its enclosed well and outhouse, it was a place of luxury when compared to any other local dwelling. That night, from the far side of our room, I said goodnight to Jim, then lay awake marvelling over how far off the beaten track I was. I fought to relax tense muscles that refused to release their grip on the day. As Jim's breath slowed into a sleep rhythm, I lay alone on my mattress, wishing for a hug and imagining a mysterious lover.

The day before we planned to leave, someone had offered to donate land suitable for the clinic. If they hadn't shown this commitment, MSF would not have allowed us to begin work there. As we drove out of the canyon in the two Land Cruisers, I looked forward to the shower that would wash away the five days of grime layered on my skin. But climbing the mountain pass, the vehicles began slipping sideways on shifting layers of melted snow and dust the consistency of talcum powder. Sand mats, sand, wood and stones provided little traction. Finally, Jim gave up. Under his direction, Zia carefully executed a five-point turn, and the second driver followed suit. We rolled down to the nearest village, and a young boy directed us to the elder's compound.

Over tea, the grey-bearded man offered to slaughter a goat. We thanked him for his generosity but declined. He refused our offer of food. In a back room somewhere, Reza negotiated dinner and a couple of rooms for the night. Payment must have occurred in private so everyone's honour could be maintained.

Just before retiring to bed, the elder's son led me to a straw-covered area in a barn where I heard the stamping hooves of big animals that I couldn't see. In a back room somewhere, Reza negotiated dinner and a couple of rooms for the night. I peed on straw.

After I finished, he spoke. "It is a good idea if you stay in your room tonight. At night, our dogs guard the compound against robbers."

The next morning, Zia knocked on the door of the room where Jim and I slept. He said good morning in a hushed tone. It was pitch dark. On frozen ground, it only took minutes to summit the pass. The challenge came later. The Utah-like savannah was covered in knee-deep powder. The tracks that had guided us on the way out were just dimples in the snow. Ribbons of snowflakes that sparkled in the sunshine careened out either side of the vehicle. All of a sudden, we hit something hard. The tires spun. We were hung up on a barely visible, hard-packed snowdrift. The Land Cruiser looked like a tortoise stranded on a rock, its legs completely useless. Piling out of the cars, we grabbed two shovels, pots, pans and sand mats and set to work freeing the stuck vehicle.

Over the next two hours, we clambered out of the Land Cruisers five more times to repeat the stunt. As the winter sky faded from blue to grey, we scooped harder and faster. Oh, how I wanted that shower! Thankfully, we did reach the office in Qala-I-Nau before sundown, when thieves and kidnappers came out in droves.

Three weeks later, we again requested accommodations from Oxfam. During the abbreviated radio exchange, the manager warned Reza that more staff would be on site. Oxfam was delivering free food to local inhabitants. He reassured us that we were welcome to stay, but before we could specify any details, the connection dissolved into static.

I looked at Jim. "Let's take a chance." He shrugged, then nodded. Again, we packed for a wilderness camping trip.

When we arrived, the sleepy village looked like a movie set for Rambo III. Steaming horses, donkeys and camels, covered in heavy blankets instead of saddles, were hitched to every bush, tree and post. A stallion stamped a hoof, dust turning his chestnut brown coat to grey. Multicoloured pompoms lent bridles a festive air. Litres of corn oil and bags of lentils sat in dusty, mended paniers of qilim weave or carpet pile. Bags of wheat were thrown on top of them. Men with straggly beards and dust-stiffened hair reminiscent of dreadlocks assembled in small groups. Over top of traditional shalwar kameezes, they wore multi-pocketed vests and patus. Kalashnikovs hung from shoulders or were propped against trees. Swords and sheathed knives dangled from leather belts.

The crowd's eagle eyes examined us as Zia slowed the Land Cruiser to a stop near the Oxfam guest house. Jim sent one team member to the compound to confirm our accommodations for the night. My stomach fluttered with a thousand butterflies. A donkey's hoarse braying expressed the tension I felt. Two horses pawed the dry ground as a rooster careened between their legs. I scanned the crowd. Were they friends or foes? The women we had seen on the previous visit had disappeared. I tightened my chador around my face, arranging its drapery to cover myself. Stretching, I released a kink in my neck. If someone had offered me a burka right then, I would have gladly pulled it over my head to become invisible, just like Kareem's mother had described.

As I exited the vehicle, I inhaled the musky scent of unwashed men. My brain was repulsed, yet my nipples tightened against the touch of soft cotton. Remaining near the vehicle, we left the doors wide open in case we needed to make a fast getaway, even though every one of us knew that a man on a horse could travel faster than a Land Cruiser on this terrain.

Young boys in mismatched layered clothing squatted and played games with rocks and sticks. A man with kohl-lined eyes lounged in a hammock strung between two trees, his makeshift bed for the night providing protection from snakes and scorpions. I stared as his hand moved to his thigh. Fascinated, I dragged my eyes away.

Suddenly, the crowd shifted. Zia and Jim slunk back toward the vehicle. Cigarettes dangling from their mouths, they waved us down. I crouched behind the door, my heart hammering against my ribs.

A shalwar-less man, about twenty years old, was shoved into the open area between us and them. Above his head, he waved a Kalashnikov like it was a toy gun. His bare legs flaunted chiselled calf muscles that flexed with each step. Through slits in his torn kameez, taut, dust-smudged buttocks winked at us. His belly protruded like a sixteen-week-old pregnancy, and his wide-based gait suggested that he might be high on opium or have a neurological deficit. Catcalls and whistles dared him to do something that was incomprehensible to me.

The bare-bottomed man planted his feet shoulder width apart. As his trunk jerked, the weapon flailed overhead and a giant scrotum and flaccid penis peeked from beneath his kameez, then flopped against his thigh. Jim and I raised eyebrows. We would wait. A sudden movement might cause him to shoot. I recited a desperate prayer. I had come to Afghanistan to help. I wasn't ready to die. Flirting with fatalism, I handed Allah all responsibility. It gave me comfort.

Cocking the weapon, he pointed it at us, then toward the sky. Several jeers erupted, and he aimed it at us once again. I froze. Please make the door sturdy enough to withstand a gunshot. Kidnapping I could understand, but why kill us? What a waste of quality merchandise! Squinting through the crack between the car body and the door, my eyes traced the rifle, trying to piece together whether the gun's safety catch was engaged. Where was it? Only once had I shot a gun, a .22-calibre rifle in target practice in Churchill, Manitoba, during polar bear season.

"The safety, is it on?" I projected my voice like I used to do in choir practice so that Jim and Zia, on the other side of the car, could hear me.

"Tza." Zia shook his head. Inhaling a long drag from his cigarette, he flicked the newly defunct butt to the ground. A lone smoke plume twisted upward. He dabbed his neck with a checkered handkerchief. Then, with a huff and a kick at a small stone, he gracefully strode toward the gunman with a confidence that I would have found impossible to muster. As he closed in on the young man, he murmured soft tones that I had previously heard him use to calm high-strung horses. "We are here to help. The gun, it is nice. You show it to me?"

He was risking his safety for ours. My heart lurched as I stood transfixed, and a quote from a psalm came to mind: "Though I walk through the valley of the shadow of death, I will fear no evil..." What gave him such courage?

In truth, he knew guns. As a child soldier conscripted at gunpoint when he was fourteen years old, he had been forced to choose between murdering a defenceless man or his child-soldier buddy, who faced the same conundrum. The third option was to be killed. After assassinating innocent men, the two boys hid together in terror, fearing that Allah would punish them for such heinous sins. But the lightning bolt never arrived, so Zia perfected his tactics and survived for years in the bush. He told me that his modified bullets burned through metal and created fire inside Russian tanks. As men escaped, he killed them one by one. He immobilized convoys by incapacitating the first and last vehicles, which made blasting every remaining one easy since mines were everywhere and they were afraid of leaving the road. That is what I understood, anyway, from evening conversations on the road with this gentle soul whose sound judgment I had come to value.

A loud guffaw rang out from the group, then echoed across the canyon. Others joined in bellowing counterpoint.

Zia, his palms skyward, approached the younger man. He nattered soothing sounds as the gun barrel tracked him.

"*Ta-ta-ta-ta-ta.*" The sudden machine gun–like sound caused me to jump. For a split second I thought it was real, but Zia was still walking away from us, tall and graceful. Someone was good at imitating.

Zia touched the man's shoulder. "Your gun is beautiful. Can I see it?"

The partially clad fellow puffed out his chest and proudly handed over his weapon like a boy might share a treasure. A second later, Zia had exposed its unarmed magazine and chamber.

"Someone get this man a shalwar!" Zia's voice dripped with disdain. Grimacing, he placed the troublesome rifle into a bystander's outstretched hand and gently pushed the boy into the snickering crowd that swallowed his nude fanny.

"Stupid people. What a dangerous prank!" Zia spat the words softly while his face remained impassive. Anyone out of earshot would think he was commenting on the weather. He wore the same mask that he had employed at Taliban checkpoints the previous year, when his animated voice had turned subdued and his face became forgettable.

Some minutes later, we drove through the entryway of the Oxfam guest house compound. Craving solitude, I was disappointed to see fifteen local Oxfam employees carting boxes, milling around trucks and conversing in small groups. More of them were working in the offices. Where could I go? Where would I sleep? I refused to share a room with a bunch of Afghan men. I simply didn't want to know what happened in the dark.

What concerned me more than our sleeping arrangements was the capacity of the lone outhouse, with its tatty canvas door. Outhouse etiquette that I had learned on the previous visit involved standing a few metres away from the hut, coughing loudly two or three times, then listening for an answering hack. If there was none, I entered. Not wanting to make a mistake, I coughed every few steps until my little finger hooked the curtain aside for a peek. Inside the hut, a plastic jug with a long spout provided water for washing afterward. I preferred the wad of heavy-duty pink toilet paper that was tucked in my pocket. After finishing, I hiked across the compound to the hand-pumped well.

The compound's outer wall was so low that the hundreds of eyes from surrounding hills, tree branches and rooftops peered over it. Every nook and cranny in Oxfam's compound was visible except inside the rooms, which had all been taken. Dejectedly, I just plunked myself down in full view, pulled my diary and pen out of my blue day pack and began writing. I would have loved to have taken a photograph of such wild men, but I was petrified of causing a riot—these villagers probably believed that photos stole souls. I shut them out, and the day's events filled page after page. Too soon, the evening call to prayer rang out. By then, the eyes of the watchers had dissolved into the greyness of dusk, and my heart beat calmly once again. I read the time on my watch, a gift from Kareem. How I wished that he could tell me more about his life now and help me understand the behaviour of these men.

Our communal dinner that night was mutton pilau with dal and vegetables from our pantry supplies. Our team joked excitedly as we gathered in a room to watch a DVD of an Italian romance on Oxfam's new television set. Within months of the Taliban's defeat in December 2001, DVD players, televisions and cellphones flooded Herat's bazaars as Afghanistan entered the twenty-first century. The year before, none of our local Bala Morghab staff had ever seen a movie. As a departing gift, we had viewed *Titanic* in secret one evening, and for a couple of hours, they were whisked away, spellbound by the magic of film.

In the Oxfam guest house, the movie began. No one spoke. After two minutes, the image of the pirated DVD pixelated. A technician doggedly pushed the fast forward button, coaxing the image back to life. The film froze so many times that I began fidgeting. Why was I watching a boring film when I could be outside enjoying the night sky and writing by lantern light? A few minutes later, the image blacked out, yet the sound continued. Urgent, sensual voices cried out, then faded to a murmur as I imagined two lovers tearing off each other's clothes. When grunting began, the sound suddenly cut out. The technician pushed multiple buttons, but the DVD failed to resuscitate.

Taking advantage of the pause, I stood up, mumbling goodbye as I stepped between bodies that lounged on mattresses, some of them cozied up together. Men caressed each other's hair or thigh. I had been told that before marriage, some Afghan men had sex with men. Zia once told me that he chose to sleep alone in the car when we were on road trips. When I asked why, he had recoiled. In his eyes, I saw something raw and painful. I imagined his story as a child soldier, and we never mentioned it again.

As soon as I closed the door to the movie room, muffled cries of pleasure erupted. Gosh, had I been too impatient? I placed a hand on the doorknob, but something held me back. Had the operator blacked out the image because Afghan men don't watch sex scenes with women outside of their families, and especially not a single woman who was their boss?

A month after that trip, we traded out one Land Cruiser for a Russian Jeep and added a Kamaz truck to our convoy so we could transport building supplies to Jawand. The materials had been held up for weeks at the border. Finally, we had what we needed to replace the tent clinics with a permanent structure. The evening before we were to return to Qala-I-Nau, Jim, who at the time was in Qala-I-Nau managing the logistics for this trip, that flash floods had washed out local roads. He said that the Jawand canyon was probably impassable and, as our security advisor, he directed us to delay our departure by a day.

On departure day, our three-vehicle convoy drove out of town before sunrise. The creek was swollen. The Kamaz truck's high clearance and long wheelbase made crossing it a cinch. The Russian Jeep descended and ascended steep-sided creek banks like an intrepid beetle. Once, it lost traction on the way down and was submerged up to the running boards, its tires spinning uselessly. It sputtered, then silently bobbed in the river. Quickly, the Kamaz truck towed the featherweight out. Zia powered the Land Cruiser through the water on a different path, successfully making it to the other side. Once he did, he called Jim on the HF radio to update him on our travels. Jim's harried voice came through interspersed with static. He directed Zia to place the air and oil filters on rocks to bake in the sun. As the Jeep innards dried, we ate a breakfast of hardboiled eggs, bread, sour cherry jam, cream and black tea.

My attention was snagged by Dr. Seuss–like flowers bobbing in the breeze across the canyon.

Zia grinned. "Doktar Murreen, photo?"

"Yes, photo, I walk. Not far." I pointed at the exotic flowers.

Zia nodded. Even though he had never taken a photograph, he had a good eye for detail and often guessed my subjects.

As I sprinted away, Jim's loud, anguished voice on the radio during another check-in began to fade. Figuring out what to do when he was physically present was challenging enough. Relying on other people's explanations sounded as excruciating to him as a bad toothache. What he didn't seem to realize was that his anger and impatience triggered more mistakes. Witnessing the dynamic made me cringe, and I felt compelled to do almost anything to escape it.

Across the canyon, I stood among flower stalks, their composite blooms nodding above my head like tiny purple fireworks. A shrill whistle pierced the air. BJ waved. The Jeep's cough reverberated off the canyon walls.

The Kamaz driver asked if I wanted to accompany him. Up to then I had always travelled with my maharam, but that day BJ and I were tired of being cautious, so I clambered aboard, the massive front seat spreading out like a bed in front of me. I gawked at the view through the front window like a kid might when seated on Daddy's shoulders.

A flash of electric blue, green and violet iridescence streaked by, disappeared, then returned again.

The gentle Kamaz driver pointed at it like a boy entranced by a new object. "Khonum Murreen, look!" A tiny kingfisher with a cascade of vibrant colours and a black pirate's stripe across his eyes swooped by me.

"Yes, it is beautiful. In English, it is a kingfisher." The little bird darted from window to window, hovering momentarily.

"King-fisher. In Kaa-naa-daa, you have this bird?" The delightful pirate reappeared right beside the driver, then veered away.

"In Kaa-naa-daa we have a bird like this one, but it is not so beautiful." For a second it landed on a branch ahead of us, as if waiting for the lumbering truck to catch up. As its head tipped sideways, the metallic violet, gold and blue in its feathers glittered like gemstones.

As the bird flashed along beside me, I wondered if he had travelled from India or Nepal. For several more minutes, the driver and I grinned like kids playing a game of I spy. At the mouth of the canyon, our little friend sped off. Sad to see him go, I waved.

As we crawled toward the pass that had previously waylaid us, I prayed that the road on the other side wasn't washed out. On the way up, the little Jeep coughed and choked but kept moving. On the next uphill, it sputtered, vibrated violently as if having a seizure, then sat there silently, looking glum. The Jeep driver's face mirrored my annoyance. Time was slipping away. He opened the hood and once again lay the innards out to dry. Why were they wet again? We hadn't driven through any more water. Zia spread a patu on the ground and slipped underneath the vehicle while the Jeep driver tried to restart the engine. When their manoeuvres failed, they radioed our office in Qala-I-Nau and waited for Jim.

European poppies, hazy bluebells, sunflowers and white Queen Anne's lace dotted the surrounding hills, a scene reminiscent of a Monet painting. As I squatted on the road to have a closer look at the tiny bells waving in the breeze, Jim's razor-sharp words cut the air. Zia had just admitted that the Jeep's engine had actually been completely submerged in the river, a fact that he had previously omitted, likely to avoid Jim's fury. Irate expletives from the speaker peppered the air, sounding perverse in such a beautiful place. I too shied away from his temper. It triggered my own childhood fears of not being good enough.

Reza, Zia, BJ and I exchanged rueful grimaces, grateful for the distance between us and the source of the outrage. Reza interpreted Jim's words and stifled a giggle each time the Jeep driver made a clown face at the radio. He carefully omitted all insults and curses but everyone understood "fuck." Adhering to Jim's orders, Zia extracted, cleaned and dried various Jeep parts. He smiled sadly as he washed his hands with a bar of soap and rinsed them with water from a pop bottle. He had promised Jim that we would arrive in Qala-I-Nau before sunset. He so wanted Jim's respect yet had trouble dancing with his own harsh inner critic, which reminded me of mine.

"Zia, we'll make it." My hopeful reassurance sounded hollow even to me. He lit another cigarette.

I walked down the road to find a place to pee. Often the Afghan landscape is so barren and flat that a private spot is impossible to find. And even if you do come across one, a shepherd or a boy inevitably ambles along, anxious to greet you. Men had it easy. Squatting or standing, they just turned their backs to others. Women in burkas crouched in their private tent right beside vehicles. The possibility of land mines precluded scampering up the hillside away from the road. That day I ran down the path, veered onto animal tracks, then crouched behind a medium-sized boulder.

When I returned, the Kamaz driver reappeared from behind his truck, and the Jeep driver was squatting near his gutted vehicle, his back toward us. BJ stood glumly beside the Land Cruiser. Our group's merry mood had been crushed, like a balloon popped by a pin. Usually Jim's temper caused my heart to pound, my breath to speed up and my sweat glands to spin into overdrive, but that day, after Zia hung up the radio, I laughed. Here we were, a group of smart, able-bodied people who were amazingly adaptable and good at solving problems, cowed by someone else's inability to manage their emotions.

I crouched again by the field of bluebells that nodded sombrely on the slope. As I examined their petals, the Jeep driver stood up, and my inner thoughts flew out of my mouth. "In Canada, men stand. They don't squat." I stifled a giggle. I had just voiced my private musings about Afghan men's urinary habits!

"Hmm, why standing?" The Kamaz driver's tone implied curiosity, but he wore a horrified expression.

I shrugged. "Maybe it is faster. I don't know. I ask BJ." I translated the conversation for BJ and will never forget his what-the-fuck face.

Giggling, I plowed on: "Afghan men squat. Foreigners stand. Why the difference? Are there advantages of standing over squatting?" Women would pee all over themselves if they stood. The more I spoke, the louder I howled. Good thing my bladder was empty!

Rolling his eyes, BJ reluctantly joined the conversation. "It is what we're taught. It's the custom. It's easier to stand. Quicker too." His smile dissolved into a fit of laughter.

The Kamaz driver chortled. "Don't you piss on your clothes?" Imagining expats and Afghans in a pissing contest had me in stitches, and my stomach muscles cramped.

Zia raised his eyes and smiled, a lit cigarette hanging from his lip.

The Jeep driver grinned. "Khonum Murreen, why laughing?" I held my stomach so it hurt less.

Reza translated for BJ, then contributed his own thoughts: "Maybe they practise."

BJ guffawed. "First we check the wind. Only pee with the wind, never against it. Otherwise it sprays your shoes." At this point, everyone was snickering.

"If you squat, you do not have to worry about the wind." The Kamaz driver looked at his shoes, then at BJ's. Then he stepped out into the mass of bluebells. Crouching, he picked a handful of the small flowers, bit one off and smiled, as if relishing the flavour. "Khonum Murreen, look at the flowers! These flowers, you can eat!" He bit off several more. "They are delicious! Try some."

I snapped a photo of him, blossoms spilling from his lips. BJ shook his head. He wasn't going to risk a taste. I strode out into the meadow, snapping more photos. I plucked a flower and nibbled the edge of it. The taste reminded me of mountain sorrel: citrus with a bitter tinge, yet lettuce-like too. Harvesting a few more, I doused them with purified water and tossed them into my mouth.

We set off again. Near Qala-I-Nau, the sky turned pink. The radio crackled. Jim asked where we were.

"Five minutes away," Reza lied. We all smiled.

Fifteen minutes later, we drove through the compound gates. The sky was a light blue. Jim's face was stony, just like my father's used to be. Ignoring his sputter, I walked away.

CHAPTER FIFTEEN

A SURPRISE

"Life is either a daring adventure or nothing."

— *Helen Keller*

"You take photo?" As Zia turned to face me in the back seat, his eyes shimmered with the kind of delight that a boy might demonstrate when giving the best gift ever to someone who mattered. His grin was so wide that his weathered thirty-four-year-old face seemed to crinkle into cascades of tiny smiles. Four car lengths ahead of us, in a field of dry grassland dotted with asters, poppies and Queen Anne's lace, stood ten naked golden-haired camels shimmering in the sunlight.

We were returning from having set up our second clinic in a village called Khairkhane. Negotiations had been difficult. On our last day, we had settled a land dispute. Our accommodations had comprised a set of rundown rooms beside the tent clinic in which windows and doors were simply holes in mud walls. Each night before settling in, we had shooed away roosting bats and mice that had sought refuge during daylight hours. Mornings, I awoke at sunrise to fists pounding on the wooden door in the compound's exterior wall. Sick people wanted to be seen at the clinic, having walked through the night so they could return home the same day.

Too tired to do anything in the vehicle as it crawled in and out of deep tire grooves in hardened mud, I had let the soulful female singing and the beating Afghan drum from the cassette deck wash over me—that is, until we stopped near the dreamlike dromedaries. The early afternoon sun squeezed every last drop of water from the desiccated, scrub-like desert, creating a surreal scene. I scanned the land nearby for a shepherd or a dog. There wasn't one. Several times I blinked, subconsciously trying to clear the haze. The beasts stared down their snouts, appearing almost princely in their nudity. Could they be wild?

"Yes, good idea! How beautiful they are!" I quivered in anticipation while cursing the midday sun. If only it was early evening, when the setting sun caused colours to pop, textures to sharpen and

We really did ride camels bareback! With some help.

eyes to glow. At midday, the harsh light washed out fine textures and dulled the complex hues of the hairy coats and the tall grasses that the beasts nibbled, their jaws chewing in a cockeyed, sideways motion. Screwing a polarizing filter onto my lens, I hoped for the best.

Over the previous few months, Zia and I had gravitated toward one another. He was sharp, security conscious and knew the area intimately. Each morning, he shared local security information with me that he had collected from truckers at the bazaar. That information influenced the routes we chose. Being suspicious of any interpreter, he had insisted on giving the information to me in Dari since I was the only expat who understood the language.

Alone in a vehicle one afternoon, he had explained his distrust of interpreters. "Khonum Murreen, when the bombing by America happened and MSF left Afghanistan, I drove foreigners to the Turkmen border. The foreigners had a letter from MSF saying that I drive them to Ashgabad. I brought my passport but, without a visa, the guards did not let me cross. They aimed their guns at me and pushed me back. So the foreigners drove two of the Land Cruisers away, and I parked the other one near Bala Morghab. We hid the

Russian Jeep in a compound after removing its engine, which we buried elsewhere. Then we walked some hours to the village. The Taliban came to my house expecting to steal cars, but they saw none. I told them nothing. They threatened my family." In the quiet of the evening, his voice had sounded husky, his face twisted. "I was afraid for my family, so I drove the Land Cruiser to Qala-I-Nau. There were bombs. *Zzzzzzpkhahhhhhh!*" His hands clapped together, then flew apart. "When the foreigners came back, I picked them up. We had saved all of the vehicles, but they did not know all that I had done, because other people said it was their idea." He grimaced. "When the Americans came, why does MSF not give visas to Afghans who help them?"

A lump formed in my throat. "It is difficult." What could I say? It had to do with where you were born? I made up some excuse that I don't recall. It probably described how expensive visas were and how often they had to be renewed.

Although he had taken the same English courses as our other staff, he understood only about half of what was said, and when it came time for him to speak, English words seemed to stick in his throat. One evening just before walking home, he had asked if I would practise English with him during our travels. Overjoyed, I had said yes while I searched his face for the reason behind his change of heart.

"Soon, you leave Afghanistan. Other foreigners speak only English. I am a very good driver and mechanic, but my English is so bad. When other Afghans speak English, they get better work. For me, work is always the same. If I speak English, foreigners know I give good information and have good ideas. Maybe I get a better job." He turned away from the light, and his expression dissolved into the darkness.

Although I had told no one, I was sure that he was aware of my liaison with Kareem in Bala Morghab. Only once since leaving had I had the chance to visit my friends in that village. It had been a sad occasion. We were handing the clinic off to a local NGO who insisted on shrinking it to suit their budget. The remaining staff were crestfallen. That evening, anticipating a heartwarming chat with my friend Kareem, I had walked into the guard house to find Zia perched cross-legged right beside him. A few minutes later, he left us alone. How many others knew? Kareem told me of his plans to return to his land. His weak wife was strong, but she had not yet conceived.

I told him to be patient. Her body needed two years to recover from the last baby. His worry lines had softened.

Where Kareem was thoughtful and refined, Zia was street smart and wily. Both of them were survivors. While travelling, Zia and I often sat in the vehicle after dinner with doors and windows wide open so anyone could join us if they wanted. Sometimes we perched on doorsteps under the stars. Language practice with him covered travel, education, war, family, marriage and the burdens of being the eldest son, of providing for the entire family. When I quizzed him on words that he had promised to learn, he often froze. What memories paralyzed him?

When I asked, Zia had shrugged. "Words in English are difficult. Maybe I say the wrong word or pronounce it badly."

"Every day, you have heard me make many mistakes in Dari. When people tell me the right word, I learn. Sometimes I forget it and they tell me again. With time, I don't forget." I spoke Dari like a child, but that wasn't important. Learning the language was a way for me to uncover what mattered to Afghans, to understand different perspectives, to appreciate nuances. It was a bridge straddling the gulf between us that humanized all of us and helped me do meaningful work.

Inhaling through a cigarette, Zia looked into the black expanse above, which was filled with twinkling stars that I imagined were laughing at our foibles. His thoughts were miles away. Finally, he spoke: "I feel shame. Shame for being wrong."

I was well-practised at wrestling with shame, having internalized Dad's harsh self-criticism, just like he had from his father. As a teenager, I had been desperate to escape this criticism, so at seventeen, with Dad's help, I cobbled together scholarships that covered university expenses. I vowed never to give that wretched gift to anyone. In university, I taught myself to risk, fail and try again. Even now, my fear of failure sometimes sneaks in when stakes are high. Usually, I decide to take the risk anyway.

"To learn English, you must practise. Not trying to do something is the biggest mistake. Every mistake teaches us something." I looked straight ahead and spoke into the night, hoping to give him privacy to mull that over. I heard the rustle of his turban, the crackle of a cigarette and an exhale. The earthy odour of tobacco smoke wafted by.

"Jim wants you to learn English." I knew how much Jim's respect meant to him.

"I like working with Jim. I am a good driver and mechanic because of what he taught me. He is a good man, but his anger is too much. Behind every rock is 'fuck.' When he is angry, I want to give up. Sometimes nothing I do is good enough." At their best, Jim and Zia worked like a well-oiled machine, but the resulting happiness was short-lived.

In the field, I slowly approached the camels on a diagonal, like a birdwatcher observing skittish fowl. I had no faith that the camels would stay put. I wanted to take a stunning photograph, so I snapped the shutter repeatedly, using the maximum magnification of my 35 to 120 mm zoom lens. One camel's docile brown eye blinked lazily, his eyelashes as long as the fake ones used by sorority girls in the 1950s. How I wished for a 400 mm lens right then—the flowering landscape reflected in his eyeball would surely have been an award-winning image. In unison, their long necks dipped, their lips nibbling succulent weeds, their worn, yellowed teeth pulverizing grasses, woody plants and even thorns before swallowing with a gulp. A baby camel sidled up behind a larger one. Nuzzling her flank, he ducked between her legs for a quick drink, but she bit him and he slunk away. Change was painful.

A few metres away, Zia's brain looked like it was on fire as clouds of smoke billowed from his nose and mouth. He grinned self-consciously. "Smoking is a very bad habit. Only thirty-four, and my face looks too old!" Several times in the past, we had discussed the hazards of smoking, such as cancers, heart and lung diseases and wrinkles. He said that he wanted to quit but couldn't. He wasn't ready yet. What would he have become if alcohol had been legal!? He told me a story about travelling to Ashgabad, where he had drunk too much alcohol and wound up bringing an unwelcome gift home to his angry wife. Our team called Ashgabad the City of Love, since *ishgh* in Dari means "love" and *abad* translates into "city" or "settlement." What traumatic memories caused him to escape in those ways?

"These camels, are they wild?" I glanced over at Mr. Bashir, our interpreter, who looked contemplatively at the creatures.

Azaad, not azad. He corrected my pronunciation of the Dari word for "wild" and for "free," and I repeated it until he nodded approval.

"No, they are not wild. See the rope around that one's head?" He pointed to the largest camel. "The shepherd may be tending other animals nearby. No one here steals someone else's camels, even when the shepherd is a day or two away." As barbaric as Sharia law was, thievery really did seem relatively uncommon. I imagined someone trying, then getting caught. His hand falls off the chopping block. A bloody stump is left.

Mr. Bashir, a quiet and thoughtful teacher, had replaced Reza as our team's interpreter. During the 1980s, he had been an officer in the Afghan army and fought against the mujahedeen. On Mr. Bashir's first trip, Zia had pointed to an irregularity on top of a hill and, with a laugh, had bragged about being a wily mujahedeen. As Russians buried mines, mujahedeen spied on them, later digging the munition up to use against the Afghan army. The tension had mounted until Mr. Bashir humbly acknowledged what fierce warriors the mujahedeen had been. Exchanging grins, they had gazed out opposing windows.

Mr. Bashir's smooth, silky tone complemented Zia's brashness. He was an expert at negotiating. Once, while our team ate breakfast in the forest, an Afghan had waved a gun and accused us of trespassing on private property. Mr. Bashir had fearlessly approached him. They discovered that they knew someone in common. They shook hands, then sauntered off, deep in conversation. About twenty minutes later, Mr. Bashir reappeared, bearing a gift of black tea. We had run out.

I always sought Zia and Mr. Bashir's feedback as I sifted through options of what villages to explore for our next clinic locations. Only after hashing out a plan with them did I present it to Jim or Clarence.

Clarence, our project coordinator, was our newest team member. He and I had travelled together only once. I had initially balked at this soft-spoken man's rigid ideas and public school accent, fearing that he would hamper our ability to successfully negotiate in a culture that required understanding, acceptance and heaps of flexibility. In my opinion, the only way to create sustainable projects in Afghanistan was to wrestle and pound guidelines designed in Geneva or Amsterdam until they fit into the Afghan outback. In Khairkhane, Clarence had proved my suspicions wrong. He and Mr. Bashir had acquired everything that we needed.

I scanned the horizon just in case one of those huge Afghan dogs bounded toward us, teeth bared and ready to protect his flock. Treeless hills under steel-blue sky replicated all the way to the horizon.

"Do you ride camels?" Zia spoke from the corner of his mouth, his lopsided grin cradling a cigarette from which a dull grey cloud swelled and was swept away in the breeze. Strutting toward a camel, he reminded me of Marlon Brando decked out in a cockeyed turban and shalwar kameez.

"No, never." Turning toward Clarence, I translated the question, all the while noting the vacant look on his face, as if he was lost somewhere in the past. From what demons did he run?

He laughed and his face lit up: "No, I have never ridden one."

"Neither have I. Do you want to?" I beamed bravado that I didn't feel while trying to peek underneath his shield of shyness. Whatever lay beyond it remained invisible.

"I haven't ridden one in some time, but you never forget." Mr. Bashir, with a nostalgic glint in his eye, described how he had challenged other kids to ride wild or ill-tempered animals bareback as a rite of passage through childhood. "All foreigners learn how to drive. All Afghans learn how to ride animals. When you practise as a child, you do not forget."

"You are right, Mr. Bashir. In Canada, most girls and boys learn to ride bicycles. When we are old enough, we drive cars because almost every house has at least one of them. Only children who live on farms ride animals." In Bala Morghab, farmers had dug trenches across roads so they could irrigate crops on the other side. Only our MSF team, with its vehicles, thought this was problematic. Everyone else rode animals.

"Clarence, what do you say?" I wasn't sure how I felt about riding camels. As a suburban kid, I had never developed ease with animals. Only a few times had I ridden horses, always at my older sister's birthday parties. With a hammering heart and clammy hands gripping the reins, I was always terrified that the horse would tear off down the track and dump me on the ground.

Clarence nodded.

I answered for both of us. "Okay, show us! You ride first."

Rocking back and forth on his toes, Zia looked like he was ready to pounce. He ground the cigarette butt against the sole of his leather shoe, inspected it for sparks, then flicked it several yards into the tinder-dry grass. Why didn't he put it in our trash bag or throw it on the road?! It would take only one spark to create a roaring inferno in a place like this!

Crouching, he slowly cat-walked toward the camel that was wearing a rope bridle. Offering it imaginary treats, he got close enough to make a grab at the cord. His arm swung forward like a baseball pitcher and, just in time, the camel pivoted away. Zia's hand returned empty. While maintaining eye contact, Zia collected long stalks of grass. He approached its flank and offered the succulent grass, all the while clucking and pishing like Harry Potter speaking Parseltongue to snakes. The snout gingerly approached his hand, its lips tugging at the offering. Zia's other arm moved stealthily toward the rope. With a sudden snakelike gesture, he grabbed it. Rope in hand, he gave the camel a moment to sort out what had just happened. Patting its hindquarters, he muttered sounds similar to those that Kareem had used with animals. The camel began folding its knees beneath its body, then lay on top of the leg pile. From behind the animal, Zia grasped the skin of its hump and sat down on the butt, which sloped downward at a 45-degree angle. Gripping with his knees, he muttered in camel-tongue and patted the animal's flank. Rocking back and forth, its knees bending opposite to the direction that my brain predicted, which caused me to cringe, it rose to stand on spindly legs.

"As a boy, many times I ride camels!" Straddling its backside, legs dangling on either side of its bulging belly, Zia guided the camel to turn to the right, then to the left, again and again, like a skier on a slalom course.

While Zia danced with his camel, Mr. Bashir, with no fanfare, slipped onto another one that had no bridle. After it rose to standing, the two old soldiers egged each other on like school chums, cantering, galloping and leading the animals in patterns that reminded me of dressage competitions.

"Doktar Murreen, it is your turn to ride!" Zia returned at a gallop, exhilarated and huffing. The camel snorted. Me ride a camel bareback? Good grief! My stomach fluttered and my fingertips began to tingle.

Clarence winked mischievously.

"Zia, I know nothing about riding camels. I know about driving cars and riding bicycles. I have ridden a bicycle thousands of kilometres, but never have I ridden a camel. You must teach me." Did he think that I could easily master it? How on earth would I stay on its sloping rear end? A few metres away, I watched the camel kneel. My palms felt clammy.

Grinning widely, Zia dismounted. Rope in hand, he walked toward the camel's head, then turned around to face me, his back toward its rump, yellowed molars that groaned and crunched as they pulverized its meal. "It is easy. I show you. Stay away from its mouth. Camels bite." If so, wasn't it cavalier to stand with your arse facing a camel's teeth? How I wished that it had a muzzle.

"Stand behind the camel." He pointed to the camel's rump while muttering in camel-tongue. "Closer." He watched me inch over until I stood directly behind its butt. Although my rational brain knew without a doubt that when its knees were folded, the camel couldn't possibly kick me, a skittish, primitive part of my thinking apparatus felt compelled to avoid all risks. Sweat ran in ribbons down my ribcage.

"He cannot kick you. And right now, he cannot bite you." Zia's reassuring smile gave me some confidence. He continued muttering to the camel. Having my fears plainly expressed by him was sobering. Even though everyone probably had the same fears on their first ride, it felt like he was reading my mind, like Kareem used to do.

Silently, I recalled each of Zia's movements. Then I tried mimicking them. Crouching over the camel's butt, squeezing my thighs together and pressing my hands into its hump, I prayed that I would stay on when it see-sawed up to standing. As its sloping bum dipped down, I leaned farther forward and slipped backward. Squeezing my knees harder, I tried to sit straighter like Zia had done. I slipped again.

"I am falling. What do I hold onto?" By this time, I was stretched across the animal's butt, like I was humping it. Zia had made it look so easy!

"Hold onto the *dumba*." He pointed a cigarette at the camel's hump. "Your knees must be strong."

How do you hold onto a big, flattened oval mass of jiggling blubber covered in slippery fur? And what does keeping your knees strong mean? I had to look like a fool! But really, who cared? I was a first-timer, and like it or not, I was in the schoolyard learning a new trick. Breathe and you'll do fine, I told myself. What's the worst thing that can happen?

Squeezing my chest muscles together, I tried using friction against the hump's scraggly fur. "Like this?" Would I be able to hold this chest curl for the entire ride?

"Doktar Murreen, hold onto the hairs and the skin." Mr. Bashir chuckled while looking mighty comfortable as he mimed what I was to do.

The camel and I rose for the second time, my knuckles prodding tentatively at first into the skin because I didn't want the camel to whip its head around and bite me. When it didn't, I dug in deeper until I held onto a handle of folded skin, one in each hand. Still I slid, then I jumped off, ready to give up.

Zia kept hold of the rope. The camel and I had gone nowhere. Again, he commanded the camel to kneel. "Tsa, I help you!" Slipping one leg over the neck of the creature, he sat in the dip between neck and hump, facing backwards. His hands rested comfortably on the fat mound. Completely at ease, he simply hung there. "Get on again! If you start to fall, hold my hand. I catch you." He sounded like he was teaching a child, but hold his hands? Afghan men didn't hold women's hands!

Gritting my teeth, I clamped my knees once again around the golden tush as I squirmed my own right up against it. Then, still unsure about what I was supposed to do, I pretty much contracted my whole body, fingers digging into the skin, chest muscles creating friction against greasy fur, hips and thighs hanging on. Zia still sat comfortably, his head tipped, as if wondering why I was stressed. Our knees almost touched as we tipped upward, back and forth in a jerky see-saw pattern. Noting our shadow, I giggled. We looked like a pushmi-pullyu from Dr. Dolittle! Sauntering among the other camels, I watched their lips hoover plants at their feet. Clarence snapped a photo of us. The camel wandered majestically around the herd. Was Zia leading it? I certainly wasn't. Zia watched me. Our eyes met. I blushed, then looked away as I tried to calm down my body.

Zia crouched and peered into my face. "Khobe?" Trying not to breathe in his scent, which had suddenly caused an alluring warmth deep in my pelvis, I pointed to a hoopoe, a beautiful crested black and white bird that was swooping toward a tree. Facing an Afghan version of Marlon Brando with only a camel's hump separating our crotches felt way too intimate for the prim Afghan version of myself. Then again, what was the harm of enjoying the moment as long as I didn't lead him on? It was just a camel ride. Closing my eyes felt safer. A little slip backward and my hands moved up the hump inches from his.

When I glanced up, his expression was tender: I wanted those hands to hold me, but I threw away that thought. I was just lonely for physical touch. Did he sense the raging fire inside me? I saw his. A camel's hump and a world of cultural differences separated us.

"Yes, good! Very good. But my camel riding is so bad." I shook my head and chuckled. That laugh felt wondrous. Riding a camel bareback with an attractive man was a rush.

Zia's eyes glistened.

Clarence and Mr. Bashir could have been sharing a cup of tea on the hump between them. I snapped a photograph that, so many years later, still brings me joy.

"Yes, enough?" Zia was still trying to see what lay beneath my mask, and I was doing my darnedest to hide those secrets.

I grinned, allowing him to see my gratitude, how happy I was and that I cared for him. He was a lovely man. "Yes, very good. Thank you! I am very happy."

Clicking his tongue, Zia reached forward, and my heart lurched. He patted the camel softly and smiled tenderly. Our eyes met. He knew.

The animal rocked to a kneel. I slipped off.

"Khonum Murreen, you rode a camel! You learned camel-riding in Afghanistan!" Zia tapped the stately beast's behind to release him.

"Yes, you teach me very well. Thank you!" I felt light. What a ride!

CHAPTER SIXTEEN

AN AUNTIE

"Commitment is what transforms a promise into reality."

— *Abraham Lincoln*

Had our guide lied to us and pocketed the cash? We had left the village of Regi at 4:30 a.m. and driven an hour to get to this deserted hamlet, where we now stood waiting. It was 6:30 a.m. and there was no sign of the promised horses, nor any inhabitants. In the changing hues of sunrise, Zia's statement from the night before replayed in my head: "In Afghanistan, always there are horses." He had spoken with such confidence.

"Mr. Bashir, Clarence, it is late. Maybe no one is coming. I think we start Plan B." I paused. Our mood was sombre. "Maybe the villagers still look for an old mare for me to ride!" I winked at Mr. Bashir. My poor riding skills were a standing joke. The goal of this trip was to assess whether or not it made sense for MSF to set up a tuberculosis (TB) program in the area. Plan B involved hiking to seven of the nine hamlets described by locals as nearly abandoned. It would take all day, but I loved hiking. We had heard about these ghost towns for months but only recently received permission to investigate. On the map our travel plan had looked simple.

The previous afternoon we had set out on a reconnaissance trip to see if we could drive to the hamlets, but we took a wrong turn and ran out of daylight hours. Looking through my binoculars from a distance of several kilometres, we saw the canyon that locals described. A Land Cruiser could not negotiate the narrow paths hugging the cliff-like walls on either side of it. Horses would be our best option. That evening, back in Regi, Zia and Mr. Bashir sent our newly hired guide to arrange horses and asked locals for estimates of walking and riding times for our proposed trek.

The tales I had heard about these nine remote hamlets involved a mysterious coughing sickness that moved from person to person, killing old and young alike. There was talk of poison in the air and bad spirits called djinn, reminiscent of early nineteenth century European explanations of illness before the discovery of germ theory.

I was pretty sure that TB was the culprit. It would be especially challenging to treat in nomads.

The year before, I had taught Kareem about TB because he had doubted the importance of his wife completing nine months of treatment for a persistent cough. She had previously stopped the medications because they upset her stomach. The cough had returned. Hers was a classic story that contributed to the worldwide problem of drug-resistant TB. To illustrate my points, I had drawn diagrams of lungs and germs and created a tale about a villainous TB germ whose aim was to become a superbug. I wanted Kareem to repeat it to others. In the end, his wife did complete the treatment. In Afghanistan, decades of war, malnutrition, poor medical care and the ease with which people acquired dubious-quality medications, which anyone could seemingly prescribe or sell, was the perfect set-up for rampant, drug-resistant TB.

We settled on Plan B. Zia drove us twenty minutes farther and parked beside the only two trees on a dry plateau where clumps of thorn bushes grew. From there we had a twenty-minute walk to the lip of the canyon. Zia and Aalem, a young interpreter, would remain in the Land Cruiser. We would check in with them every hour, using a portable VHF radio. They would relay the information about our progress to the MSF office in Qala-I-Nau using an HF radio. Back in Regi, Jaafar waited at the compound of the German agricultural aid organization where we had exchanged food for two bedrooms. He would stay in radio contact with Zia and be ready to help out with a second vehicle if needed.

Minutes later, our guide fell behind.

"Foreigners will never walk to seven villages in such heat. It is too far!" He moved like molasses. His lethargy and leaden words weighed me down. I wanted to run away from his poisonous aura, but instead I rolled my eyes at Mr. Bashir and simply shook my head. I could almost feel steam billowing from my ears.

"You agreed to walk. Now move." Mr. Bashir's genteel voice had a steely edge.

Our guide whimpered. "Walking downhill is easy, but I will need a horse or a donkey for such a long walk."

Exiting the car, Zia strode up to him like a father ready to discipline his son. "You said that you arranged horses. They did not arrive. You agreed that you would walk, if needed. Now walk! Stop being such a woman!"

I chuckled silently even though calling our guide a woman was a flagrant insult to me. It was a common Afghan expression. I decided right then that Zia needed to witness the strength of an independent woman, so I picked up the pace. "The foreigners will do this trek even if you cannot. We hired you to be a guide. You must be one."

He grumbled. "My lungs are weak. My breath is difficult when I walk up hills."

Mr. Bashir reached out an upturned palm, his voice a silky steel. "Give me your water and your lunch. If we hire a donkey in one of the villages, the cost will be subtracted from your fee. We pay you only after we return."

Handing over the requested items, our guide smirked.

We descended a steep, zigzagging path into the deep shade of the gorge, where the breeze felt air-conditioned. Red rock formations and tinkling water from an unseen source reminded me of Natural Bridges National Monument in Utah. Dry leaves brushed against my shalwar. I felt at home on the trail. Every few steps, our skinny guide coughed. For our own safety, we had opened all of the windows in the car despite the early morning chill, and now we kept our distance from him.

In the silence, four gunshots reverberated down the canyon. Although I was accustomed to the crisp *rat-a-tat-tat* of AK-47's, I still jumped. Afghan villagers used them at weddings and Eid celebrations, and sometimes they shot a gun to attract attention, since no one had phones.

I stopped for a second. "Mr. Bashir, why the shots? Did the horses arrive?"

He shrugged. "Here people use guns too much. Maybe the horses came. Maybe not."

Clarence radioed Aalem to ask if the steeds had appeared.

Aalem responded. "No horses here, but we can drive back to the village to see. With horses, you can travel faster, and we won't have to wait so long."

Clarence's eyes met mine. What foreigner in their right mind would send their staff toward the sound of gunshots?! If the horses had arrived, surely the gunmen could ride them to Zia and Aalem, who would then notify us. If men with guns were squabbling among themselves, we should keep our distance.

From a pocket, our guide fished out a flattened pack, extricated a cigarette, flicked a match and inhaled deeply. I held my tongue. Zia had told me that he was a cheat, but no one else dared visit these haunted hamlets.

Our guide's dishonesty and self-pity repelled me, so I stalked off, darting through thorns that tore threads from my shalwar and kameez. I spoke quickly as I passed Mr. Bashir. "I do not trust him. There have been too many delays. We must walk quickly. We do not accept any excuses. You manage him and make sure that he does not run off. When I look at him, I feel too much anger."

Mr. Bashir nodded. Grabbing a crooked walking stick that someone else had left against the canyon wall, he used a switchblade from his pocket to whittle the end into a point. When he offered it to our guide, his voice was firm. "You must stop complaining now. Today we walk to seven villages. If you want to be paid, you will finish the trip with us."

Deep down on the floor of the canyon, our guide crept after us like Gollum in *The Lord of the Rings*. Clarence brought up the rear in case the weaselly fellow tried to escape. I heard a thick wad of phlegm being horked up. It splatted on the ground. I gagged and imagined Clarence slipping on it.

Ascending the far cliff, I forced my breath into a slow rhythm. Elders in each village would confirm our trekking time estimates. We had to make it back to the vehicle before sundown. If needed, we could skip a village or two. I did a quick inventory of my knapsack's contents: a baseball hat, five litres of frozen water, naan, hardboiled eggs, almonds, sour cherry jam and cream. The sweater at the bottom seemed ludicrous during the day, but deserts get mighty cold at night.

As we crested the far side of the canyon, we looked back across to where we had started. The distant white speck that was the Land Cruiser parked beside the two puny trees was surrounded by an expansive, royal blue sky. Today would be a scorcher.

Ten minutes later, we approached a thin, grey-haired man who sat like a yogi in the deep shade of a mulberry tree. His surprisingly white turban gleamed against a dust-coloured cluster of compounds. Hand on his heart, Mr. Bashir greeted him, then asked for the village elder. The weathered man's eyes looked peaceful. He removed a toothpick from his lips, then rose from his cross-legged pose. Placing a patu on his shoulder, he readjusted his turban and slipped on scuffed rubber shoes streaked with mud. Then he walked in the direction of the houses.

Mr. Bashir pointed his walking stick at the disappearing figure. "We wait here. He will bring the elder."

Kicking away half-dried mulberries, he spread his patu on the ground, then spoke softly. "Doktar Murreen, today I call you *khale*. Today it is best if we tell no one that you are a doctor. If villagers know you are a doctor, they will bring too many sick people for you to cure. Refusing to treat them will be difficult, so we would have to stay here overnight. Will you agree to be an educated auntie, only for today?"

I studied his face. The closest medical care was from an illiterate pharmacist in Regi, a long day's walk away. If we refused, would they become violent? My fingers drummed against my thigh.

"Perhaps you wish to stay here tonight... I prefer to return to Regi." Mr. Bashir, a man who rarely advocated, pushed his point. Clarence nodded.

On other trips when we had travelled by vehicle and I had not hidden my profession, villagers had shown me relatives with long-standing paralysis, mental illnesses and genetic malformations. I had nothing to offer them except a prayer. They had seemed to hope that I would pull miracle cures from my bag.

"Okay, if it is best. Today I am Khale Murreen." Being a doctor had been my ticket to leading the team. An ill-defined tightness hung in my chest. I could always change my mind.

The peaceful man returned, walking beside a shorter, wiry gentleman whose shaggy salt-and-pepper fringe peeked out at odd angles from beneath a white turban. Had he just been roused from a nap? Something about his demeanour struck me as dignified. Glancing at Clarence, he approached Mr. Bashir, a hand on his heart.

After the greetings, the elder raised an eyebrow, an invitation for Mr. Bashir to explain our sudden appearance in his village.

"We are from Doktoraha Bidun-e-Sarhat, a medical organization working in Badghis Province." He used the local name for MSF. "This is Mr. Clarence, the head of the organization, and Khonum Murreen, an educated khale who advises our work." I nodded. The elder focused on Mr. Bashir. I swallowed a bitter taste.

"Today we see only ten people. Our goal is to collect information to know if we can help your village. Later, we come back only

A rugged canyon in Badghis Province, similar to the one we traversed.

if we can help. Today we can offer no treatment." He sipped tea that a boy had served. "We heard that people in this village have died from cough or breathing problems. Is this true?" Mr. Bashir laid back against a pillow that the boy had placed behind him on the mat.

The elder glanced at Clarence. "Is he a doctor?"

Mr. Bashir shook his head and lied without a flinch. "No, today we have no doctors. We are here to gather information for our organization. On our next visit, if we come back, we bring doctors."

Although I felt invisible, I was grateful that no one was demanding anything from me.

The elder sighed. "Yes, many people have cough. They are sick and need help. There is no clinic in our village. Many people have died. Will you build a clinic here?"

Mr. Bashir's face radiated empathy. "We understand that people are sick, and we would like to build a clinic, but today this cannot happen. Our organization must first understand the sickness. Different illnesses have different treatments. Today we visit seven villages. Only after visiting all of them can our organization make a decision about building a clinic."

"How does that help us?" His vacant stare and disdain mirrored the distrust that many villagers had of foreign organizations that had not honoured promises. Then he let out a lengthy sigh, almost a groan. "Yes, many people have cough." If I were in his position, I too would want a concrete solution to offer my people.

"We hope to convince our organization to help you, and we need information to do that. If we understand the problems in your village, we can give the right kind of help." Mr. Bashir's expression was earnest. The elder's frown softened. "Good. What do you need?" He sipped tea, replaced the cup, then waited.

Mr. Bashir glanced at me.

"We would like to see people with cough." I paused as the elder sent a boy to the cluster of houses. "How many people live here?"

Using the tip of a wooden staff with a curlicue handle, he drew a circle in the dirt. "Before the coughing sickness, two hundred people. Now, only one hundred. Many children died from weakness. I lost my wife and sons." He shook his head and stared into the circle, his attention lost for the moment.

As Mr. Bashir expressed condolences, I extracted my one-page survey from my blue backpack. I recorded the population and estimated deaths over time as Mr. Bashir read the first question. The elder answered and I scribbled notes.

"Living in a village where so many people die every day is very difficult. The village loses its life." His rheumy blue eyes teared. He dabbed them shamelessly with the tail of his turban.

"We will see villagers with cough. I hope that our organization can help you." I would do my best.

Off to the side, Clarence used hand signals to organize the first seven people into a line.

The first man stopped briefly to disgorge a projectile of frothy, yellow phlegm that resembled a dead jellyfish. My breath caught for a second before I slowly exhaled the nausea, thankful of being upwind. He was a smoker, and his cough had lasted five years. Was it chronic bronchitis or our mystery illness?

A mother roughly shoved her ten-year-old daughter toward me. The child resisted. The mom grabbed a shoulder and propelled her so we could see her profile. A step in her mid-thoracic backbone was consistent with a collapsed vertebra. With no history of accidents or wounds, TB of the bones was certainly possible. I forced a smile. "Thank you for bringing your daughter. She has a very difficult problem." The fracture would ruin her life even if MSF helped her. TB medication could stop other vertebrae from being infected, but surgical stabilization of the deformity, a treatment that MSF did not provide, would probably be necessary to avoid eventual nerve damage and possible paralysis.

The mom's eyes flashed. "If you do not cure her, she cannot marry!" Her eyes bored into mine. I sensed guilt and rage, beneath which lay sadness. Creating a buffer for myself against her thorny bitterness, I feigned incomprehension and asked Mr. Bashir to translate. It was going to be a long day.

Mr. Bashir explained that, as an interpreter, he didn't make decisions for the organization, that he only relayed my words. I reiterated our message about what we could offer, that we hoped to help. It felt inadequate.

The mother lashed out, her voice desperate. "My daughter must marry! And you do nothing for her?!"

Mr. Bashir, like me, seemed to swallow tears, but his soothing voice sounded confident. "I am sorry, khale. We can do nothing for you now. In the future, we hope to offer medicine. You must wait. Every day, we will pray for your daughter." Muttering under her breath, the mom pushed her daughter, who stumbled. The elder raised his hand, offering peace.

Another mother guided an adolescent covered by a head-to-toe chaderie with tiny blue flowers. Directly in front of me, she opened her chaderie in a way that shielded her body from Mr. Bashir. Turning her dark brown eyes and inky black hair to the side, she pointed at her neck, where an angry, red crater with raw edges festered. Straw-coloured fluid oozed from it, one drop clinging to her olive skin. The previous year they had walked twice to the pharmacist in Regi, where they had bought injections, pills and creams, but nothing had made it better. Next year she would marry. Could we help her?

"This looks like TB. It is cured by taking medicine for six months. Only a small scar will remain." I turned to the mother. "Thank you for bringing your daughter. I hope that we can help you and others in the village."

By then, a crowd of thirty had congregated near Clarence, several of whom squatted in the shade as if watching an outdoor theatre performance. Clarence held up five fingers.

Mr. Bashir pointed to the group and spoke loudly. "We will see these five people, then we go to the neighbouring village. When we return, everyone will be seen." No longer did he say "if," but I couldn't face correcting him.

The elder stood and waved a hand at the identified group. "They can see only these people. Today they have no medicine, but later, they may come back to help us." Turning toward the other group, he looked like a traffic cop trying to hold back a crowd. "They do not see you today." He sat down heavily.

When I turned back to the group of five, it had become seven. I shrugged and sliced a hand across my neck the way scuba divers communicate that they are out of air. Those seven villagers ranged from teenagers to sixty-year-olds. All of them had coughs that had lasted much too long. The men smoked. Several had lost weight, and some of them coughed up blood. TB was the likely culprit.

As we left that village, I placed a hand on my heart and looked into the elder's eyes. I made eye contact with as many others as I could. They looked hopeful. Would MSF answer their prayers?

Our guide coughed, then swallowed and smacked his lips. The elder escorted us beyond the last house, where he thanked us again. Trooping down the path, I glanced back, taking a mental snapshot of a distinguished man surrounded by alder-like trees whose hand still lay on his heart and whose face radiated hope.

When we were out of sight, Clarence dug the VHF handset from his backpack and conveyed our progress. In this faraway place, the radio seemed magical.

After a few sips of refreshing water from a pop bottle in which a chunk of ice still floated, we trudged along the sun-dappled trail. Dry grass swished against our legs, and papery leaves rustled in the wind as birds chirped in counterpoint.

At first glance the second village looked deserted, but telltale tufts of green grass grew near the well where the earth was wet. After a brief conversation with Mr. Bashir, our guide disappeared down a dirt path, flanked on either side by two-metre walls.

Mr. Bashir stroked his beard. "Our guide lived in this village until five years ago. He said that his family of seventeen died from TB, everyone but an older brother and him. He has gone to get his brother, the elder." He gazed into the distance, and I saw his lip quiver. I knew so little about him.

No wonder our guide had wanted to come with us! And boy was I glad that we had kept our distance from him. In the shade, I drank thirstily, then quickly hid the bottle in my knapsack so no one thought I was rude.

Five minutes later, a gaunt man with a cane accompanied our guide. He estimated that the village had lost 75 percent of its population over the previous twenty years. Only one hundred inhabitants remained. Both our guide and his brother had been treated for TB in Iran. They still had difficulty walking uphill. They could have multidrug-resistant TB or scarred lungs from untreated infection.

"Seeing their family and the village disappear must have been heartbreaking. How does he know it is TB and not something else? Did they have tests in Iran?" TB was one of the great masqueraders of other diseases.

"People have cough, weight loss, sometimes coughing up blood and, at times, fevers. Our guide went to Iran, where a photograph of his lungs was taken and he spat into a cup. The same day, the doctors told him that he had TB and gave him many medicines for six months." In the still air, Mr. Bashir wiped sweat from his forehead with a checkered handkerchief.

"Please ask him the survey questions." I dug out an English questionnaire, ready to record answers.

More women than men lived in the village. An older lady covered in a pale beige chaderie approached in the shadows, carrying a tray with a steaming teapot and six overturned glass mugs that glistened with wetness. After rinsing each cup with hot tea, she filled them to the brim. I guzzled two cups of her brew as village women gathered around Clarence. He made several unsuccessful attempts to move away from them. Usually, women stood in groups several metres away from men. What was the deal? As the group swelled, their excited chatter floated over to us. Clarence's beseeching expression asked Mr. Bashir for support. I snickered. He looked so forlorn facing a problem that many men would welcome! He would sort it out.

Mr. Bashir welcomed a beefy forty-year-old woman, who stood in front of us. She peered so openly that I felt undressed. "Are you Afghan?"

Really? She thought I was a ballsy Afghan woman who travelled with men? Was I her first foreigner?

"No, I am from Canada." Fascinated by her boldness, I wanted to know her story.

Mr. Bashir chuckled in a fatherly way. "She is an educated khale who helps our team."

"Are you together?" She looked at Mr. Bashir and then at me as she rubbed her two index fingers together, a symbol that Kareem had used when we had explored the mysterious notion of friendships between sexes.

"No, we are working together. I have two wives, and she will not accept to be my third one." Mr. Bashir's eyes twinkled as he trashed our cover story, in which Clarence and I were a couple. I smiled at her. Third wife? Never!

The lady's eyes creased into folds. Between crooked lips, her tooth stumps glinted a dark brown. "Good! I was married once. He was a good man, but once is enough! Never again. My husband, he is with Allah." She laughed sonorously as her strong fingers dug into my shoulder. I liked her gumption. When we had finished asking her questions, she turned away and began smoking a water pipe, known locally as a *shisha*. Smoker's cough, TB or both?

The stories in the third hamlet were similar, but there, widows lived with their kids, away from everyone else. Locals said they were tainted, so I asked to visit them. They lived together in one large compound that had no exterior wall. They shared housework, child-rearing and gardening. They weren't allowed out of the compound, and the elder who accompanied us refused to give us permission to enter it. We conversed over the fence.

A stooped woman in a ragged dress, a shalwar and a torn chador told me that she was nineteen years old. A two-year-old was strapped to her back. Two toddlers followed her every step. "Please help me?" Her low-pitched whisper was so wretched that my heart twisted. Neither she nor her children had a cough. We moved on to question others, and she followed, her heartbreaking story spilling out of chapped lips. Her husband had recently died, and she wanted to escape this life in which awaited only long years of sadness. She was too young for this. Please, could we take her away? I smiled and muttered kind reassurances, all of them meaningless as the ache of helplessness wrung my gut. None of the widows or their children had coughs. For the moment, my hands were tied.

At noon we came across the perfect spot for a picnic, in the shade beneath a stone that stuck out from a cliff like a shelf. The rocks emitted so much heat that I felt like a loaf of naan in a tandoor oven. Eating in the village was out of the question because we didn't have enough to share and we wanted to minimize our exposure to TB. Mr. Bashir handed our guide his lunch and pointed to a rock downwind of us. Fifteen minutes later, our shade had evaporated and it was time to move on.

The fourth village looked prosperous compared to the others. Flowers and vegetables sprouted in gardens near well-maintained houses. A jovial young man was introduced as the village elder. Pale roots marred his sable beard and hair. He looked spry and well-fed. I guessed that he was forty-five years old. Had all of the older men in the village died?

Beside him, Mr. Bashir looked ancient. The elder offered us tea at his house. A rest would benefit the team, but TB spread so well indoors—especially in the pervasive mud dwellings with tiny windows and doors built to conserve heat in winter and coolness in summer. I preferred staying outside, but Mr. Bashir needed a reprieve. We could always ask to drink tea in a courtyard. As we turned the corner, my angst evaporated. A large open window overlooked a courtyard garden where a breeze blew the mane of a muscular black stallion.

Inside, Mr. Bashir crumpled onto a mattress. "We are very happy to have tea and a few minutes of rest. Afterward, we will see people with cough outside where the light is best." He looked like he might take a nap.

Through the window, a small crowd watched, as if we were on television.

"Both of my wives died from coughing, one right after the other. Perhaps they were too weak. The stronger their cough, the weaker they became. My three sons and daughter stayed healthy and strong like me." He looked sad, his dyed hair stark against his pale skin. Suddenly, he clapped his hands, and I almost spilled my tea. "Now, I look for another wife. I dye my hair black because I want a young wife, one that is very strong." His eyes shone with hope, and his booming laugh filled the room.

"In the village that we just visited, young widows want to marry again. They are beautiful. You might consider them?" I thought about the security that he could provide the nineteen-year-old and her children.

"Ah, but she must be a *dokhtar*. Only if no dokhtar will have me, will I choose a widow." He smiled mischievously, as if contemplating which candy to taste.

Mr. Bashir peered down at me. "You know what he means?"

I nodded. Of course, he wanted a virgin. Asif and Kareem had explained that the word "dokhtar" meant both virgin and daughter, as if those words were inseparable. I still recall Asif asking if I was a virgin and me playing innocent, saying that of course I was a daughter. This man had no business marrying a virgin! But of course he would and when he did, I hoped that he would provide her with a comfortable and caring life. Many families would willingly exchange their virgins for what he had to offer.

Still, I wanted him to marry the widow. "If you want to attract a young wife, you must dye the white hairs in your beard. A widow would not mind a *riche safet*."

His deep, round laugh rang out. "If she doesn't like my beard, she will like my wealth." He was probably right.

Mr. Bashir joined in. "Perhaps it is best if you find an educated wife like my khale." He cocked his head sideways at me and smiled innocently.

"Your khale is lovely, but she is one of a kind. There are none like her here. How much is her dowry?" He grinned.

"Unfortunately, she is not available." Mr. Bashir took a long swig of tea.

"How much?" The elder pressed. The hair on my arms rose up as if ready to fight him. Was he serious?

Mr. Bashir just shook his head and repeated the same answer. "It is time to see the people waiting. Would you like to do it from here?" He studied my face. He had my back.

With a shudder, I turned toward the crowd. For a split second, I pondered the life of a woman sold against her will and saw a tunnel with no escape. I would die trying.

When we were finished the interviews, we had more evidence of TB. The elder joined our trek up the hill, and we stopped in his melon field.

"Such beautiful melons!" Mr. Bashir caressed one of the smooth, round, golden fruits lying on the ground. He and the elder snickered, glancing at me, as if trying to ascertain if I understood their lewd references. I played innocent, ignoring their description of round-ness, size, pallor and heaviness. Whatever!

From behind a tree, our guide appeared on a donkey. Clapping his hands, the elder expressed how delighted he was to loan a donkey to a tired man from a neighbouring village. Nearby was a large, black handwoven tent made of goat hair, the kind that Kuchi nomads passed between family members. In it, the elder's daughter-in-law had set out a snack of tea and chunks of pale green melon that dripped with sweet juice. She and I sat shoulder to shoulder in the shade of the tent while the men lounged cross-legged at the other end of the plas-tic tablecloth. The view from the plateau was stupendous, ridge after ridge of pinkish-brown hills intersecting cobalt blue sky. The canyon far below looked like a ragged cut in bone-dry earth.

She told me that she was hoping to become pregnant with her first child. She had always lived in this village, having only once trav-elled to Regi to visit the pharmacist. Giggling, she asked me the usu-al questions. No children? How could that be when I was so old? I had lived in many towns and travelled to so many countries. My goodness! Why would I do that? Wasn't I lonely? She held my hand to her face. Her enraptured expression and tinkling laughter had me wondering how she interpreted a story like mine.

When we rose to leave, she asked if I would spend the night. I thanked her and politely declined, then waved goodbye and began the descent. Her questions spun in my head. Was I running away from commitment but didn't recognize it because I had lived that way for so long? Did I want to reside somewhere permanently or was I satisfied with my life? Leaving people behind was tiresome, but new adventures had always added an exhilarating secret sauce to my life. Was that still true?

As we began yet another ascent, Mr. Bashir interrupted my rev-erie. "Khonum Murreen, I feel jealous of you." He paused.

"Mr. Bashir, I am just a khale. Why are you jealous of me?" I teased him but I knew.

"That beautiful woman sat next to you and held your hand. I would love to have been you!" His gentle eyes laughed. I smiled. Sex was power.

I saw a white speck far below across the canyon. "Clarence, can I have the radio?" I pressed the transmit button. "Bravo-1, do you copy?"

Aalem answered affirmatively.

"We see you. Do you see us?"

Zia's voice crackled. "Kujo hastid?"

"On the hill between V4 and V5." Mr. Bashir, Clarence and I crowded together and waved our arms in wide arcs.

"We look everywhere but do not see you. Are you well?" Zia's voice sounded tired from baking in the sun. "It is hot, but hearing your voice makes us happy."

I signed off, thankful of their dedication.

In the valley, a man on the path told us that he was the elder of the next village. He and a friend were on their way to harvest melons in a field several hours away.

Mr. Bashir turned on his charm. "Do you have three minutes to answer questions right here?"

The man accompanying the elder seemed to study my face for a moment, as if trying to recall a memory. "Did you visit Shahr Arman?" I nodded. Mr. Bashir answered: "Yes, we surveyed that village a few weeks ago."

"I spoke with you there. You are doing good work. Allah is with you." He turned to his companion. "Help them. I will wait." He promptly plunked down on a rock and was immediately absorbed in watching the scenery. His words warmed my heart. So often our contributions seemed minuscule when compared to the monstrous needs that greeted me at every turn. After answering our questions, the elder gave us the name of someone who would organize patients in his village, then he hustled on. The information from his village and the next one pointed once again to TB as the villain in our story.

At 5 p.m., we stepped into the deserted streets of the last village. When we knocked on doors, no one answered. We criss-crossed the village twice in search of participants. Finally, Mr. Bashir pointed to a window several metres away. Through it, we saw a couple hurriedly packing.

Mr. Bashir called out. "Khale! Khale!" They ignored us. As we approached, he called louder and louder. Finally, they stopped and looked up. The woman mumbled impatiently, then launched into an explanation.

"Tomorrow at first light we leave for our melon field. We are packing for some months. There is one other family left in the village. You can speak to them." Her tone was brisk.

Trekking uphill from a village below, our guide rode a donkey loaned to him by an elder.

Mr. Bashir countered in a chummy, relaxed voice as he crouched down to sit on their shaded doorstep. "All day it has taken us to walk many, many kilometres. We ask that you answer only a few questions. Only a moment or two and we are done. We promise to leave you hours to pack." His weighty sigh convinced even me of his fatigue.

The wife stalked off, then reappeared with a carpet and two thin mattresses, but Mr. Bashir waved her away. "This is unnecessary. You are busy. We will not even take tea, just a few moments of time."

The wife apologized and disappeared again. The man and an older woman sat down. They had planned to leave the previous week, but the older woman, his mother, had been ill with weakness and fever but no cough. Now that she had recovered, they were rushing to tend to the crops, which were their main food source. Everyone in the village was semi-nomadic like Kareem's family had been. People were generally healthy. No one coughed. If we wanted, we could walk for a day to the fields or return in two or three months. I scratched the village off of my list.

The man left, but the old woman and Mr. Bashir continued chatting. She had a chicken. Would he buy it for the equivalent of $3 US? He negotiated half-heartedly, then nodded. She disappeared behind the house, returning with a stick balanced over a shoulder, a ball of twine and a squawking bird. Heads bent together, they discussed how to attach the bird to the stick. After five minutes of planning, they laughed as they bound its feet together, then tied the bundle to the pole. The bird flapped its wings trying to escape. Mr. Bashir wound more twine around its legs, then slung the pole over his shoulder. The bird bobbed at the far end, its beak harmlessly pecking air. She wished us a safe journey.

At the lip of the canyon, Clarence pulled out the radio. "Bravo-1, Bravo-1, do you see us?"

"Copy. Yes, we see you! Please, you must keep walking. The car has been like a sauna today. I asked Zia to turn on the air-conditioning but he refused." Aalem was probably the youngest child in his family.

After a scuffle, Zia's voice crackled. "The engine, I turned on twice. It is important to save fuel, but Aalem complains too much. He is so weak! We are very happy to see you!"

Aalem whined again and Clarence interrupted him. "Now, we go into the canyon. Over and out."

As we descended, I felt like a slice of bread slipping into a toaster. Long shadows from boulders, trees and bushes decorated steep, zigzag tracks through green vegetation. Goat and sheep scat guarded the entrance of a cave that we passed. I pointed to hundreds of dark holes above us. Mr. Bashir said that people lived in those caves. Crossing the dry riverbed, we walked in the cool shade of a humongous natural stone bridge. I drank the last of my lukewarm water. Halfway up the other side, we stopped to speak with a woman and her daughter who were returning from an unsuccessful trip to Regi. The pharmacy had been closed. What could we do for them?

Mr. Bashir explained our work, then whispered solemnly: "We have no medicine. Today we pray for you." Dissatisfied, she huffed and continued her descent.

When we were near the top of the canyon, we paid our guide, who adeptly turned the donkey around and began retracing his steps.

After nine hours of walking, we stood on the plateau once again. The Land Cruiser, decorated with six blooming hollyhock stalks that waved at us from the flagpole holders on the roof, sped toward us. The noise of the engine was jarring after such a peaceful walk, but Zia's beaming face, as he stepped from the vehicle, was a delight to behold.

This Afghan horseman stopped to water his horse. He greeted us, then quickly moved on. His goal was to arrive at his destination before darkness descended and bandits came out.

CHAPTER SEVENTEEN

A STONE WALL

"Only from the heart can you touch the sky."

— *Rumi*

As I walked into the German aid agency's living room in Regi, a dozen Afghan men sat up from cozy, lounging positions. They straightened shalwars and kameezes, as if caught red-handed. I felt like a mom entering a room of adolescent boys. After having spoken to so many people on our day-long trek, I craved solitude so I could regain some of the energy that I had expended. Like us, they had been granted accommodations for the night. In rural Afghanistan, guests are rarely turned away.

I had been looking forward to quietly unravelling my thoughts of the day, sorting through them and making sense of the few about which I still brooded. What about the girl with the step deformity of her spine, whose life lay out in front of her full of harshness and rejection? What would happen to the sorry group of segregated widows? And how could I ensure that I was never kidnapped or sold when doing this kind of work? I trusted Mr. Bashir, but he wouldn't always be there.

I eyed the crowd in front of me. I had no energy for another innocuous comment or question that gave them no insight into what they really wanted to learn, which was how a single woman spent her time. These circular conversations always made me dizzy and raised questions about the purpose of the interaction. I wasted lots of effort trying to intuit the real meaning of their Dari words and their nuanced body language. I expended more energy on hiding my opinions behind placations so I might appear compliant with their preposterous rules. I just wanted to let down my hair and have an honest conversation. I could accept if they were gay or bisexual, had cheated on their wives, had killed someone or whatever other nefarious stories were held in their pasts. But would they demonstrate the same acceptance of me?

Caked with salt crystals and Afghan dust, my kameez could probably have stood up on its own. Grit was lodged in the creases of my skin and glued the hairs of my nose together. When I wiped my face with the end of my chador, a beige streak marred its whiteness.

An entire thermos of gnat's pee, as my grandmother would call it, helped clear my foggy brain. My muscles started to relax. Had I peed only once that day or was it twice?

Through the double doors to the courtyard, I watched a couple of twenty-year-old men in cotton sarongs pour buckets of water pumped from the well over their muscular torsos and wished I could do the same. Guffawing, they piled shampoo bubbles over each nipple, proudly showing off their foamy breasts. Then they cupped well-endowed groins with their hands and provocatively thrust their hips. There was no way that I had the cheekiness to stand in a wet shalwar kameez clinging to me like plastic wrap in full view of this crowd. Just the idea of a woman bathing would tantalize their imagination—according to Kareem, Asif and others, Afghan villagers bathed once weekly, before a Friday night frolic with their spouses.

It wasn't fair that they got to be clean when I didn't. Mumbling to no one in particular, I left in search of shade outside, where I put pen to page. As I scratched words in my journal, Mr. Bashir came over, his chicken now dangling limply from the carrying stick. "Your penknife, please." Wishing he had one of his own, I grumbled, opened the pouch and pulled it out. He stepped a metre away, held the bird upside down and with one stroke, expertly slit its carotid arteries. Then he angled the twitching chicken, whose legs moved as if running, so that its blood sprayed down onto the dirt and flowed into a puddle.

Wearing a worried expression, Kabir, Zia's brother, hefted a spade. He was our cleaner and cook when we travelled. "Khonum Murreen, the food we have is not enough for guests. More than twenty sleep here tonight!" Had he known in advance, he would have bought extra meat in the village, but it was too late.

"What is the meal tonight?" I made half an attempt to engage him, but I really didn't care.

"We have enough spiced lentils, cumin rice, zucchini with onions and tomatoes. This chicken is the problem. Our guests will eat less than a mouthful of it!" He scuffed his sandal in the dirt and searched my face for answers. I had none. How was this our problem? They weren't our guests!

The last few drops of the fowl's blood landed in the sangria-coloured puddle. The chicken was scrawnier than the two sad turkeys that we had failed to fatten for Christmas the previous year in Bala Morghab. It might serve three not-so-hungry people. My knife sawed through its tendons, joints and gristle. The head rolled away from the body, landing with a thud on the hard-packed earth. Zia's brother shovelled the remains into a hole, scraped the tainted earth in after it, then smoothed everything over with fresh dirt.

Placing my hand on Mr. Bashir's shoulder, I made my decision. "Mr. Bashir, this is your culture. Our team must have enough to eat. In Canada, in a situation like this, the guests and hosts would contribute to dinner. You know your culture better than I do, so you will solve this problem better than I can." No one would walk away hungry. The problem was that a meal of rice and lentils was poor man's fare and MSF, a wealthy organization when compared to any Afghan one, was expected to provide better than that.

Regi had no restaurants and the bazaar had closed. We could probably buy an animal from another household, but that seemed too extravagant. I turned back to my journal. Little by little, words filled my page.

In the background, voices mumbled. I heard *hamom*, or bath. A bath would definitely be nice. While I filled a second page with thoughts and memories, Mr. Bashir approached me, an arched eyebrow giving him a mischievous flare. "With your permission, we go to the spring to bathe. There, we stay until much past sunset. Only after we return from bathing do we eat. By then, many guests will be sleeping. No one will be offended. We will tell them that we have an important appointment. Bathing after such a hot day is necessary." He winked.

"Good idea," I lied. His solution seemed backhanded, dishonest somehow. Wouldn't it be easier to apologize, saying that we hadn't expected guests and that we were happy to share what we had? Why would they be upset about that? But this was up to them. I definitely supported bathing in the spring. It would feel awesome!

In the Land Cruisers, we beelined to the mouth of the canyon and parked beside boulders the size of the vehicles. Hefting snacks and thermoses of tea to a flat spot a short distance from the trucks, we rehashed the day, and Mr. Bashir and others congratulated themselves on their plan. A carpet and cushions were laid out. Jokes began as tea was poured. No one was above an Afghan joke that made fun of a big nose, a mouth that could fit an entire fist, slanted eyes that vanished when someone laughed and hands so gigantic that no one would share a plate with their owner. Sipping a cup of tea, I felt the cooling evening air touch my cheek, like a calming breath after an adrenaline surge.

"You go first." Mr. Bashir looked at Clarence, then at me, as if undecided which one of us took precedence. I had visited the spring once before but hadn't bathed in it. Too many men had milled about.

"Come, I'll show it to you." I pointed out the path that squiggled uphill and ended at a rocky overhang where a tiny jungle of green plants proliferated in deep shade. The spring was a few metres below. We headed directly to the greenery because I wanted to show him the scraggly junipers, philodendron-like vines and fern species growing from between rocks and in cracks in the cliff face. Mosses coated every surface, from which miniature pear-shaped droplets of dazzling colours dripped onto thirsty ground near our feet. The air was scented with moist earth. It was like a tiny rainforest in a desert.

Descending a few metres, we reached a stone wall that was wide enough to conceal three people my size behind it. It stood at neck height. On the uphill side, warm water gushed out of a crevasse at waist height, like a fountain. A symphony of sounds tinkled as it splashed onto rocks and stones at different heights before disappearing into thirsty soil.

To me, bathing outside is pretty self-explanatory. What pointers did Clarence need? Wanting to provide at least one helpful tip, I showed him a convenient spot to put dry clothing, a rocky hook for his towel and a moist stone for soap, which helped prevent sand and pebbles from adhering to it. A small plastic cup sat on a flat rock, ready to pour water over the bather's head.

Clarence tapped a stone with his finger. "You go first. I'll go next." He looked briefly into my eyes, then turned on his heel and skipped down the track. The carefree happiness in his step was contagious. Had he enjoyed the day as much as I had?

I clutched my plastic bag of shower supplies. Scrubbing off several days of grime would feel amazing! Behind the wall, I laid out my clean chador, shalwar, kameez and undies. I placed soap and shampoo on the soap dish stone. Then I surveyed my surroundings. As Kareem once said, peeping Toms could be anywhere. By then, my memory of Asif's hungry eyeball had become comical, even though it still fired up my ire when I was feeling hampered by patriarchal norms.

Far below, a shepherd tended a large flock of sheep, their fifty or so fat bottoms jiggling in a discordant dance. Two boys looked down from the lip of the canyon, their tiny forms too far away for me to identify details about their clothing. To my left, high on the plateau above, a man led a donkey that resembled a walking grass hump. Leaning forward, I saw our tiny, toy-like team lounging on the carpet, Clarence just joining them. Reza handed him a cup of tea. Above me, swallows dove in wide arcs or perched in holes in the cliff. I squinted upward and saw no one looking down from rocky ledges higher up.

Privacy was more of a concern for women than for men. When men noticed each other bathing or toileting, a self-conscious goofy grin or a mutual nod could turn their discomfort into a non-event, or perhaps a bonding one. In Canada, I might have the same experience, but in Afghanistan, female nudity was complex. I had no interest in discovering what an Afghan male might do if he saw me buck naked. When teaching health care workers how to take blood pressures, I had once bared my arm in public. Never again! The pharmacist had almost orgasmed on the spot, marvelling again and again about the pearly white tint of the skin of my upper arm.

I shook out the chador I had worn for the last three days and hung it on the rocky hook. It would be my towel. Next, I had a decision to make. Do I remove my clothes and risk being seen? Or bathe in them and do a quick change at the end?

I was no novice to skinny-dipping. That first time in Vermont so many years ago had been magical and freeing. I had stripped off my clothes, run along the beach and splashed into my boyfriend's arms. Every part of me had come alive! But in Afghanistan, who knew what the consequence of being caught would be.

I imagined being stark naked behind the little stone wall, secretly watching men go about their lives. What would someone do if they saw me? I pushed the thought away. Mr. Bashir and Zia would protect me, wouldn't they? I slipped down my shalwar, stomping it in the puddle at my feet, the warm sand scouring my callouses like a pedicure. Still wearing my kameez and carefully concealing my entire body behind the wall, I considered the sequence of events if someone came up the path. Would I have time to cover myself?

Of course, Mr. Bashir would waylay anyone who made a move to head my way. He might offer them tea and a snack. He would tell the intruder that our team was waiting their turn, instilling shame if the newcomer didn't also wait his turn. If the intruder kept going, Clarence, Mr. Bashir or Zia would call out. And just in case they decided to play a joke at my expense, I would check frequently. I would have about three minutes to get dressed.

I poured warm water over my dust-stiffened hair, the rivulets tickling my scalp and neck before they seeped into my kameez. As I lathered shampoo on my head, bubbles tumbled down in long frothy streaks. I closed my eyes and inhaled the floral scent. I massaged my temples, then the nape of my neck. It felt so good! I rinsed and rubbed my eyes so I could glance in all directions. Little had changed. I inhaled deeply, feeling my body expand, and then in one movement I pulled the dress over my head and stamped on it in the puddle. I grabbed the bar of Lux soap and set about cleaning the crusty spots. My fingers scrubbed away salt crystals, dead skin and any microscopic hitchhikers.

I spied on our team below. Reza's voice drifted up. He was still making fun of Jaafar's massive body. Did he never tire of that? The two boys on the plateau were still specks, and the man with the donkey had disappeared out of sight. I twisted around to look above and to the sides. In the twilight, people headed home.

I stroked my abdomen and the nearby shadowy patches on my thighs as I rinsed away all the angst from the day and imagined it flowing off me down the cliff. I pinched my nipples just for the pleasure of waking them up. Memories of the day flowed. Our horses had indeed arrived in the village when the gunshots had rung out, but Zia only found out at the end of the day as we drove back through that hamlet where we had waited in vain. So our guide wasn't a total cheat. I was happy with what we had accomplished. I would recommend that MSF create an innovative TB program that empowered villagers and hopefully was sustainable at some level. It would be a cool project for someone else. I didn't want to remain in Afghanistan much longer. One day, I might become incapable of reintegrating into Canadian culture. Recalling the glee on Zia's face when he drove the Land Cruiser toward us at the end of the day, its hollyhock decorations billowing in the wind, I felt a tenderness. I fought against desire.

Rosy pinks and cool blues filled the sky. A star twinkled. It was time to finish and let others take a turn, but I stalled. With no reason to ration hot water and our intention of staying out until after sunset,

I convinced myself to stay a moment longer. Crouching down, I let the water massage me. I relaxed, letting go. I trembled. Everything looked beautiful and dreamy at the same time. Casually, I stood up and dried off. I pulled on a fresh kameez, then tried as always to keep my shalwar dry as I stepped into it. Winding a clean chador around my head and shoulders, my heart felt like it wanted to burst out of my chest!

From behind the little stone wall, I stepped onto the path, feeling like a princess in a fairy tale. Skipping down the trail to the lyrics of "Climb Ev'ry Mountain" from *The Sound of Music*, I called out, "Clarence, it's your turn."

The team glanced over at me for a split second, then continued their activities. Reza joked with Jaafar. Aalem sat alone like an ostracized younger brother, amusing himself by skipping flat stones across the sand. Mr. Bashir wore a lazy smile, as if enjoying a memory or two. Clarence collected his shower supplies. Zia alone caught my eye. Cigarette poised on his bottom lip, he stared brazenly at me, resembling a seductive gangster piecing together a baffling puzzle. I smiled. If I wasn't careful, I might cause trouble.

My farewell party that year was a team picnic in an eleventh-century fort on a hill about a ninety-minute drive outside of Qala-I-Nau. We climbed to the top of the fort and enjoyed stunning views of the land far below. Next to the only trees in the area, we pitched a tent and celebrated our team and what we had accomplished. My picture was taken with just about everybody—with a catch in my throat, I promised to send them copies from Canada. I didn't know if I would return to Afghanistan.

CHAPTER EIGHTEEN

A REBEL

"I alone cannot change the world, but I can cast a stone across the water to create many ripples."

— *Mother Teresa*

Throughout my time in Afghanistan in 2002, a Canadian surgeon and MSF colleague in Herat who I admired encouraged me to apply to the Master's in Public Health program at the Johns Hopkins Bloomberg School of Public Health. He and I used to meet each morning to strategize, and I wanted the skills that I saw him use. I hoped that they would make me more efficient. With degree in hand, I returned to Afghanistan several more times. Between 2005 and 2009, I was based in Kabul.

Nancy Dupree's description of Kabul in the 1960s, where she had taken restful vacations amid its ancient buildings and flowering gardens, and Momo Rahim's stories about miniskirt-clad female students at Kabul University stood in a stark contrast to the Kabul that I saw in 2005.

Through bullet-ridden, tumble-down walls, the guts of mosques, palaces, shopping centres and apartment buildings were conspicuous. A concrete stairway in an apartment building led skyward, abruptly ending nowhere. Expats rented refurbished mansions in Wazir Akbar Khan, the embassy district of Kabul where armed security agents patrolled the streets and we went jogging in groups. We paid more than $4,000 US per month for our accommodations, an exorbitant fee in a place where bread cost 10 cents and a local could eat dinner for $1 or less. Traffic jams choked the streets. You could spend an hour and a half driving from one side of town to another, your driver squeezing between cars with only centimetres to spare, as if competing for an unknown prize in a daily race against time. So much diesel exhaust from generators and trucks tinged the air that I blew black ash from my nose every night and developed a wheeze when I ran, even though I had never before been diagnosed with asthma. That level of pollution would damage anyone's lungs.

One day, a female physician colleague held a cellphone to her ear, her face crinkled in distress. Clicking it off, she moaned. "My son is hurt. I must drive to the school to pick him up." Her voice trembled. At the time, I was working with several Afghan physicians for an American organization that helped the Ministry of Public Health in Kabul implement and evaluate strategies to improve women's and children's health.

"I hope he is okay." I tried to find compassion for this physician and mother who had worked so little over the past few years, but I was too preoccupied with her pile of unfinished reports. Would our organization receive the next allotment of funding to continue our programs? Most days that month, she had either left early, shown up late or taken a day off. Her son had been sick several times and so had her five other children. Her in-laws had visited for weeks. She had cooked and cleaned until late at night, trying to satisfy her mother-in-law and her husband. Like many doctors, she often worked privately in an evening clinic.

At the office, her concentration had been poor. Unfinished projects had piled up. Too often I walked by her empty desk and found her chatting with an officemate or texting on her cellphone. I felt like a high school teacher overseeing an adolescent who agreed with me, then dodged any request that I made. Trying to be sensitive to her struggles, I had adapted my expectations to her evolving circumstances, delegating tasks to others or doing them myself when that was possible. But my leniency had improved nothing and, quite possibly, she did even less work. Every day, her chaotic life seemed to encroach on her work tasks.

To date, she had rejected every one of my suggestions. She had refused to ask her husband to help because men don't do women's work. She couldn't fathom saying no to his family. She had declined to hire help. And she had refused to take any medicine to help with insomnia because she was afraid of not waking up when her children cried or becoming addicted to the substance. I was at a loss.

Yanking off her stethoscope, she spoke vehemently. "My son fell down and scraped his forehead. The nurse said he is bleeding. I must take him to the hospital. She says not to worry, but he is my son! I always worry about him." The force with which she flung the stethoscope and a notebook into her oversized leather purse hinted at a more complex story.

Why was she so worried about an abrasion or a cut? Although I couldn't relate as a mother, I had treated countless anxious women. Hers had a panicky flavour. As a doctor, she must have stitched up hundreds of wounds. Was her husband violent? Did her son have other problems? Were deep wounds manifesting as panic attacks or post-traumatic stress disorder? Perhaps she simply worried about losing her only son, the sole family heir who, in the not so distant future, would bear the weight of supporting the household as she aged. Her story triggered in me a tremendous gratitude for birth control and fair Canadian laws.

I tried to think of something helpful to say. "Facial lacerations often look worse than they really are. They bleed so much. I will pray for him and for you." I added the last three words as an after-thought. No longer did I express sorrow for other people's circum-stances. Early on, Afghans had told me that communicating my sad-ness about their situation benefited no one, that instead, I needed to do something to improve it.

Shutting the metal buckle with a snap, she hefted the enormous purse over her shoulder, her torso tipping sideways with its weight. Reaching for her burka, which was hanging from a hook, I imagined unspoken words on the tip of her tongue. She sighed like the weight of the world pressed down upon her.

"I am a doktor married to a doktor! In Afghanistan, a woman's life is so difficult, even when she is educated like me and a doktor." She spat the word "doctor" like she was angry at it, as if the desired prestige that the title had to offer hadn't materialized. Instead, she was just a woman with an untenable number of problems to solve. "West-ern women are so lucky! Without children and a husband, your life is simple! And if you have a husband, he does some of the laundry, clean-ing, cooking, errands and rearing children. In Afghanistan, men expect their wives to work all day as a doktor and then work all night as a wife and a mother! It never stops!" Her well-enunciated words cut the air:

I had heard other Afghan doctors voice similar complaints. But I disagreed that a foreigner's life was always easy. Her sample was skewed. Independent, adventurous expats travelled solo to Afghan-istan, often leaving family behind because of safety concerns. Every foreigner I knew toiled long hours into the night. Our organizations eked more work out of us by providing cleaners, cooks and guards, who liberated us from spending time on household chores.

I suspected she didn't know that countless Canadian women struggled to divide their attention among their diverse roles. As a group, female doctors often give too much to everyone else, until they have nothing left for themselves. Even without kids, I had felt exhausted at the end of a day of caring for a never-ending stream of patients. Like Humpty Dumpty, I had longed for someone to lift me up and put me back together again. Of course no one did, so I had to learn to say no.

Afghan doctors like this woman had the potential to become true trailblazers, but she, like so many others, seemed paralyzed by the medieval rules. I imagined that the price of trailblazing would be violence, rejection and pain in the short term, like other women had experienced elsewhere. I watched as she fitted the cap of her burka onto her head and smoothed the inside-out garment that flowed down her back.

"One hundred years ago, women in Canada and America stayed at home to cook, clean and raise children. They did not have careers and could not vote. At the time, laws favoured men. But women became angry. A large group formed. Their goal was to change the laws so women could vote. After many difficulties, they succeeded. Decades later, women got together again. This time they argued for birth spacing so they could choose when they became pregnant. They wanted careers and money like men had. We called this women's liberation. Each time women fought was like a revolution. Women took risks. Some of them got hurt, but they were determined that life would be different. Some husbands became angry and forced their wives to quit. Only after winning those fights did it become easier for Western women. Starting this kind of change requires courageous women who believe in a goal and risk their own safety."

I am forever grateful for those suffragettes and women's lib advocates who had paved the way for my unorthodox life. When Mum confided that she had lost part of herself in marriage and motherhood, I assumed that most women did. So when blessed with other talents, why would I bother to attach myself to a man and bog myself down with kids?

I stopped lecturing and scrutinized my colleague's face instead. Would she fight for the sake of her daughters? Or would she become another mother-in-law mired in misogynous tradition?

She picked at the stitching of the burka. "I did not know this. To Afghans, Western women have always had easy lives."

"Sometimes I think that Afghan women want foreigners to fight this battle for them. If we lead this effort, you cannot win." Burned-out expat women with post-traumatic stress disorder already littered this battlefield and, despite their efforts, changes had been maddeningly slow. "You must join other Afghan women and risk creating the change that you want. Foreign women can help you, but we cannot lead it. I do not know if now is a good time for this revolution. You must decide if you do this quickly or create slow and steady change that might benefit your daughters or granddaughters, not you. Katra, katra, daria meche." The well-known Afghan proverb meant "Drop by drop, a river is formed."

She shook her head, her hand primed to pull down the burka like a window shade.

"I hope that your son does well, that you worry for nothing." I hesitated for a split second but felt compelled to continue. "Last week, on many days you left early. The translation you work on now, I need it finished by end of day tomorrow. Maybe after that, you take a vacation."

Her eyes narrowed. "Why vacation? Tonight, after the children are sleeping, I work on it, and tomorrow too. It will be finished tomorrow." She sounded determined. Was work a break from a tortured home life?

I had met several strong Afghan women in Afghanistan, and had heard of others. Would any of them join such a cause or lead it? An Azerbaijani doctor we had failed to entice to work in our clinic in Jawand had courageously followed her heart to Afghanistan, married a village man and was probably still shepherding sheep and goats high up on the plateau in a life that was either a dream or a nightmare. I pictured her galloping away in the night, her hair flying every which way as she joined this revolution. Dr. Saachi and the midwife in Bala Morghab both wore the pants in their marriages while enjoying motherhood and careers. Would they take part? I had lost touch with them; the internet and cellphones had only recently become available in Afghanistan. Several potential change-makers employed by the Ministry of Public Health in Kabul seemed very busy. Would they rise to the challenge?

I wondered if the ballsy wife of a rural health care worker, who I had met only once, would join in. I had treated her nose infection that had worsened despite her husband's ministrations. She had met me in her living room, cradling a white bundle swaddled in embroidered cloth, her chador pinned over her mouth, nose and cheeks. Her shiny green polyester dress was gathered in the front, ready for an expanding waist or a receding one. The dust-smudged, lacy white pantaloons of her shalwar peeked from beneath the dress. A rip in a sleeve had been sewn by hand in tiny stitches. She wore a silver and lapis lazuli necklace, earring and bracelet set. Sitting down beside me, she reached for my hand.

Mohamad, her husband, had sat down beside her. The loving look she gave him warmed my heart. When she dropped the tail of her scarf and stared brazenly at me, I almost gaped at her beefy red, swollen nose. Everything else about her looked normal.

I confirmed the medicine that Mohamad had used, which I had already guessed. Her husband drove me bananas! At the clinic, he made the same mistakes again and again, even after we had discussed the correct approaches many times. And each time I quizzed him, he had parroted the right answers. I felt like I was wasting my time and had even considered firing him.

Her husband shot me a worried glance.

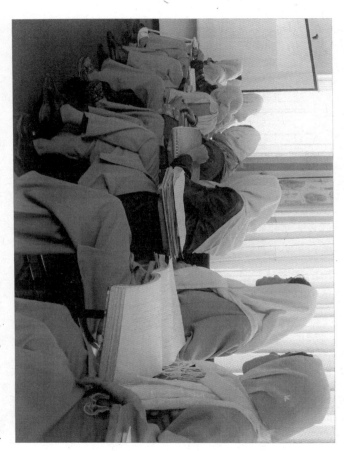

Midwives in training. Will they foster changes in family rules for women or stick with the status quo?

I pointed to my nose. "This problem is from fungus. Fungus comes from animals, maybe the cow, goats or sheep. It is important that you wash it two times each day and use a different cream." On a scrap of paper, I wrote the name of the cream and detailed instructions. "For this problem, cream is better than pills. Injections from the clinic will make it worse." Rural Afghans commonly believed that injections were better than pills and pills were stronger than creams or lotions. "This problem is not dangerous. It can be cured. In two weeks, your nose is perfect!"

After telling me stories about her family of origin, and her first meeting with Mohamad—when they had fallen in love under the chador while looking at each other for the first time in the mirror—she asked me to stay for dinner, which I refused. As I rose to leave, she grasped my hand and pulled me back down.

"No, not yet! Please take one photo." She smiled sweetly.

I nodded. They held hands and looked lovingly into each other's eyes. She asked for another one of her husband cradling little Mohamad.

"One more!" She handed the baby bundle to me and pointed to herself and Mohamad. I took the shot and the warm bundle beside me cooed. Mohamad grabbed the camera and, after learning where the shutter release was, he snapped an image of me with his wife. Then she did the same, clapping with delight.

"One more!" She motioned to her husband. "Sit!" She posed again. Wasn't ten photographs enough for a memento?

Suddenly, she twisted, and as fast as a monkey she grabbed Mohamad's turban. Placing it on her head, she patted her hair and hooted with so much glee that her entire face turned as red as her nose. His hair looked like Einstein's. Her eyes beamed as her body shook with waves of laughter. Beside her, Mohamad smiled sheepishly.

I was laughing so hard my belly hurt. My finger released the shutter a few more times. Not once did he attempt to recoup his turban.

"Good?" I was asking for permission to take the photos after the fact.

"Bale!" She sat up straight and defiant. Bale meant "yes." He nodded.

They crowded around my camera pointing to the back side, expecting a screen to reveal the image. My maharam, who waited outside, had a new digital camera like this.

"The photo, where is it?" Although still giggling, Mohamad was quickly becoming sober.

"I send it to Pakistan. In one month, I give it to you."

In the images I eventually sent, Mohamad's turbaned wife sits proud and playful. Beside her, he looks like he cherishes her spunk. One day, she might outgrow him.

He nodded. "A secret. No one to see it. You give only me the photos."

The Afghan suffragette and I high-fived.

Who will lead the Afghan Suffragettes?

CHAPTER NINETEEN

POWER AND POETRY

"You yourself are your own obstacle, rise above yourself."

—*Hafiz (attributed)*

"Dr. Murreen, what do you do with your time when you have no relationship?" Dr. Qabeel, my co-instructor in Herat, often began conversations abruptly. Uninvited, he frequently jumped into personal questions with both feet and no apology or lead up. Then he would chuckle at his audacity.

Did Dr. Qabeel think that a single woman had nothing to do? Or that her evenings and nights were filled with illicit sex?

In 2005, Qabeel and I taught and launched five teams in the western provinces, as part of a national survey whose results would steer primary health care spending. Qabeel was my second Afghan co-instructor. The first one, a nervous, prematurely grey-haired man with a slew of physical complaints, had simply disappeared on the second day of the course, leaving me with fifteen flirtatious male students who didn't know any English. Qabeel had been a godsend. With a firm handshake and a decisive voice, he had taken charge of the boisterous group. In the centre of the room, he had taught like a conductor, skillfully navigating the antics of one of the ring leaders, forcing him to wait his turn while giving time for the more well-behaved to answer.

In the car after work, our hired driver, a lecherous man who kept eying me in the rear-view mirror, was taking us to Takht-e Safar, a park outside of Herat built by a Sultan during the fourteenth century. I had never been there and loved nothing better than exploring sites outside of the dusty city with its honking horns. Disliking our driver intensely, I didn't argue when Qabeel chose the front seat.

I had already told him that I was happily single with no kids and had begun recounting a few highlights from my previous trips to Afghanistan, including how I had learned Dari.

With a glum expression, he had studied my face, then abruptly interrupted my story: "You are brave, maybe too much brave."

That shut me up. Too brave, huh? Did he find the topic boring, or was this his attempt at taking control of the conversation? Male physician colleagues from Kabul were a different breed. They jousted to conquer. I found them annoying, preferring instead the respectful men from my previous trips.

On other outings, Qabeel had shared that he was happily married. His first language was Pashai, a Central Asian tongue that he bragged was more difficult to learn than any other. Why was he so rude? It felt like he was trying to squish me into a pigeonhole that was way too small.

In the car, I responded to Qabeel's question. "I spend time with friends walking in the mountains, cycling, skiing, swimming and kayaking. I go to movies, restaurants, concerts and theatres. Sometimes I visit my family, who live far away. Travelling for work teaches me to see events and issues from different perspectives. I have learned that many ideas can be right."

"And you prefer that to marriage and making a family?" His eyes darkened, and his ample forehead crinkled. "When you are young, it is impressive to do those things, but for you now is a good time to have a family." Despite being a decade younger than me, he exuded a certainty that seemed to justify him seizing the role of uninvited mentor.

The suburban landscape sped by in a blur. If the right person came along, would I consider marriage and kids? Marriage? Absolutely. Kids? No way! Creatively carving a novel path through life and reinventing myself periodically had filled me with joy and inspiration. My twenty-year-old self had sighed with relief after turning the last page of M. Scott Peck's *The Road Less Traveled*. I wasn't the only one! I loved to trailblaze, even when unsure of my destination. I was always scouting out others who lived on the edge in a niche of their own making. I had already rejected three marriage proposals, telling myself that the world didn't need any more people and that my legacy would be something more exciting.

Qabeel had more to say. "First I thought maybe you did not like men or that you were one of those religious women. A nun, right? Then I thought maybe you had difficulty communicating, or some other serious problem. In a marriage, communicating is challenging, but it is good that there is always another perspective. By sharing your life with someone, you can learn a lot." He paused, his eyes snagging mine for a split second. It was hard for me to believe that

Dari is a beautiful, poetic language. Speaking it sparked the artist inside me.

he listened to his wife's perspective, or anyone else's.

"But now I think that you are, hmm, what is the word, picky. That's it. He does not have the right nose." He scowled, pointing to the driver's bulbous hooter. "Or his hair is not perfect." He pointed to his own baldness. "Or maybe you are picky about other things." He paused as the car swerved around a curve. "I can find you a good husband, a good Afghan husband."

I smiled in spite of myself, acutely aware that Qabeel loved to tease. Waiting for the punchline, I scoured his face for a flicker or a twitch. In high school, acting had been one of his favourite activities. Who could trust an actor with a huge ego and a chip on his shoulder? This far from town, finding another ride would be tricky, so I was cautious not to offend him. I didn't know exactly where we were, and my $40 Nokia phone had no GPS.

"Thank you for such a kind offer. One day, I will meet a good man, one that fits into my life." In my previous relationships, I had either compromised too much or was too rigid, like Mum and Dad. I had witnessed great relationships but had no clue how to create one. Did he know that a third of marriages ended in divorce? Did he realize how small a parent's world became when kids occupied every waking moment?

The news report on the radio mentioned a skirmish somewhere else, and then a man began singing.

Qabeel interrupted my thoughts: "Dr. Murreen, what is the cost of marriage in Canada?"

Gosh! I had no idea. Was $25,000 US inexpensive or expensive? Some couples spent $100,000 paying for hotels, meals, alcohol, rings, gowns, tuxedos and whatever else. Weddings were big business.

"The cost of marriage in Canada is very different from Afghanistan. When a man asks a woman to marry him, he gives her a ring made of diamonds and gold. He does not pay money to her parents. The tradition in Canada is for the woman's family to pay for the wedding ceremony and a big party where guests bring gifts." I had never paid much attention to how the costs were split.

"A gold ring, I understand, but what, what is a diamond?" His knowledge of English was extensive, but every now and then, I got to add a new word to the dictionary in his head.

Diamonds had never come up in previous conversations, so I didn't know the Dari word. "A diamond is a clear stone like glass. It is very expensive. Specially trained people cut diamonds precisely so they sparkle. People also use diamonds to cut glass."

"Ah, *almas*, very expensive. How much does this ring cost?" He looked at my fingers. The same silver Hopi ring that I had worn on every Afghan trip still decorated the fourth finger of my left hand.

"Maybe the cheapest is $200, but they can cost many thousands of dollars." Once, when looking through a Neiman Marcus catalogue, I had seen an engagement ring for $50,000. What possessed people to buy such things? In Afghanistan, it would be an invitation for a thief!

"It is not so expensive. Is there always a ring?" With his head cocked to the side, he looked devious.

"Most times the woman receives a diamond ring. Sometimes the couple agrees to spend money on something else instead, like a house. At most weddings, the husband and wife receive a ring made of gold or platinum." I knew couples that didn't buy into the concept and considered rings to be a waste of money.

"I paid no afghanis for my wife. We met in medical school. She is from Bamian and I am Laghmani. After two years of marriage, we have twins, a boy and a girl. It was her decision to stay home to care for them. Two children is enough." He looked out the window. His family probably had a decisive vote on whether she stayed home.

Did she regret giving up her career?

He stared pointedly at me. "Dr. Murreen, when you marry, do you accept nothing in return?"

I fiddled with my ring, a vestige of an expired relationship. Years ago, I would have said yes. But would I if I found the love of my life? "Oh, I don't know. The man would have to be very special. There is something heartwarming about receiving a ring from a special man who promises to spend his life with me." As I clasped my hands, my ring dug into my finger.

A herd of goats cantered by. I thought of past lovers. The gains from committing had never been worth the sacrifices.

"Suppose you found someone that you loved very much. Would you then?" He coughed and looked down for a second, then his solemn eyes delved into mine. "Someone, maybe someone like me!"

He couldn't be serious! Fifteen minutes outside of town was a bad time for a row!

My shock at his comment must have been plainly visible on my face because suddenly he grinned like a Cheshire cat. "It is a joke, a joke!" His laugh sounded strained. His wily flip-flopping gave me a headache. Trying to sift any truth from his words exhausted me.

Snickering, the driver nodded. Knowing no English, he was probably making up his own version of the story from our body language and snippets of Dari conversation. What stories would he tell his friends?

Thank God, Qabeel was kidding. Part of me wondered if he wanted to entice a Western woman to forgo a dowry or an engagement ring just so he could throw it back into her face and brag about winning later. I didn't grace him with an answer and breathed slowly, trying to relax my neck and shoulders. It was sobering to realize that at my age, most Afghan women were grandmothers.

"Marriage is wonderful and the children are a delight! To lead a full life, people must enjoy family, not work all of the time." Removing a pencil from behind his ear, he spun it around his thumb like Kareem used to do.

A man from Nepal once told me that life is a train. People climb on, stay for a while, then step off. No relationships are permanent. That was the story of my life. My train had housed many visitors.

We passed a turbaned man standing beside a large pyramid of cantaloupe-like melons.

"Stop!" Qabeel cried. "We must buy a melon. Herat is known for its very sweet melons!" He grinned suggestively, and the driver braked. Both of them guffawed at the innuendo, just like Mr. Bashir and the elder had done.

Qabeel got out, bent down and grasped a large melon, sniffing it for ripeness. Repeating the actions several times, he finally settled on one and asked for the price. Disgust overcame his features. "It is too expensive." He turned his back on the vendor and told the driver to go. The salesman came running, the melon in his arms. "Having a foreign woman in the car is expensive. I had to walk away to get a good price!" Still, he had won.

As we pulled away, he fired off another question, his expression boyishly innocent. "Dr. Murreen, sometimes you talk of men you call friends or a man's female friends. Afghan men use both words for male friends, but I never hear you talk about female friends. In Canada, a man who is married to someone else can be my best friend. From Kareem, Momo Rahim and Mr. Bashir, I understood that the two Dari words meant "friend." I had never heard an Afghan woman refer to a man as her friend.

"In Dari, maybe there is no word to describe a woman's male friends. Are they not boyfriends? *Rafirq is rafirq and dust is dust.*"

"What do you call a man who is your friend?" His eyes probed my soul as I realized that boyfriend and a male friend probably sounded identical to him.

"A man who is my friend is not my boyfriend. A man who is more than my friend is my boyfriend." It sounded like a riddle even to me.

"How do you know if he is a friend or a boyfriend?" He raised an eyebrow. Was he serious or playing games again?

"You just know. There is only friendship, like between two women, nothing more." I hesitated to mention sex because a conversation about sex with two men I didn't know that well might cause trouble. His eyes tried to sift through my thoughts like Kareem used to do. Kareem I had trusted. Even then, I had hidden many opinions behind a neutral mask.

"What is nothing more? Do you mean they do not have sexual intercourse?" Enunciating the sanitized terms with precise diction, he gaped at me as if goading a reaction.

"Yes." I opted for simplicity, even though committed relationships could take many forms. I mulled over how fiercely Afghan families protected virginity and what a highly valued commodity it was. On the radio, a seductive voice crooned a melancholy tune, the tap of a *daireh*, an Afghan drum played by women, providing rhythm.

In the parking lot at Takht-e Safar, a young boy asked for money to protect the vehicle from thieves. Qabeel asked for the price, then got the kid to describe in detail what he would do for the money. The kid's overly zealous tone hinted at a lie, and Qabeel accused him of being a thief, then simply walked away, leaving the deflated boy in the dusty parking lot with its load of cars parked higgledy-piggledy.

"You raised his expectations when you had no intention of accepting his offer. That wasn't nice." I watched him shrug nonchalantly. The poor kid was just trying to survive.

"They are all thieves. Come. The picnic area is most beautiful, and we have a sweet melon to eat!" Qabeel's finger indicated the weighty fruit balanced on the driver's shoulder, then he pointed to the picnic area where children scrambled on swings and monkey bars and nearby groups of picnickers in bright colours sat on tablecloths laid on the ground, their laughter and shouts giving the place a festive air. The majestic pine forest's green tones contrasted starkly against the dusty brown cityscape below. Sunset would arrive much too soon. I craved solitude in nature.

"Let's walk in the forest." I pointed to the tall white pines as I marched down the path.

"Let's sit here and eat melon." Qabeel indicated a grassy area near the trees.

"I want to walk." I resented his assumption that I would simply comply with his wishes.

"How long is this walk?" His voice sounded peevish, his face in a childlike pout. The hairs on my neck prickled.

"Maybe forty-five minutes." So often imprisoned in compounds, cars and offices, I just wanted to move my body and feel the wind blow through my hair. The latter, of course, wouldn't happen.

"That is too long! I bought us a succulent melon. We must eat it!" His wily smile suggested confidence that he would win this argument. "You will love its sweetness!" He and the driver snickered. Was this tired joke really that funny?

Long tree shadows stretched in stripes across the grass. In 2005, sunset no longer signalled a curfew. We had, on occasion, returned from dinner as late as 10 p.m.

The driver spread a cloth on the ground. From a vest pocket, Qabeel pulled out a switchblade, then flicked it open. With surgical precision, he carved triangles of melon. I scrolled through the list of personality disorders catalogued in my brain. Obsessive-compulsive? Perfectionist? Narcissistic? Histrionic? A combination of these traits?

"Please, taste a morsel of one of Herat's most tasty melons!" Qabeel stabbed one of the perfect triangles geometrically arranged on the thick rind. I grasped it with my fingers, then popped it into my mouth. Succulent juice slid down my chin. I leaned forward so the drip landed in the dirt instead of hitting my shirt. Musky sweetness exploded in my mouth, and pools of saliva collected under my tongue. My fingers automatically reached for another, then another. I love all fruit but durian, which gives me waves of nausea. I sang compliments to Qabeel and watched his ego swell. Within minutes, the melon was in our bellies, and the driver chucked its rind into the trees. Fertilizer, he said. Trash, I thought.

Wondering whether they would wait for me if I walked on my own, I sat on the recently vacated swings, pumping my legs like I used to do as a young girl. Qabeel joined me. The driver watched as we rose higher and higher until we were flying at the height of the topmost, horizontal bar in the swing set.

"I went higher," Qabeel exclaimed. The driver agreed.

I laughed. We had reached the same height, but who cared? I ascended the climbing bars and looked back at them from the top.

Qabeel watched but remained rooted. "Why do you do this playing like a child? You should have children instead."

I climbed higher. He refused to join in, so I descended the far side and walked away. He followed. I let the silence grow.

"It is late. We go to the car." He spoke sharply. Maybe our adventure hadn't panned out as he had hoped.

"I will walk to the edge of the forest and catch up with you." I continued on my path.

"Catch up?" He wore a puzzled expression.

"You and he walk to the car, and I will walk quickly to the forest and then back to you." I kept going.

"We wait here." Dejected, they sat heavily on a picnic bench. Although at least ten years younger than me, they seemed to be transitioning to old age more quickly.

Some time later, the car sped down the winding road, a gentle breeze ruffling my chador. In the front seat, Dr. Qabeel turned around. "Do you like poetry?"

"I love poems." On my first visit to Afghanistan, I had been introduced to Rumi.

Qabeel recited several musical verses that I didn't understand, the air in the car pulsating with his emotion. Wearing an expression of pure joy, he kissed each syllable. His voice was a man's, then a woman's, and at times, his inflection sounded younger. Twice the driver chimed in. In high school and university, I had been a science geek. I knew almost nothing about poetry.

"This poem is about love between a man and a woman." He recited another one using different intonations. "That one is sad, describing how a love between two lovers will never last because she will marry another." As another one sprang from his lips, his face melted. At the end, he just sat there in silence.

After some minutes, his attention returned to the present. "What kind of poetry do you like?"

"I love Rumi and Hafiz." In an attempt to feed the aliveness that had awakened during my first trip to Afghanistan, I had bought Rumi's *Gardens of the Beloved* and had read one or two poems each day. Later, I had included Hafiz.

"Rumi, Rumi, all foreigners know is Rumi! Afghanistan has many masterful poets. Pashto poems are much better. But Pashai is the best!" Reciting the next poem, his tone dripped with honey, crescendoing, then dying away to a whisper.

After entering Herat through its medieval gates, he spoke animatedly to the driver, moving his arms theatrically to augment his words. Turning to me, a look of delight spread all the way to his forehead. "With your permission, we stop at the book bazaar for a moment. Do you have time?" In the twilight, the dust that had settled on the ancient gate of the old city gave the scene a dreamlike quality. Storekeepers were shaking out qilims and carpets that had lain in the street all day in a disingenuous process of manufacturing "antiques."

"Okay!" I had no plans for the evening. In Herat, Qabeel and I were a two-person team. My other expat colleagues were spread across the country. All of my old MSF co-workers but one had moved on. He was a gentle soul who, a month before, I had called in a panic after having spent one night in a room that barely locked in a hotel full of Afghan soldiers. Fearful of an intruder, I had leaned the only chair in the room against the door handle. Completely understanding my fear, he had found me accommodations the next day at a United Nations guest house. I liked visiting his family. In their small village outside of Herat, I felt a sense of well-being and safety.

"At this bazaar, most of the books are in our languages." Qabeel raised his hand. The driver stopped.

We climbed out and immediately entered a maze. Stall after stall was packed with books, diaries, pens and other writing paraphernalia. A plastic sheet pulled tightly across most doorways indicated that they were already closed. We weaved through a mishmash of pathways. Dusty books that might be antiques were stacked on plywood floors. Afraid of losing sight of Qabeel, I sped up. Having twisted and turned so many times, I no longer knew where to find the car. He stopped at a cubbyhole entryway that opened into a larger room. In it, shelves lined every wall and divided the space into passageways so narrow that I had to turn sideways to get through them. Stacks of books littered the floor.

Behind a table loaded with assorted volumes, a bookseller pushed reading glasses farther up his magnificent, hairy nose. Dr. Qabeel nodded to him and began scanning the Arabic titles. Recalling Qabeel's earlier remark about expats inflating prices, I hid behind a bookshelf, hoping they would seal the deal quickly. Leafing through a book back to front, I felt illiterate. I had no idea if the book that I held was science fiction or a romance.

After flipping through several volumes, Qabeel handed one to the bookseller. He spoke rapidly in a language that I had never heard before. Their voices rose and fell as they haggled aggressively, Dr. Qabeel's tenacious tenor playing against the bookseller's adamant baritone. Herat was famous for tough businessmen. I understood only a few words: foreign, new and love. Was he buying a book for his wife?

Suddenly, the room was silent. I peeked between two books. An annoyed Qabeel counted afghanis from his wallet. He hadn't walked away. Had he wanted the book too much? Tipping his head toward the door, he glanced at me, then strode out. I followed. In the corridor, he stepped aside, his empty hand motioning for me to walk ahead. What was he up to? Puzzled, I strolled right into the book that he was holding at chest height.

"A gift." He grinned. "Old Pashto poems about love, translated into English. They are better than Rumi and Hafiz. You will see. When you are back in Canada, you remember me."

The paperback was tattered and worn, as if someone had perused it many times. The title was *Anonymous Pashto Couplets.*

"Thank you. What a wonderful gift!" I had learned from Momo Rahim that graciously accepting gifts was important for keeping the peace. I was genuinely touched, but a question nagged at me. What did he want in return?

In the car, he asked for the book, flipped through it and read three poems in a captivating tone. The driver and he chuckled. He was such a flirt!

"Now you read one." He returned his gift to me. I felt safer now, knowing that I could walk home if I felt it was necessary.

I flipped through the pages, trying to find an innocuous verse that wouldn't elicit too much desire and yearning. I didn't want him to jump over the seat and kiss me! I also wanted my own dormant impulses to remain asleep.

"The flower in my hand is wilting. In a strange land, to whom should I offer it?" I flipped to another one. "For Heaven's sake, O Moon, do not throw your beams of light between two lovers."

He gazed at the bright orb in the night sky, entranced by the here and now, a memory of long ago, or possibly a yearning never fulfilled.

CHAPTER TWENTY

IN BETWEEN

"No one outside ourselves can rule us inwardly. When we know this, we become free."

— *Buddha*

In a bedroom in our guest house in Kabul, pressure mounted in my chest. I had just returned from Herat, and Melanie, a fellow researcher from Johns Hopkins University whose room I was borrowing, was on vacation. I wasn't short of breath and didn't have other symptoms of a heart attack. I had always been fit, had no diabetes or hypertension, had never smoked and exercised regularly, so my risk for a cardiac event was low. Placing a hand on my heart, I asked it a question. "What do you want?"

In the silence, the pressure grew. Taking a deep breath, I willed the constriction away. But on the next inhale, I choked. A blanket of loneliness wrapped around me, its folds beckoning me to hide. My pen was poised to write in my journal, but only my tears spattered the page. Lying on the bed in a borrowed room, I felt stuck, like a cog in a wheel that I had chosen but no longer wanted. My previous work with MSF—providing health care to women and children in remote places—had made village life tangibly better. At least, that's what I had told myself, but had it? In 2004, an MSF team had been killed in one of the clinics in Badghis Province. I wondered if the quick introduction to Western habits had been too much for the local villagers, who had just emerged from beneath Taliban restrictions. The people responsible had received no punishment. Local government officials had not apologized. As a consequence, MSF had withdrawn services.

My current projects had less tangible longer-term benefits. That night, we were celebrating the successful completion of the national survey. Helping design the tool, then teaching and overseeing survey teams, had been a great opportunity for me to use newly acquired skills from my master's degree in public health. But were we improving villagers' lives in significant ways? Would the money have been better spent on helping people to provide food for their

Straddling two very different worlds eventually led me to an inner struggle. How do I live "in between"? Photo Bruce Lampard

families or funding schools to teach children how to read and write? When people were trying to survive, health care was often of secondary importance.

My heart felt small and dried out, like a prune. For years, as a medical doctor, I had contorted myself into molds that hadn't fit or that I had grown beyond. Was public health yet another skillset that I didn't really want, or one that I had not yet figured out how to use in ways that were meaningful to me? The adventurous creative inside me still felt stifled. An ardent task manager had taken the helm of my ship, and I didn't like her. She hampered my explorations to the point that the ember that was me barely glowed. Over and over, I had been enchanted by the charming allure of Afghanistan's story, people and cultures, and the adventurer inside me had thrived. Yet that evening, in the borrowed bedroom in Kabul, I felt mired in towering challenges and endless to-do lists. Bah! For what purpose? Afghanistan's problems were just too enormous.

Doling out my energy, skills and drive, I had accomplished some things and learned so much. Dressing up in foreign costumes, I had entered a culture so very different from the one in which I had been raised. With each return to Canada, relief had flooded my soul as I looked forward to relaxing into normalcy. And yet when I arrived there, I couldn't find the normal I craved, and the desert lured me back again. Afghanistan had been like Dr. Seuss's green eggs and ham. Afghans had taught me to see differently. Countless times, I had thanked Nancy Dupree for her wise advice of withholding judgment, remaining curious and knowing that I didn't have the right answers.

Through the bedroom window, a cool breeze blew in a medley of laughter and Indian music from the party that continued below in the front yard after I had left. Why didn't I feel satisfied? The team of Americans and East Indians who lived with me in this mansion were still whooping it up with government officials, trainees, consultants and friends. On offer were pop, wine and beer, cooled in buckets of ice, and of course there were thermoses of tea. Team members who were giddy and red in the face had disappeared often to spike their pop with rye from a stashed forty-ouncer. The secrecy reminded me of high school dances. Kebabs on a long metal barbecue were handed out by our cook. Everyone was watching everyone else, as if trying to make sense of old colleagues in a novel context.

Dancing at the party had been whimsical. To rock 'n' roll, I had let myself go. To Afghan tunes, my feet had mimicked rural women's dance steps, my fingers twisting ever-present, imaginary doorknobs. A twenty-five-year-old American student had joined me, her body swaying drunkenly to her own beat. Like me, she wore a chador around her neck and a knee-length kameez over jeans, which was common attire when inside Western compounds. When visiting Afghans, I typically wore a chador over my hair like most Afghan women did. The dreaded circle had formed, and we had danced in the middle. Then an Afghan man had ducked in, bopping disjointed shoulders while pirouetting intricate steps, twisting his wrists and swirling his fingers. Through furry eyebrows, Afghan men had peered at us. Some guests had laughed and pointed. Others had bent their heads in serious discussions, as if making deals. I would have loved to have been a fly on a nearby wall.

It was later while relaxing on cushions with other expats that I had felt so utterly alone. I had been listening to teammates' exclamations. "At the ISAF store, you can buy peanut butter and regular bread. I am so tired of Afghan bread." "That bottle of gin was so cheap! And the hot dogs!" "Isn't the Lebanese restaurant awesome!" "I can't believe that we can get Thai food in Kabul!" "And the carpet shops on Chicken Street are unbelievable!" They talked of tourist meccas where prices aimed at foreigners' fat wallets were inflated so high that Afghans rarely, if ever, shopped there. The ISAF store was run by the armies that made up the International Security Assistance Force. It catered to foreigners and only stocked Western goods. When living in such a fascinating place, why didn't they explore local cuisine, culture and politics? While in Herat, I had ached for simple, clear communication with other foreigners. However, when surrounded by them, I could no longer relate to the frivolous discourse.

Silently, I had stolen up the stairs, then softly closed Melanie's bedroom door, hoping that no one had noticed my exit. I recalled the sage advice given to me by a Buddhist nun from Australia. We had met in Thailand, where she had lived for twenty years and still felt like an outsider. Her words still ring true: "Make sure you create a home somewhere. I wish I had. Living in between is too difficult."

In the bedroom, I dreamed that I was Dorothy in the Land of Oz who, with a single incantation, would find herself at home. I imagined a peaceful place, it's location a mystery.

The Karzai government was allowing alcohol sales in Kabul, and expats drank it more freely than we had during my past trips, when the rare glass of smuggled wine or beer was served speakeasy-style in the company of foreigners. I wondered whether the murder of the MSF team in 2004 had been fuelled by the substance. Some people told me that the Taliban had hidden in Badghis Province, benefitting from the Pashtun custom that protects guests, known as *pashtun-wali*. Although I had lived in Afghanistan for twenty months, I had spent only one of them in Kabul, so I was still digesting what normal was. Kabulis were like the New Yorkers of Afghanistan. Everything there was better. I disagreed. Was I stuck in the past?

A soft rapping on the plywood of the door coaxed me from my musings. Shrinking back, I buried my face in the pillow. If I stayed silent, maybe they would go away. I wanted no witnesses to my wilted, misfit self. Usually, I wore a smile and exuded confidence.

The insistent tapping reverberated in the silent room. I held my breath.

"Maureen?" Paul paused, as if listening. "Maureen, are you okay?" He sounded concerned. Paul was a gentle soul who had just defended his Ph.D. thesis, married a fellow student and taken the helm of our research group. He belonged. A childlike voice inside my head told me that I didn't. She even sniffled. The adult me lifted my head, noting a streak of black mascara on the starched white pillowcase.

I groaned. I didn't want him to worry. "Yes, I'm okay." I spoke loudly, fighting to steady my voice. Snorting into a tissue, I used a corner of it to dab under my eyes, hoping to eliminate the raccoon-like markings that I was sure would be a dead giveaway. Cracking the door open a little, I peeked around it.

"What's wrong?" His voice was soft. He bit his lower lip. From the depths of my abyss, I peered out at him. He seemed so far away. What do I say? How could I explain how stuck I felt when I knew that he was revelling in his new position, in his new life? If I told him that I was questioning my purpose and where I belonged, he would think I was nuts! What would he know about wasting a year chasing an image that wasn't to be? He appeared to know what he wanted. Then again, to an outsider, I was a huge success!

Shrugging lopsidedly, I answered Paul's question. "I'm just feeling sad, Paul. That's all. Being the only woman on our team in Herat was difficult. I felt pretty alone there, surrounded by guys who didn't know how to interact with a woman. The doctors were more difficult to deal with than village men. Nothing specific happened. I'm alright. I just want to be alone right now, to think things through. I will feel better soon." I pasted a reassuring smile on my face, the one that I used for patients when I delivered bad news. I could hide loads of emotion behind it.

"Maybe you'd feel better if you came downstairs and joined everyone." His blue eyes encouraged me. The cleft between us widened.

For his benefit, I pretended to consider the suggestion. Downstairs among the others, I would feel worse. I shook my head. "Thank you. Right now I want to write in my journal. I'll be fine." We exchanged mournful smiles, me wanting to reassure him and he wanting to help but not knowing how. He turned around and disappeared. I lay back down on my borrowed bed.

What had been so trying about dealing with Qabeel in Herat? There had been several rough patches. When a cab hadn't picked him up, he had irately accused me of not phoning the driver, which was a lie. The driver simply hadn't shown up. The following day, while still fuming, he and the driver had discussed how many lakh (100,000 afghanis) I would fetch in the bazaar. I didn't want to know their opinion. As if I could be sold just like that! Still seething, I squashed an urge to scratch his face. Being locked up was my worst nightmare. Qabeel didn't seem to understand that trusting him had not been easy for me. BBC News had just reported the release of two kidnapped foreign females, one of them Canadian. If I was taken, would anyone pay my ransom?

We'd had good times too. On several nights, we had dined on restaurant terraces and shared stories under the stars. Even routine tasks such as paying salaries had been exciting. To get cash, we had gone to the money bazaar, known locally as the *hawala*. I had received a text containing a code and an office number. On foot through crowds of men, Qabeel and I had rushed along convoluted pathways, passing offices where bundles of $100 bills in US currency were stacked a half-metre high on countertops, as if on display. Kalashnikovs were everywhere. In the designated office, I had listened, avoided people's eyes and wondered how often robbers attacked the hawala. A quick tally of the loot in the room suggested that several hundred thousand dollars sat in the one office. The bazaar would churn through millions. Where did it all go? How much of it was counterfeit?

Qabeel and I had counted the number of bills in each bundle. Then he had divided the loot into his many pockets, his socks and his briefcase. As a foreign woman, I was already a target, so I carried nothing. He blended in so well that I almost lost him once. Shoulder to shoulder with men I didn't know, I had forced myself to breathe slowly as I scanned the beige-coloured crowd until I located him waiting impatiently off to the side. When returning to the car, he had chosen an alternate route in case an ambush awaited us. Several months later, my phone still pinged with his texts offering to find me a good Afghan husband.

What I longed for were simple, quiet evenings under the stars with Kareem or on the road with Zia and Mr. Bashir. Or the joyful events of the picnic in the eleventh-century fort with our old team. Or with a wonderful Afghan friend from my MSF days who lived in a lovely village with his extended family where I used to escape among grapevines, birds and trees. He would scold Qabeel's behaviour and we would laugh. His quirky sense of humour healed my wounds.

Living in Afghanistan had taught me to question my own culture just as much as I did theirs. Which media presented better facts? Were democratic processes, as currently implemented, as fair as I had thought? When living in a place where it seemed like a thousand years ago, reports about some modern issues sounded absurd, such as the recount of Florida's votes and the cartoon images that made fun of Muslim beliefs.

For years, home to me had been a state of mind. But what was the essence of it? Belonging? Community? Connection? Contribution? To be known for who you truly are? Belonging to something bigger was part of it. I was skilled at making new friends, fitting in and letting go. Armed with my shiny new public health degree, I had hoped to join a global group of like-minded people, but a little voice inside me still asked that age-old question: "Is this all there is?" How would I sew the many disparate scenes of my life into a unified tapestry of contrasts and similarities?

When had I felt most alive? In Puvirnituq, a tiny Arctic village in Northern Quebec, I had learned so much medicine. Inuit had taught me about their culture and about the land that I ended up exploring on foot, by kayak and on skis. Afghans had tipped my view of health and health care on its head by illustrating intrepid resilience—men walking for days to bring sick people to clinics, pregnant women surviving arduous births, and kids exuding joy in unlikely places. I had found common ground in both places, but they weren't the home that I sought. Neither was Vancouver. Friends and colleagues were scattered across the world. Where did I belong?

Lying on the bed, I felt empty. A sob escaped, then another, and another until waves of them cascaded out of me. Curling into a ball, I wanted release—but from what? Myself? Face buried in the pillow, I cried soundlessly when I really felt like screaming. I cried for me, for my mother and for lost love and opportunity. I cried for Afghans and how hard life could be.

As I rolled over, the pillowcase clung to my cheek. I stared at a crack in the ceiling. Allah, God, Buddha, Mother Nature, please help me. I apologized for asking yet again. Muttering another one of my half-baked prayers, I promised to do better if they would once more provide guidance.

Nothing shifted. No vision presented itself. So I grabbed my earphones from the nightstand and selected "Up on the Roof" by the Nylons. I imagined sitting on top of the compound in Bala Morghab, the stars smeared across the sky, twinkling and dancing as the lyrics flowed. My forehead relaxed. My body sunk into the bed.

As I let the song carry me away, the word "choice" pierced through the lyrics. It was, and is, my *choice*. On the road of life with its countless intersections, I choose where to shine the light. I couldn't languish in beauty, poetry and love without truly feeling pain, loneliness and unfairness. My home is at the edges where learning flourishes. There I belong, but I never fit in.

CHAPTER TWENTY-ONE

A CHOICE

"May your choices reflect your hopes, not your fears."

— *Nelson Mandela (attributed)*

As I contemplated my revised idea of home and the choices I had made, a memory from 2002 came to mind.

The dirt road had simply ended, even though the map portrayed it continuing on for miles. There was no other route into the valley that we were set on exploring. A man wearing a beige shalwar kameez ran uphill toward us, his grey suit jacket flapping in the breeze, his black and white strands of hair sticking out like jellyfish tentacles. Grinning like a mad scientist, he bowed deeply.

"I am the leader of our team. You are welcome to use our road. As you can see, it is not quite finished!" His name was Sahi, and he happened to be the man we sought. To explore the other side of the river in a region that locals called Tagabi Alan, we needed a local guide. The area was so remote that it wasn't even labelled on the UNDP/ProMIS maps supplied by the United Nations, our most reliable navigational aids. Sahi lived in the first village and was also a cousin of our Khair-khane pharmacist, Moqim, who was Zia's cousin and our trusted guide until we crossed the river. When travelling in Afghanistan, an extended family, or *qom*, could save one's life.

As someone from a dispersed family who was used to doing things myself, I had been slow to understand the importance of a qom. Early on, Kareem had mentioned that his strength came from his relationships with his father, uncles and grandfathers and the history of their land. Although his relatives had died at young ages, he claimed that his father and grandfather still guided his decisions. Try as he might, he couldn't understand the emotional distance separating my family and me. It took months before I appreciated that his qom, even after death, was a rock-solid platform on which he stood when reaching to whatever was next. That level of trust captivated me. Zia and Mr. Bashir had reassured me that once Sahi agreed to accompany us, his qom would guarantee our safety, housing, food, transportation and anything else that we might need.

Squinting beyond him through the dusty air, I saw dozens of village men hefting picks and spades. They called him *ma'alim*, meaning "teacher." He showed me his engineering degree from Herat University, a crumpled piece of paper that he extracted from a pocket. The boulder- and clod-filled track they were digging snaked down a steep slope of sagebrush to a raging river far below. We had a choice: walk, drive or turn back.

Our goal for the trip was to investigate if setting up a clinic in Tagabi Alan was feasible and warranted. For months, a doctor in Qala-I-Nau, whose qom lived in Tagabi Alan, had spoken to us about the region's high death rates and lack of medical care. Since Afghans often tried to convince us to set up clinics on their home turf, we needed more solid information to back up his story.

We followed Sahi on foot partway down the makeshift road. Zia tossed a cigarette butt into the dirt before grabbing a spade, his eyes twinkling. "You must shovel more dirt and pack it firmly, slanting each turn uphill so the car will not roll. Do this to all of the turns and I will be the first to drive a vehicle down your new road!" Ours was the only vehicle I had seen that day.

For the next few hours, our team patiently taught the ragged crew how to build a navigable road. Finally, Zia grinned, slipping

The "not quite finished" road in Tagabi Alan.

into the driver's seat of the Land Cruiser, his dainty hands cradling the steering wheel, his brow knit in concentration. He radiated satisfaction like a jockey might when riding his favourite horse. "I drive this alone. I don't mind dying. You walk, Khonum Murreen. You like walking very much, and I don't want *you* to die!" His blue eyes glinted mischievously. His lips formed a pensive line.

I told him that we would give up on the trip if he didn't feel safe, but he wouldn't hear of it. "I am joking, Khonum Murreen. If it is too dangerous, I tell you!" Would he? Machismo flourished in Afghanistan.

When Zia stepped on the gas, everyone sprang into action. Clarence and Mr. Bashir shouted as they pointed out where the road needed work. Moqim and Sahi called the crew over to repair defects. As he drove, Zia surveyed their work, frequently shifting the vehicle into park so that additional rocks could be removed or more dirt could be piled into sections of road that still sloped the wrong way. Near a switchback, Zia drove back and forth several times, packing the earth. I held my breath as he fishtailed around the bend, and exhaled only after the four-by-four stopped wobbling. Our closest backup vehicle was in Khairkhane, about three hours south of our location.

An hour later, we washed our hands in the swirling current of the Morghab River where it flowed around the two aging cement pillars of a bridge never built. A hanging footbridge of stick bundles lashed together by braided rope would support the weight of humans and animals. The nearby mud buildings where we had hoped to stay had disintegrated into dust. A cowboy with an AK-47, a kettle, a pot and a flask hanging from his saddle stopped to water his steaming horse, then pushed on against darkness. Zia mumbled, "As salaam alaikum." Their exchange was brief. You don't share your story with people this remote when you don't know anything about them.

Sitting on stones in the river, we drank tea and brainstormed what to do next. Do we give up and stay together, or forge on after leaving one person behind to man the radio? To Sahi's dismay, we insisted on staying together that night and camping beside the river. For safety reasons, Clarence wanted to be near the HF radio in the Land Cruiser. Sahi, our guide, refused to leave us.

After a dinner of lamb kabobs and rice, I tucked my bed net snugly under my thin mattress in hopes of sleeping apart from the snakes and scorpions who might seek heat in the coolness of night. Using a fleece as a pillow and my extra chador as a cover, I lay down to sleep, hooking a leg through my knapsack's shoulder strap for safekeeping. That night, I watched Orion cross the sky. It felt like the night before Christmas. If I slept, I might miss something.

When the Big Dipper still peered down from the dusky dawn, I saw Sahi cross the bridge. Two hours later, he returned with two donkeys in tow. By then I was lounging on a flat stone, hoping that my steaming cup of black tea would soothe my aching, sleep-deprived head.

At the bridge, Zia wished us a safe journey. I thanked him for his willingness to be the radio relay point between us and our team in Qala-I-Nau, my expression conveying one last chance to refuse.

His smile was lazy as he scanned the horizon. "I'll be fine. If I need something, I call you or Jaafar. I survived outside in much more difficult situations." I guess having a vehicle equipped with two radios, camping gear and food was luxurious to a seasoned ex-mujahedeen. I reminded myself to quit worrying.

Mr. Bashir sped across the perilously narrow footbridge as I wrestled with my childhood fear of him being swept away by the swirling water below. When it was my turn, I looked back at Zia and tipped my head, a hand on my heart.

"Never look at the water!" he called out, his eyes telling me not to be scared, that he would help in any way he could.

Breathing in, I stared at a rock on the far shore and

Crossing the Bala Morghab River on a precarious bridge made of sticks, stones and a few cables.

tried to forget about the missing handrail. I stepped high to avoid tripping on the bumpy surface. Keep going, I told myself. Don't look down. I unclenched my hands and tried to block out the roar of water moving sideways far below. If I froze and needed to be rescued, our team would joke about it nonstop. Falling was not an option. Tagabi Alan was the most remote region I had ever travelled to in Afghanistan, so it would be a lousy place to have a head injury or even a broken bone. Testing my fear, I looked down for a second. Below me, the river was cutting away the mountain. Up ahead, a footpath meandered through a peaceful valley. When my shoe hit solid ground, I breathed out a sigh of relief!

The loaded donkeys crossed last, digging their hooves into the bridge as they resisted each forward step that Sahi won through hauling on a rope. Behind them, Moqim's body was almost horizontal as he pitted his determination against theirs.

A half-hour later, in Sahi's village, a herd of horses nibbled grass. Men milled about. Sahi passed around a wide tin bowl of green grapes that his son had just picked. Moqim swung a leg over a black stallion and galloped off like a medieval knight, smoothly rounding a tree in the distance. On the return leg, he bent forward, as if whispering into the horse's ear. The stallion raised a knee, curtsied on three legs, then repeated the same performance like a dance with each foot in turn until a villager slapped Moqim's shoulder, as if admitting him into an elite club. Moqim smiled expansively, his shyness vanishing. Other horsemen galloped off as if competing in an unnamed event.

Clucking at my stunned expression, Mr. Bashir pointed to a wooden box on the ground beside my steed. Stepping onto it, I slid onto the horse's back. It stomped and snuffled. Patting its chocolate-brown flank, I attempted to mimic Moqim's confident movements, but my horse ignored my efforts and continued nibbling grass, even after I kicked its belly and smacked its flank.

Mr. Bashir rummaged in his backpack. "Maybe this will help." He cocked his head to the side.

Reaching for the leather-handled whip, I thanked him, doubt creeping into my voice.

When I whipped its butt, my horse lumbered forward. I leaned in, urging it to canter, and imagined galloping off like a nomad as we circled the tree. My return was greeted by quizzical expressions.

Did they expect me to ride side saddle, or saunter like an old mare? Could they see how little I knew about horses? Clarence grinned. Mr. Bashir hid his face behind his steed's belly. I patted my mount's neck and figured we would get along just fine.

As our caravan left, Mr. Bashir motioned for me to stay close. "You must be careful, Khonum Murreen. MSF will not be happy if you are injured."

On well-trodden trails through dry grassland, we ambled for hours, stopping at every tiny grouping of mud compounds and cluster of black goat-hair tents, where we interviewed men who were milling about, pasturing animals. Inside the tents, I visited illiterate women who were pregnant, breastfeeding or caring for grandchildren. The older women in a household delivered the children of the younger ones, and when birth complications surpassed their skills, everyone grieved the moms and babes who died. In those villages, Allah decided fate, not men or women. Family planning was scorned. After finishing their tasks, boys learned to read from the Koran. Girls cared for younger siblings and fetched water.

I listened as a young mother, twenty, described having lost three of her five children, her face twisted in grief. One had succumbed to pneumonia. The other two to diarrhea. Vaccines were a fantasy that no one understood. To believe in Allah was to survive.

Traditional doctors charged money for herbs and teas. Mullahs scribbled blessings on scraps of paper that mothers knotted into rags, then pinned onto children's hats and shirts. An elderly woman described a secret stash of injectable antibiotics and ergonovine, a drug that prevents women from bleeding to death after giving birth. When I asked to see her stockpile, she stood defiantly and refused.

In each village, new riders joined our group. People asked about news from elsewhere. At one village, I glanced behind us and gasped, my face flushing hotly, my limbs tingling with pleasure. About forty donkeys and horses snaked in single file down the valley. Quickly, I snapped a photograph, then hid the camera once again just in case they believed that photos stole their souls.

The valley ended at a shimmering waterfall. Using my baseball cap as a scoop, I poured ice cold water over my head. It trickled down my neck before evaporating. Mr. Bashir transformed from teacher to ruffian by winding a wet patu around his head. His face looked impish, but his eyes remained sad. What secrets did this old soldier bear? I only knew that his two wives lived in different towns and that one of them had children. He reminded me of a sad poet.

Pointing to the cliffs above, I imagined extensive plateaus dotted with clusters of black tents surrounded by sheep and goats.

"How many people live up there?"

"Maybe ten thousand, maybe twenty," Beside me, Sahi shrugged. He was guessing. "We can go if you want, if you have time."

Sahi estimated that it would take two to four hours to reach the top and, to make the trip worthwhile, we would have to explore farther afield. Hearing this through Mr. Bashir, Clarence shook his head. To a man like Sahi, who seemed to have all the time in the world, our decision must have seemed ludicrous. Why come this far and not finish the task?

On our return trip, the most influential elder in the region invited us into his garden for tea. MSF would need his support if we built a clinic. With a radiant smile and a hand on his heart, his wiry form led us through a garden of grapevines, roses and flowering trees. The valley stretched out below. The peaceful air caressed my cheek. Small songbirds sang duets. In the shade, goosebumps sprung up on my arms. Pulling my chador close, I sat cross-legged on a mattress beside Mr. Bashir and Clarence. We faced our host at the opposite end of a long rectangular tablecloth while men took spots on either side.

As I washed my hands in traditional fashion, the scent of cardamom wafted over us. Down the hill, smoke rose from a cooking fire. A stocky boy strutted across the tablecloth and placed a platter overflowing with fresh figs in front of the three of us. A plate of green grapes came next.

Mr. Bashir motioned to the fruit. "Take some. You must not disappoint him." Clarence and I placed a fig and a few grapes on the plastic cloth in front of us.

"Take more. You must appreciate his hospitality." Mr. Bashir plucked a handful of figs and two large clusters of grapes. I added more to my pile. He bit into a fat fig, its seeds clinging to his upper lip. As he chewed, delight flooded his face.

I spoke in a low voice: "You know that expats have weak stomachs. We wash fruit with clean water so we don't get sick."

Mr. Bashir gulped, then spoke in a loud voice. "My foreigners have weak stomachs. This one has just recently arrived, so his stomach is very weak. Khonum Murreen asks if the fruit has been washed with well water."

I suppressed a frown. He was supposed to finesse my question. I could have asked it that bluntly! Hoping to repair any damage, I conjured up Momo Rahim's diplomatic skills. "Your figs look very beautiful. Their taste must be like from heaven." Mr. Bashir chimed in something about angels.

Our host beamed. "We washed the fruit with well water that was boiled first. My well has the sweetest water. It does not need boiling. But for you, we do everything. Do not worry." His whimsical voice tinkled with laughter. I wanted to believe him, since figs don't peel easily. Well water in a place like this was probably the best we could do. I doubted that they had boiled it.

Salivating, I bit through the furry, paper-thin skin. Its soft flesh dissolved in my mouth and sweet juiciness burst out, punctuated with tiny, tart flavour bombs. I cast another one into my mouth and plucked a few more from the platter.

"How are my figs?" Mr. Bashir translated the older man's words.

After sucking the pith from my teeth, I spoke directly to our host. "They are the most delicious figs I have ever eaten! I believe that figs are now my favourite fruit."

The skin beside his deep-set eyes crinkled. "Good! Our orchard is the largest in the valley, and the trees are heavy with fruit. You must take some with you." He paused to look directly at me. "You like figs very much! Have more. You have eaten too little."

I devoured three more while Clarence nibbled one.

"Figs are very good for health." Our host squinted. "You are a doctor. What do you say?"

Mr. Bashir translated. On this trip, he hadn't seen the need to conceal my profession.

"In Canada, we do not know of particular health benefits from figs." I looked at Clarence. He shrugged.

Mr. Bashir's voice rose excitedly. "There is no benefit in Canada or in England? In Afghanistan, figs provide much goodness. Khonum-doktar Murreen, you do not know what figs are good for?" Eyebrows raised, he peered down his nose. A pregnant pause followed. Chewing, I studied his face and decided that I would win more points by staying silent.

He winked and turned back to the elder. "She knows nothing.

She is just an innocent khale." He tipped his head toward Clarence. "Our foreigners are missing out."

Tapping the tablecloth with his finger, the elder chuckled. "It is important. You must tell them."

My fingers plucked yet another fine fig.

Mr. Bashir swallowed. "Figs are good for ah… um… a man's strength… when he is… um… with his wives." He eyed me. "Is that not true in Canada?" He grinned at Clarence like a kid sharing an illicit secret. "Or in England?"

So the testicular-sized fruit in the palm of my hand was an aphrodisiac!

Smothering a grin, Moqim pretended to contemplate his half-eaten platter. No wonder they ate so many! I bit one in half and macerated the tender pulp with my tongue.

"Khonum finds my figs delicious," our host crooned, smacking his lips.

Mr. Bashir laughed. "True, Khonum Murreen has an appetite for figs."

Reaching for another, I laughed along with them. Rumours would flow no matter what I did. "Your figs are the very best! Mr. Bashir, what is the Dari word for awesome?" I watched him shrug.

"You say they are good for men. Are figs also good for women?" He translated my question. Our tablemates giggled, glancing furtively at one another. Someone changed the topic. When we departed, the sun was just above the horizon.

At Sahi's village, our attempts to contact Zia failed again. During the day, we had told him that we would camp that night by the river. At his home, Sahi voiced other intentions. "You must join us for dinner. The women have prepared a delicious pilau for you!" His eyes glimmered in the dusky light. Eating dinner with him meant spending the night—we would never risk travelling in the dark.

Since first hearing Kareem's tales of his life as a young shepherd, I had longed to overnight in a remote village and experience the magic in his stories, but doing so wasn't in MSF's playbook. However, the previous night by the river, Zia had recommended that Clarence and I stay at Sahi's house. The protection afforded by pashtunwali made it safer than camping. In his home, Sahi would protect us with his life.

Turning away from the gaggle of men who observed our every

move, Clarence and I slipped around the corner of a building where, out of sight, we set up the satellite receiver for the phone. On our fourth try, the logistics coordinator in Herat answered. Clarence explained our dilemma to the old soldier. "We think it is best for us to stay in the village because of pashtunwali. Zia will be alone in the car overnight, which is not ideal. We cannot contact him by radio. Will you communicate our plan to him?"

The barely audible voice sounded supportive. "Difficult situation. You know best. Will radio Bravo-1. Good luck. Over and out." My belly flip-flopped. I felt like a kid whose dad was letting me camp overnight in the forest for the very first time.

When we told Mr. Bashir, he picked at a mole on his neck. "Perhaps we can send food and a message to Zia."

"I will send my son." Sahi turned to provide instructions to the surly youth. I gave him a note that I had written in Roman script so few locals would be able to read it. Mr. Bashir had verified my phonetic spelling of the Dari words. The Afghan Pony Express galloped away.

"Khonum Murreen, my wives would like to meet you. Please come." Sahi's outstretched fingers pointed to a two-storey wooden dwelling across the trail.

At the compound gate, he left me with his mother, his sister and his wife, who knew a few words of Dari. They led me up an outdoor staircase. We walked into a living room with windows in all directions. Pink sheers billowed in the early evening breeze. Children clambered over women or tumbled and ran after each other. A four-year-old boy hung back behind his mother. How many wives did Sahi have?

Bold flowers in primary colours decorated everything—pillows, curtains, shelf coverings and mattresses. From the middle of the room, I could see farms, pasture lands, the stables, the valley trail in both directions and the mountains beyond. I could even spy on the men's area. Cardamom-spiced green tea perfumed the air, and little plates of green raisins, pine nuts and sunflower seeds lay on the floor between us. Picked from local trees one day each year, the pine nuts were a luxury. Once, in Bala Morghab, I had witnessed the event. Trucks left town before dawn and returned at dusk full of tired and injured men and boys who clung to sacks brimming with the prized cull. Limiting the harvest to one day was supposed to make it fair, but I heard that armed men had gathered their quota two days earlier: No one reported them. The penalty for cheating was death.

I answered the usual questions. When Sahi's wife found out that I was single, she offered to help me: "A husband can be found." Her approach to marriage was practical, a set of criteria to be ticked off a list, not a quest for a soulmate. Was I too picky, like Qabeel had pointed out? "Without children, you must be sad and lonely. Without children, where is the joy in life?"

I struggled to find common ground with them. "In Afghanistan, many women have difficult births. Some die. We want to make a clinic that keeps women healthy. This is my work." I paused to gauge their interest.

Sahi's wife translated the Pashto words of an older woman. "Women in our family do not die in childbirth. We are fortunate. But the wife of Asif, the bricklayer, died, and so have others. We pray to Allah for them. Bismellah rakhman rahim. Peace be upon him." Sahi's wife looked down, her fingers fidgeting with the handle of a teacup. "My first son died before he finished feeding from the breast." Afghan women typically breastfeed for two years. "A djinn. And Fadheela's twins died. They did not eat well." Fadheela was her sister-in-law. Djinn were bad spirits that for these communities explained diseases like tetanus and polio.

"I become sad when I hear of these deaths. Our clinic would help you."

A shadow passed across her eyes. The air in the room felt heavy. "Children bring so much joy. Their deaths, such sadness. Our organization wants to help. What do you need?"

"It is Allah's will. What can we do? We appreciate what He gives. I have a good husband and family." I watched the weight of her sorrow smother her joy. The age-old chasm separating science and religion sat between us. Recalling Kareem's appreciation of science gave me hope. Right beside her, a four-year-old somersaulted and a six-year-old clapped his hands. She hugged the smallest one. If I walked in her shoes, I would want kids too.

Two adolescent girls in long dresses balanced plates brimming with mutton pilau, eggplant with tomato and garlic, zucchini with minted yogurt sauce, cumin-scented rice and fresh naan.

Lounging on pillows, we licked our fingers. "Why are you not married?" Sahi's wife knitted her plucked eyebrows together.

Mine confused Afghans, since only married women were supposed to do that.

I told them of my childhood wish to travel to every country in the world, that I wanted to understand life and ideas from many facets. These ladies, whose qom took care of their every need, could they relate to any of my ramblings?

"When you become old, you need children to take care of you." Sahi's wife spoke gently.

So many children leave their parents, exchanging distance for unfettered growth. I had tried to stand tall each time I returned home, but no matter what I did, I transformed into that awkward, imperfect girl. "In Canada, a woman's life is different. We own land and a house, and we have money, so I do not need sons the way Afghan women do."

An older woman clucked her tongue. Other women nodded.

"Stay with us tonight. You can be our guest." Sahi's wife patted the mattress, her smile radiant, like a queen of a tiny castle.

"Thank you. I would be very happy to stay here, but I must return to my team." What would it be like to sleep in the same room with all of them? I imagined hungry babies crying and conversations continuing into the wee hours like at an adolescent's slumber party. Would their husbands join us?

Sometime later, Sahi, accompanied by his brothers and his sons, limped into the room,

"Khonum Murreen, we have a gift for you. You must accept it." Grinning expansively, he offered me a package wrapped in embroidered cloth.

"Coming to Tagabi Alan is my work. A gift is not necessary. I am here to help people." I knew that a gentle refusal was a compliment.

"Please accept this small gift from my family. You have brought happiness to the valley." A bead of sweat ran down his cheek as he let the large package fall into my hand. "Open it."

I undid the ribbon and opened the fabric. Inside was a simple white cotton dress covered in embroidered flowers, like those on the pillows and curtains.

"Hold it up for us to see." He mimed the instructions. When I did, he frowned. "Ah, it is much too small. There is no time to make a new dress. This is the only one. Perhaps you give it to your daughter."

A collective cry sprang from the women as they exchanged horrified glances. His wife spoke for them. "But she has no children!"

He looked aghast. "What is life without children? You must marry and make a family. It is important. See?" He motioned to the crowd of lovely people in the room. Having a throng around me all the time would drive me nuts.

"Ah, it is so beautiful! I give it to my niece." There, hopefully that settled things. I began rewrapping the present.

"Wait! There is another gift." With a slightly harried smile, he handed me a large, soft bundle wrapped in pink nylon. "Open it!" His voice rumbled with eagerness. Sweat slid down my torso. How I wished for Mr. Bashir's measured advice!

From the package, I withdrew an embroidered velvet chaderie, a burgundy cape like the one worn by Little Red Riding Hood. Rimmed at the front by a thick, gold border of bead brocade, the rest of the velvet was stitched in multicoloured patterns. It was a proper Afghan covering! The knot in my stomach suddenly tightened again. Although it was beautiful, what did he expect a foreign woman like me to do with such a thing?

"We had only a short time to make your gift! So the material is not perfect, and there is not nearly enough stitching for you. If you stay longer—two or three weeks—we make a beautiful chaderie with stitching by hand and many flowers." He bowed his head. "You stay with the women tonight, okay?" His tone suggested that the decision had already been made.

I thanked him and shook my head, stating with finality that I would return to my team.

He argued. I stayed firm. When he picked up the oil lantern, his eyes looked sad. I thanked his disapproving wife and followed his shadow down the staircase.

In the stable where the men had congregated, I scrunched my nose against the reek of cowboy and horse sweat. My thoughts drifted back to the soft, peaceful room full of bright colours and fresh breezes. Twenty squatting riders slurped tea, their hawk-like eyes following my every step.

Sahi whispered, "See, for you this is not comfortable." He motioned to a dark hole of a room like the ones we had rented in Khairkhane, where bats sometimes roosted and spiders crouched in corners. "Do you want to sleep inside? Or outside?" Outside, gaping men wrapped in patus lay on bare ground or sat in groups. A patchwork pattern of oil lanterns illuminated the pitch-black night.

"Outside. The sky is beautiful." I pointed to the earthen courtyard surrounded by mud walls.

Sahi ordered two boys to move a Pakistani cot to the centre of the compound. His son placed a starched white sheet and a thick polyester blanket at the foot of it. On the ground, on either side of the bed, they unrolled a thin mattress.

Sahi bowed, then nodded at the raised bed. "For our lady guest!" Pointing to the two mattresses, he gestured like a master of ceremonies. "For Mr. Clarence and Mr. Bashir. We all protect the honour of Khonum Murreen."

Lying there fully clothed, including a chador, I marvelled at how the Milky Way appeared to jump out of the sky. A star slid across the darkness and winked out. A satellite blinked. As my body sank into the cot's netting, Frank Sinatra sang "Fly Me to the Moon" inside my head. My thoughts drifted, and I didn't know if I was dreaming, lying awake or somewhere in between. In the background, male voices muttered. A cough followed a snort. Heavy breaths rattled in windpipes. Horses stamped and whinnied. A rooster crooned morning. Cassiopeia spun around Polaris.

In the dark, I heard shouts. A door creaked, then banged shut. Hooves thudded against the earth. More mutterings. Were we being attacked? In the silence, Mr. Bashir whispered, "Two horses escaped. Men went to find them. Go back to sleep." His clothing rustled, then his breath became regular.

Later on, whispers interrupted my dreams. I opened my eyes as the last stars twinkled in the dawn sky. Stretching my cramped legs, I contemplated weaving a path through sleeping men's forms to the pit toilet. I rolled over to find Mr. Bashir watching me. Clarence was folding his sheet. Gentle snores filled the air.

Sahi, his eyes puffy, offered Mr. Bashir two bundles wrapped in checkered cloth. "Figs and freshly baked naan for you! Khonum Murreen enjoys figs too much! Now you enjoy many more of them." He offered each of us a steaming mug of milk. "Fresh from the cows!" He beamed. "You must not leave with an empty stomach. Drink fresh milk and you are strong for an entire day of travelling!"

"You are too kind. Did you sleep last night? Did you find the horses that escaped?" I was going to miss being spoiled like this.

"Oh, yes!" He smiled. "I hope they did not keep you awake. A second horse escaped as we searched for the first one. Now they are both safe." He motioned toward a field near the women's house. At the doorway to his compound, we thanked him once again and I shared my hope that MSF would decide to build a simple clinic in the valley.

On the path to the river, out of earshot, we radioed Zia. His voice was higher pitched than usual. "Where are you? It is so very good to hear your voice. Last night, I was worrying too much! All night I was awake!"

Had he received our message and the food? No. Had he heard from the Herat team? No. Our logistics guy in Qala-I-Nau had told him to stay put. Thank God! But how terrible for him that the Pony Express had broken down. Had Sahi lied? We promised Zia figs and freshly baked bread.

That morning, as I skipped down the path, my heart felt huge. Mr. Bashir's rich, baritone-timbred chuckle rang out behind me. Travelling with such loyal companions to places so far removed from modern times was bewitching. I was reminded of the main character in James Mitchener's *Caravans*, who had exchanged a privileged American life for a simple one among Afghan nomads. I would convince MSF to help the people of Tagabi Alan. No other organization would dare venture there.

Three hours later, we arrived at Moqim's house in Khairkhane. He wanted me to meet his wife. The others waited in the car. When we left, his parting words replayed sweetly in my ears: "Travelling with you, Khonum Murreen, I learned so much. My daughter, I will send to school. Before spending time with you, I did not think it was important."

CHAPTER TWENTY-TWO

FREE SPIRIT

"I know but one freedom and that is the freedom of the mind."

— Antoine de Saint-Exupéry

In a Kabul hotel in 2005, a wall of black velvet split the room in two. Gender segregation at weddings was normal, men in one room and women in another. As more women congregated, the rumbling of conversations intensified, as if a host had cranked up the volume. Sparkling sequins, mirrors and silver threads enlivened boldly coloured ball gowns. Heavily outlined eyes and dark red lips popped against backdrops of pale foundation and rouge. Hair, piled up like beehives from the 1950s, glittered as if bedecked with fireflies. Dangling earrings jangled. Wearing our usual cotton shalwar kameezes and chadors, Melanie and I resembled drab custodial staff. Her driver, Rahim, had invited us to his nephew's wedding, and we hadn't considered buying outfits for the occasion.

I wore this style of outfit for all occasions in Afghanistan, even weddings. Photo Krishna Rao

An unknown woman kissed our cheeks and called out to an adolescent girl, the older lady's bosom threatening to pop the bows of her frilly pink bodice. From the girl's pocket, three bottles of nail polish materialized. The matron held the flasks of fuchsia, rose and scarlet next to Melanie's wrist, then to mine. Winking suggestively, she raised the scarlet one.

The girl's left eyebrow lifted. She shook my finger. Could she paint my nails? I nodded. During my manicure, she, accidentally dented, then smeared the polish with a napkin. Fidgeting through-out, she wiped most of it off, then began again. Once groomed, my fingertips looked like they had been dipped in blood. Fluttering them to hasten drying, I suppressed an urge to tidy up the blotches of lacquer staining my cuticles.

"You left your children with your husband and came to Afghanistan?! It is so far from them!" I translated the words of a woman in a baby blue and white gown that reminded me of Australia's magnificent blue wren. "And your husband is fine with this?" Her tone suggested disbelief.

Twirling her wedding band, Melanie shifted from one foot to the other. "Yes, for many years, I took care of my children. Now that they are older, my husband enjoys spending time with them, so I am here in Afghanistan for some months." I marvelled at her courage to stress her marriage like that. Would their hearts grow fonder or become distant? Living in Afghanistan changed people.

My experiences there altered the way I interpreted issues. Early on, I realized that common beliefs about Afghan women held by many Westerners were just as false as those about us borne by Afghans. We weren't all promiscuous sluts. They were not all down-trodden, unhappy, forcibly married and scarred. Western news reports were particularly frustrating to me because reporters portrayed their information as general truths when, so often, they had only spent a few weeks in the country and had witnessed a biased sliver of someone's reality through an interpreter.

My views on feminism had evolved. I had been wowed by the strength of some Afghan women, the way they used their power in subtle ways to get what they wanted. I realized that I had armed myself with a thick veneer that blunted a softer side of myself, a strategy for succeeding in a male-dominated world in which strong women leaders wore tough armour. Ignoring my emotions was easier when wearing pants or suits.

In Afghanistan, I couldn't be a token male, even when I tried. One time, Kareem had asked me for a keepsake, a photo of the two of us both wearing a patu and a turban so no one would know that I was a woman. He taught me how to wind metres of cloth into a proper headdress and ensured that I covered my brightly coloured kameez with the beige patu. Later, when he saw the photo, his fits of laughter had barely allowed him to eke out a sentence word by word: "You look like a woman, not a man!" Holding my aching belly, I had gasped for air. In Afghanistan, I inadvertently wound up exploring a part of myself that I had lost.

Rahim's nephew, a twenty-year-old, was marrying a bride five years his junior, which was an entirely different scenario from the first wedding that I had attended in Bala Morghab, just after John and Vicky's departure. That first time, the beat of the daireh had lured me next door into a dark house brimming with women and girls in traditional dress. The fourteen-year-old bride had sat Madonna-like beneath a veil of white lace, her eyes downcast. Her mother was crying. It felt like a funeral. When everyone suddenly disappeared, I hastened back to the office to an amused interpreter who explained that I hadn't offended anyone and that the party had moved to the groom's compound, where I should expect a joyful event. Apparently, the bride was supposed to look sad in her parents' house out of respect for them. To my surprise, at the groom's home, we did sing and dance in the sunshine.

At the Kabul wedding, it was once again my turn to be grilled. "No children?! Aren't you sad?" They pushed beyond my usual answers. "A husband protects you. He keeps you warm at night." A matron shot a sly look at another lady in a yellow gown with lace appliqués that reminded me of a wedding cake. "We choose your husband! A good Afghan man!"

"Thank you." I smiled, trying to sound grateful. "I am happy without a husband." I repeated the story that I had told a hundred times. Their eyes and fingers pointed at Melanie, and I read that they didn't buy my belief that spinsterhood gave me freedom. Our conversation dragged on.

Marriage, a ceremony that I had avoided, was the glue that bound Afghan society together. It strengthened families. There, adult children took care of their parents and single women had no rights.

In fact, single women were a liability that caused trouble. How could I explain that I was drawn to follow an unorthodox path that had no clear destination? I was living my journey, figuring things out, just like my great-grandmothers had done when they moved across the ocean to Dawson City in the 1890s.

I signalled to Melanie that our ninety minutes were up. Weddings could carry on for hours, sometimes days, and we had work to finish. The bride had yet to show up, so Melanie shook her head, her finger drawing "30" in the air.

An hour later, the bride, wrapped in fine lace and pearls from chin to satin slippers, appeared on the arm of a groom wearing a black tuxedo. Flower girls and maidens in pink guided the cathedral-length veil trailing behind her. The groom steered his precious cargo, beaming with every pirouette. The room murmured: "She is so beautiful." "They are made for each other." "How fine their children will be!"

Forks clinked on glasses. Someone made a toast. "Congratulations! You are the perfect couple! You will have many fine children and a long, happy life!" Raising glasses filled with orange pop, we toasted them. Women with knowing smiles congratulated each other. "Matchmaker, Matchmaker" from *Fiddler on the Roof* looped in my head.

Through the velvet divider, a boy's head poked out, like a prairie dog surveying the Saskatchewan grasslands. Beside it another one appeared, then a third and a fourth. Abruptly, they vanished, as if plucked from behind.

Waitresses, straining under trays piled high, presented us with cumin-scented pilau, spinach with paneer and fenugreek, eggplant sautéed with tomato, garlic and onions, and other delicacies. The groom fed the bride pilau. The bride fed him a kebab. A couple of mouthfuls later, they stood up, spoke intimately with a select few, then disappeared into the velvet barricade. I signalled to Melanie. We couldn't leave before eating!

Partway through the meal, a lively Afghan beat overtook the chamber music. My foot tapped. The beat swallowed the conversation. Raising arms above their heads, two middle-aged women swivelled as they pulled others onto the dance floor.

I nudged Melanie. "Do you wanna dance? Women dance together at weddings." To me, prancing with a partner was more fun than doing it solo.

Emphatically shaking her head, she looked like a deer in head-lights. "No, I-I don't dance!"

"Come on, it's easy. You just move to the beat." I reached for her arm. She snatched it away, her butt scooting back in the chair like the stubborn donkeys on the footbridge in Tagabi Alan. Music had always spoken to me, lifted my spirits and calmed me down. Moving to it felt natural.

On the dance floor, I joined other women, swinging a hip and rolling a shoulder while picturing our cleaner in Bala Morghab danc-ing bewitchingly at our Eid celebration on Christmas Eve that year. He brilliantly performed a sultry one-man show, playing a mother, a shy adolescent girl and the man who pursued her.

Another woman and I mimicked each other, our shoulders and hips almost touching, then flying apart. We experimented, daring each other to twist a little more alluringly. Hands twirling, shoulders rolling and hips swinging, my body seemed to lead my mind.

A woman shimmied her shoulders, and her large breasts swayed horizontally. How did she make her entire body vibrate like that? Behind her, the black velvet curtain was pockmarked with curious expressions peeking through gaps in the fabric. A camera flashed. Beside Rahim, two men in suits standing brazenly on our side of the velvet surveyed us from afar.

I shut my eyes, my feet two-stepping to an Afghan tune. A few minutes later, I smelled a musky scent. I cracked open an eye just enough that a fuzzy image of a guy with straggly salt-and-pepper hair appeared. He wore a shiny brown suit and, to my surprise, he was dancing right in front of me! His lined face, capped with greasy hair, came close. I backed away. Given the strict Afghan rules re-garding gender segregation, his forwardness made me wary, even though it would have been fine at any Western event. Wide-eyed, I looked at Melanie. She shrugged. Hoping that he would lose interest, I ignored him, pivoting away so many times that I felt dizzy. By the curtain, Rahim clapped and smiled. The guy was probably his rela-tive. When the song stopped, I stepped away.

His oily face approached. His voice rumbled, "Why so shy?"

I shook my head, pasting a smile on my face. I wasn't shy. I didn't like him.

A man in a black suit cut in. My feeble smile probably failed to convey my gratitude. His hair was clean, and he gave me space. The rock 'n' roll music lubricated my limbs. Eyes followed us. The song finished. He thanked me and moved into the crowd.

Women closed in. Nearby, a well-endowed lady in a creamy gown shimmied at high frequency, jiggling all over. I tried to mimic her, but my body just didn't do that. We giggled. She demonstrated in slow motion. I tried again, then gave up. Closing my eyes, I imagined looking down on the guests from above. Suddenly, I was alone in the middle of a circle. I stepped to the side, but someone nudged me back.

Everyone was facing the black curtain, so I did too.

John Travolta's doppelgänger in a white suit à la *Saturday Night Fever* was gyrating toward our circle, his pelvis thrusting as his gymnast's legs stepped rhythmically, his sturdy shoulders shifting back and forth. Wearing the sultry expression of a tango dancer, his eyes focused on mine as he choreographed from deep within. I closed my mouth and hoped that I hadn't drooled onto my kameez as his delicious form strutted closer. Swallowing hard, I felt flushed all over. My limbs danced woodenly. What should I do? Did he intend to dance with me? Was I the sample foreigner for everyone to try on?

Well, two could play at that! With a big inhale, I shifted perspective. We arced together. We stepped apart. He winked. We traced each other's bodies, with our hands never touching. His breath brushed my ear. I mirrored him and smiled deep inside. It felt like a tango looked, but the beat differed. He cocked his head and we both spun around. Was he twenty-five or younger than that? The song ended. With a nod, he vanished.

I gasped. People clapped. A hand patted my shoulder.

Afterward, the pulsing Iranian disco music felt weighty. I gulped cold tea and was watching Melanie speak with her hands when off to one side, a flash of red dazzled my eye. I turned. A woman in a skin-tight scarlet dress kicked off her three-inch heels. Tossing waist-length curls, she skipped in a complex rhythm while speaking at me in rapid-fire Persian.

"I don't understand." I shook my head and stared helplessly at the mermaid-like thighs and breasts bound tightly together by the shimmering dress.

Flinging her abundant mane, she repeated words that sounded like a machine gun. I shrugged, suddenly irritated. I needed simpler terms spoken slowly. What was she trying to tell me?

Her hips in their red hot wrapper cocked to the left. Buoyant mammaries bounced to the right. Back and forth they toggled. She was a stunner! I glanced from face to face, searching for someone to translate her words, but everyone simply watched expectantly. Was I supposed to dance with her?

The singer's wail followed a Persian scale. The sassy mermaid's enormous eyes and well-manicured hands beckoned to me. Fascinated, I stepped forward, my hands fluttering in twisting movements above my head, like I had learned in the countryside to a different rhythm. Beside her, I felt like Jane of the jungle. A young woman from the sidelines whispered in my ear while moving two index fingers up and down, one facing the other.

Was I in a dance competition? Had I challenged her honour by dancing with her betrothed? Was the prize the man in the white suit?

My brain yelled at me: "Let her win! Let her win! We don't want that reward!"

Women and men chanted while clapping to the beat. I tried to feel the rhythm, but my body danced like a flat-footed hippo, the beat a mystery to it. Cameras flashed. I felt like Cinderella after midnight.

A rock 'n' roll song began, boosting my energy. The mermaid slung her shoes over her shoulder and smiled. Our competition had ended, but the man in the white suit didn't drop to a knee and carry her away.

Tapping my shoulder, Melanie pointed to her watch. Hours had vanished.

In the black limousine on the way home, Rahim grinned so widely that his molars glistened. "Khonum Murreen, your dancing is sooo beautiful!" His hand drummed the steering wheel as he repeated his words again and again. During dinner at his house a month or so before the wedding, we had hooted and guffawed at scenes in wedding videos of people dancing beautifully, making faces or just plain goofing off. His wife and daughters had announced each scene as if they had memorized the entire recording. I would be in the next one.

Dropping us at the driveway, he briefly spoke with our two guards. They promptly opened their phones, eyes dancing with infectious delight. What were they sharing? I heard only a few of Rahim's words, "Khonum Murreen... dance... very beautiful..."

"Khonum Murreen, congratulations!" They both grinned at me.

"Oh, thank you," I nodded, hand on my heart as was the custom. Then I stopped. What?! "Excuse me. Congratulations for what?"

"We find you a good husband." They beamed like my grandfather used to do when telling me stories about panning for gold. Weddings were where Afghan matchmakers did their best work.

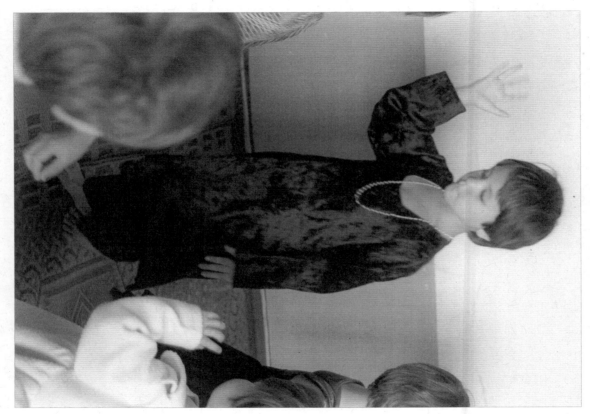

Young village girls were encouraged to practice dancing at tea parties and weddings. The hope was that a husband would be found when other women witnessed their skills.

EPILOGUE

In a rented cabin near Coquihalla Mountain in British Columbia, Mike, my partner of fourteen years, and I drink the last bit of coffee from our stovetop espresso maker. Outside, the sky is a robin's egg blue. After layering up, we step into our skis and trudge up the mountain in zigzag patterns, skins on our skis providing friction. When I squint, colours of the rainbow glisten off snowflakes. Sweat soaks my pullover, and I strip down to a T-shirt.

Fuelled by dried fruit, homemade cookies and dark chocolate, we reach the summit, where the trees are frozen into snow-encrusted spirals that remind me of candy canes. I pull a thermos of mint tea from my blue knapsack and we empty it. The hot sun dries my shirt.

To my left is a cliff. On my right are slopes of sparkling untracked powder. We yank the skins off and lock our bindings. That's when I think about avalanches, snow-covered boulders and tree wells. What if? I've learned to cradle that fear gently, and trust myself. I let go of a big whoop as we float over the terrain, side by side, carving swooped turns in the snow. I catch an edge and land face first, then blink away snowflakes from my eyelashes and wipe others from my cheeks. Squirming like an overturned beetle, I shift my weight onto my knees before skiing behind Mike through the trees.

At the bottom of the hill, we gaze up. My ski tracks are lopsided and marked with a glaring splat halfway down. My grin is so wide that I feel my face splitting in two. "That was fantastic!"

We high-five. Who wouldn't love that feeling?!

While eating a sandwich, a memory of my happy-go-lucky mother materializes. She died six months previously, at the age of eighty-five. Three years before her death, we hiked up a mountain together in Hawaii. She was beaming. She would have loved to stand right here and view the simplicity, the power and the beauty of this wild place. Over the last several years, we had visited her often to help care for my ailing father. When he was too weak to walk more than a few steps, I decided to conjure up small adventures for him. At the time, he didn't trust that an electric scooter would make it up the hill to their house, so his life had become the size of the block on which they lived. The day after we arrived, Mike and I had him bombing around town, waving to people like he was driving a Ferrari.

After Dad died, Mum travelled a lot. When Mike and I accompanied her, we hiked, foraged for berries and mushrooms, kayaked and ate great food. Once, we rode in a helicopter with no doors. That was the day I suddenly realized that my "conventional" mum was anything but. In fact, we shared a quest for adventures that she had kept hidden from me. I wasn't a misfit after all. As a widow, Mum seemed to rekindle the gutsy part of herself that she had lost in marriage and that as a child, I had seen and understood.

An image of Kareem surrounded by ancestors whis-

Backcountry skiing in British Columbia with my partner, Mike.

pering in his ear popped into my head, reminding me that even when we feel lonely, we are never alone. Whatever I had become was fed by people I met and by my roots from diverse places.

Since 2002, when MSF handed over the Bala Morghab clinic to a local organization, I had wondered how Kareem's life had unfolded. At the time, he had no address, email or cellphone. Just recently, his cousin had sent me Kareem's mobile number. It took a few months for me to work up the courage to text him. How would he perceive our friendship twenty years later? In 2021, the Taliban had walked into power in a matter of days, their threats and accusations causing Afghans to close Facebook accounts, sever ties with foreigners and leave their home country yet again. Girls no longer went to school. Would the Taliban harm Kareem if they discovered our liaison? The consequence of being labelled a spy was death.

In the first text, I mentioned my name and asked if the number was correct. In subsequent texts, we exchanged gratitude for the experiences we had shared, and what we had learned from one another. I still want to know more about his life. By now, he might be an elder like his dad. Maybe he has grandkids. I hope his children are still alive, and that he provided them with a solid education. If he had a daughter, what would her future look like now? Even in the absence of Taliban laws, restrictions for women in rural families are often more severe than those for their urban counterparts.

Back on the mountain, Mike and I watch a lone skier carving a path next to ours. He waves. We raise cups of tea. It's time for another run.

In Vancouver, Mike and I own a small home that has room for guests. My office is a safe space where physicians call to get help when facing challenges. I never did stop learning. Professional coaching skills help me guide doctors to use their strengths, decide what they want, ask for what they need and thrive, rather than burn out. I still like helping those who suffer be their best.

Writing this book has helped me trust myself when the going gets tough, and to remain committed to a path with an opaque destination. Before visiting Afghanistan, I was close-minded about what might come of interacting with people there. Having spent years in the country, I now treasure my experiences and relationships with Afghans whose ways of seeing life and events differed so much from mine. Acknowledging and confronting my fears, judgments and discomforts gave me a deeper understanding of myself, what matters to me and what is possible. I believe that by reaching across a chasm and joining hands for a time, we saw value in those differences and developed a deeper understanding of what it is to be human.

ACKNOWLEDGMENTS

When I first sat down to write this book, I thought it would be quick and easy. How wrong I was! I am extremely grateful for the unfaltering patience of the many people who supported and guided my learning in such an iterative way. With each revision and reflection, the story I really wanted to tell unfolded.

First, I thank the many Afghans who invited me into their lives, gave me their friendship, and shared their ideas and culture. By accepting my rudimentary language skills and my impressions as an expat Canadian, they created a welcoming environment that shaped the adventures I have described. Their approach to life inspired me to write from my heart.

Mike, my partner, demonstrated unerring patience and support during my early forays into writing, when his gentle nudging caused me to reluctantly acknowledge the merit of recrafting the work again and again—even when I thought it was good enough. It wasn't. His confidence that the work would one day become worthy of publication kept me going, as did his support during times of disappointment.

The idea of writing this book began in conversation with Jane Warren and Kevin Patterson. Early on, Jane encouraged me to narrow my story when I wanted to tell everything.

I am deeply grateful to Betsy Warland, who provided sage advice on writing a memoir. She guided me to identify themes that unified my narrative, and she encouraged me to approach writing as a "quest to discover" when the final product seemed opaque.

I am also grateful to Jim Gifford, Patrick Crean and Ian Mulgrew, who generously gave me feedback that helped me shape the story into one that I hope readers will find entertaining and evocative. I thank Robert Mackwood for helping me navigate and understand the world of publishing.

It has been a great privilege to work with the publishing team at Caitlin Press: Vici Johnstone, Sarah Corsie and Malaika Aleba. I also thank Pam Robertson for her careful reading and attention to detail, which provided finishing touches to the manuscript.

I have enormous appreciation for those who read chapters at various stages, offered feedback and cheered me on, and to those who shared their own journey of writing and publishing. Special thanks to Mike and Del Hayden, Tom Hayden, Bonnie and Michael Klein, Brian Goldman, Cathy Cameron, and my fellow students in writing workshops.

ABOUT THE AUTHOR

PHOTO MIKE HAYDEN

Maureen Mayhew earned a medical degree from McGill University, a master's degree in public health from Johns Hopkins University, a fellowship in research methods from the University of British Columbia and a certificate in life coaching from the Co-Active Training Institute. She has practised medicine in eight provinces and two territories of Canada, as well as abroad with Médecins Sans Frontières and other international organizations. Currently, she volunteers for MSF as a peer support worker. As a UBC clinical professor, she has instructed on topics in global health, refugee health, remote health care and primary care. Her research has been published in peer-reviewed scientific journals and portrayed in two educational films. She has published articles about her experiences in Afghanistan in the *Canadian Medical Association Journal* and contributed to the collection *Outside the Wire: The War in Afghanistan in the Words of its Participants*, edited by Kevin Patterson and Jane Warren. Her passions include travelling to far reaches of the globe, active forays into nature, stunning photography and learning new things.